An Introduction to Christianity

ROBERT T. ANDERSON

PETER B. FISCHER

Michigan State University

HARPER & ROW, PUBLISHERS, NEW YORK

AN INTRODUCTION TO CHRISTIANITY

Library of Congress Catalog Card Number: 66–11260

Contents

II. *THE CHURCH*   27

III. *THE BIBLE*   64

IV. *MAN*   98

V. *GOD*   127

VI. *JESUS THE CHRIST*   163

VII. *THE CHRISTIAN FAITH AND WESTERN SOCIETY*   193

Preface

The purpose of this book is to bring the doctrines of the major Christian faiths to an audience not necessarily familiar with any of them. It grows out of several years experience of trying to do just that in the classroom.

We are aware of similar efforts of our colleagues who have put their insights into writing and we have been grateful to them for the use of various texts over the years. Nevertheless, in our particular experience we have come to feel that a text could be tailor made with the particular constellation of virtues that have seemed to be most appropriate and effective in a nondenominational undergraduate introduction to Christianity.

We have found, for example, that required introductory courses in the humanities have eliminated the need for extensive historical surveys of the Judeo-Christian tradition, so although some historical background is provided throughout our discussion, our focus is doctrinal rather than historical. We have also found that we meet our students at a very elementary level in their study of religion and we have accordingly made a very conscious effort to simplify the outline of this text and to explicate in straightforward, clear prose. We have also tried to make the student familiar with the best scholars in the field without overburdening him with too vast a barrage of unfamiliar names. Although many introductory texts today omit a treatment of the Bible as such, we do feel that the Bible, as the source of Christian doctrine requires particular treatment. With the availability of many excellent paperbacks for supplementary reading, this comprehensive text is purposely concise to allow for the use of optional readings.

Two particular qualities extend the usefulness of this text to nondenominational schools. The work tries to be comprehensive in its treatment of Christianity. In selection of opinions it tries to avoid what the authors think Christianity ought to be in favor of what experience demonstrates Christianity to be. Consequently it is not persuasive in its approach. It avoids offensive comparisons between positions and seeks to be descriptive rather than normative.

A very brief list of suggested reading is appended to each chapter to point out directions in which the student may turn for additional related material. All biblical quotations are from the Revised Standard Version published in 1952.

The authors have divided the book so that Professor Anderson has written the chapters on the Bible, Jesus the Christ, and the Christian Faith and Western Society, and Professor Fischer the chapters on the Church, Man, and God. The introductory chapter was written in common, Professor Fischer writing most of the first half, Professor Anderson the second.

ROBERT T. ANDERSON
PETER B. FISCHER

AN INTRODUCTION TO CHRISTIANITY

I

Introduction

DEFINITIONS OF RELIGION

Religion is so large a subject that no single definition will describe all it has meant to civilizations and to individuals. Across the world in all ages religion has been so universal that some people have ventured the supposition that it is "natural" to all human beings. It has been only in the very recent period of history that many people have said they could find a happy and useful life without religion.

If it should be true that religion is natural to man, that there are no unbelievers and faith is universal, then the question would not be "to believe or not to believe," but only "what to believe." For example, it has often been argued by political scientists that communism is a form of religion with its own prophet and with its own doctrine, religious loyalty, symbols, ritual, and other religious patterns. Any value that a group or an individual cherishes above all other values then can be called "god." There are democratic faiths and nationalistic faiths apart from traditional religious faiths. In the year in which World War II broke out, Reinhold Niebuhr gave a lecture on God at the University of Michigan. In it he said something like this: "Religion is the implicit sense of life's meaning. All men have some sense of the meaningfulness of existence and cannot live or think or act without it. In that sense all men are religious. I have always held it to be foolish, therefore, for teachers of religion to persuade people to be religious. For one thing, it is foolish to do that, not only because all men are religious, but because it is not necessarily a good thing to be religious. In the modern world, I know of no man more religious than a young Nazi, but I don't like his religion and if I had to choose between that religion and skepticism, I would choose skepticism. No one is good for being religious. The question is, what God do you worship? No one is really cruel until he is religious, for all cruelties are ultimately religious cruelties."

This comprehensive definition of religion would include the large portion of mankind that dissociates itself from traditional religious bodies and change the terminology of the current debate on the relevance of religion. Many would object to so broad a definition.

Some descriptions of religion are in terms of sudden commitment, a "leap of faith," and others in terms of a gradual cultivation of a "way of life." For example, the Danish theologian Kierkegaard likened believing to swimming. As long as a person wades and insists on keeping even a toe on the ground, he will never learn to swim. He must entrust himself to the water. Faith is like swimming with deep water beneath the swimmer. Mystics have again offered the image of a ladder, or a mountain which one climbs step by step toward God by means of careful practice and exercise. A favorite way to describe religion has been by means of

the road of life. In the *Pilgrim's Progress,* the pilgrim goes
through life full of spiritual dangers, temptations, and obstacles.
"The way" is one of the oldest words for religion. It was used by
the Chinese. Jesus says, "I am the way," and the early Christian
community is referred to in Acts as followers of "the Way."

But of course it is true of all vast areas of culture that specialists
project the terminology of their own special fields of study into
their definitions. Thus an anthropologist in the tradition of
Emile Durkheim may assume that society personifies itself in god
as its own image or symbol. To him the function of religion is that
of strengthening society, maintaining its institutions, and generally
assuring stability and coherence to the social body. Or a psycholo-
gist in the tradition of Freud may insist that god is projection of
the image of authority, of the "father-image" formed in a person's
childhood, into the realm of the absolute. Philosophers, from
Hegel's time on, write about god as "absolute spirit" or "eternal
energy," or as a "principle of concretion." In the day of hallucino-
genic drugs, there are, no doubt, those who also think of religion
in terms of the effect of chemical reaction upon the activity of the
brain and point to the ancient use of *rauwolfia serpentina* in India
and the ritual consumption of peyote by the Native American
Church by way of illustration.

Martin Buber, in distinguishing religion from philosophy, defined religion as "essentially the act of holding fast to God. And
that does not mean holding fast to an image that one has made of
God, nor even holding fast to the faith in God that one has
conceived. It means holding fast to the existing God. The earth
would not hold fast to its conception of the sun (if it had one),
nor to its connection with it, but to the sun itself."[1]

There are many ways of speaking of religion or defining it
quoted in literature. For example, an old Greek skeptic said that
"fear created the gods," and some feel that this contention is

[1] Will Herberg (ed.), *The Writings of Martin Buber,* Meridian, 1956, p.
108.

supported by the statistic of increased church attendance in times of war or other danger. With this may be paired the negative valuation of religion as an escape valve of individual psychological pressures or as the "opiate of the people." Another psychologized definition would identify religion with "the power of positive thinking." Whitehead's statement is often quoted: religion is what a person does with his solitariness. Unamuno suggested that religion is to speak the truth always, especially when it hurts most. Henry Nelson Wieman defined religion as that quality of the universe that makes for growth and Paul Tillich defined it as the search for ultimate reality. There have been definitions in terms of value, such as the search for the highest good or relation between the ideal and the real. It is to be noted, however, that these definitions are a typical outgrowth of modern Western civilization. Ancient religions had only partial relation to ethics and often no relation at all to what we call "morality." One of the most commonly quoted definitions of religion is that by the German nineteenth-century Protestant theologian, Schleiermacher: religion is the "feeling of dependence" of man on a higher power. None of these definitions comprehend in one statement all that religions have been; and the smallest common denominator of many religions is of the smallest value in understanding what they are about.

Besides formal definitions of the pure essence of religion, it is good to realize at the start of our study that the expression of religion is always culturally colored. If the expression is by intellectuals, it will take the color of some prevailing philosophy, such as idealism, existentialism, or pragmatism. The vocabulary of the early Church Fathers is often Neo-Platonic and their philosophical mantle cannot be separated from the substance of their thought, which is Christian. Later medieval writers again will use Aristotle's way of expression and Aristotle's arguments.

But intellectuals have always been in the minority even though theologically the leaders. The majority of Christians, like the

majority of adherents of any religion, are people of little philosophical training. Their religion is culturally colored, but the
coloring comes from such sources as ancestral customs, legends,
and local folklore. Some of these will give the particular religion
its fringe phenomena, such as mixtures of magic, astrology, and
various superstitions. Some will gradually develop into traditions
of popular belief so strong that the church may incorporate them.
The Auxiliary Saints of the Middle Ages, the prayers to whom
were supposed to protect a person from a toothache or a sore
throat, are an example. Erasmus in his *Familiar Colloquies* poked
fun at the popular superstitions thinly coated with Christianity.
They are still derided by intellectuals and humanists, but remain a
firm part of popular religion. Local festivals, local and regional
saints, and local practices distinguish one group within the same
church from another. German Catholicism differs from Mexican
Catholicism. European and American Protestant churches differ.
The social and cultural environment and inheritance is part of the
religion of the people. Those who search for a definition of
religion by essential features of abstract nature often forget this.
Religion does not appear in a cultural vacuum. Yet this textbook
will seek to isolate some of the essential features of Christianity.

CHRISTIANITY AND THE WORLD RELIGIONS

There are about half a dozen major religious faiths. Members of
each one are sometimes concerned about the "uniqueness" of their
religion. Is it really the best of all religions or does it look special
simply because they were born into it? Familiarity is of course a
great factor. Very few people have a real firsthand acquaintance
with more than one religion. Students of comparative religion
sometimes take the scientific attitude of classification, description,
and noncommittal comparison of several religions. This approach
stresses the similarities, differences, and comparable categories of

religious belief and behavior. The question of "uniqueness" does not come in for discussion at all. Logically, every religion, as every person, is unique. People who profess certain religious beliefs would be less than loyal if they did not believe that their faith was better than that of anyone else. The same may be said of members of political parties and other groups.

There is no simple way to answer this question for everyone. Perhaps our attempt has merit insofar as it tries both to show that Christianity is indeed a religion with features standard to most religions and that Christianity is in part significantly and decisively different from other religions.

What follows is an attempt to present the first part, that is, an outline of the common themes of the various religions of the world and how they find expression in the major world faiths. The rest of the book will deal with the Christian religion and demonstrate how Christianity expresses general and unique themes.

One early theme is the initiatory pattern of rebirth. In the Fourth Gospel of the New Testament, Jesus is quoted as saying, ". . . unless one is born of water and the Spirit, he cannot enter the kingdom of God" (John 3:5). Nicodemus asks the natural question, "How can a man be born when he is old? Can he enter a second time into his mother's womb and be born?" To this question most religions of the world would answer emphatically that although one does not literally return to the womb, he must do so symbolically. The death of the old self and the birth of the new self is a standard feature of religions both primitive and advanced. For example the highest castes of India undergo a puberty rite through which the novice is born again (the "twice-born") into a position as a brahman. There are rites which symbolically transform the initiant into an embryo and others which suggest a new birth from the womb of "mother earth."[2]

[2] For a splendid documentation and expansion of this theme see Mircea Eliade, *Birth and Rebirth, The Religious Meanings of Initiation in Human Culture,* Harper & Row, 1958; especially chaps. 1, 2, and 6.

In primitive religions, as the boy is to die to boyhood and rise to the new life of manhood, he is symbolically killed, eaten, or burned, and passes through a region of darkness which may represent the belly of a monster or the womb. Thus the tomb and the womb, death and the new life in preparation are joined together. In the Christian Church Fathers one finds such comparisons in the image of the baptismal fountain. It is both the tomb in which the catechumen buries his earthly life and the womb in which the new life, the eternal life, is born. The new religious status is indicated by giving the initiate a new name, a standard practice in several tribal religions and also in Christian churches which give the new name, the "Christian" name at baptism. The new name is an indication that the novice is now a new man. A parallel phenomenon is the giving of new names to monks and nuns who take lifelong vows. Only baptized persons can participate in the full worship service and the intimate ritual of the church. The early Christian churches would allow the catechumens to be present only for the first part, the instructive part of the worship service. Then they had to leave and the baptized alone continued with the liturgy of the faithful. One could suggest further parallels, such as the varied blood baths ritually performed to give spiritual strength to the novices and the saving power attributed to the blood of Christ as the slain "Lamb of God" by some Christians. Baptism and the Eucharist are associated with sanctification, both symbolizing a radical change in the status of the believer.

A second theme of religion that is nearly a universal feature is the orientation or cosmic axis. Ancient Greeks had many shrines and temples, but the one which was from time immemorial consulted for the will of the gods and which became the most widely accepted was the Temple at Delphi. The Temple of Apollo made God's answers accessible to men. Communication between the divine wisdom and human need made this place the most sacred of all the places on earth. It made the good life possible in the face of destruction, homicide, and other tragedy. The central spot, marked by a stone, was referred to as the "navel" of the earth. The Greeks believed that here was the central point of the whole earth. Similar examples can be given in Mecca for the Moslems, and one thinks immediately of the spatial orientation of medieval churches and cathedrals: one entered from the west, and faced not only the altar in the church, but also the tomb of Christ in Jerusalem. The center of spiritual orientation that gives meaning to life is also the geographical center of the world! What would seem more natural? Without the center of orientation, there is chaos, insanity, and death. The symbols of the center are numerous and are found in both primitive and advanced religions:

All myths which stress the Tree of the World, the Cosmic Mountains, pillars, stone columns, or ladders that link the earth with the heavens express this fundamental idea; that a "center of the world" exists, thanks to which communication with the heavens can be accomplished and around which the totality of the habitable world extends. The "center" is the place where a split in the ontological level was effectuated, where space becomes sacred, therefore pre-eminently real. This also means that the universe is created from its center and extends from a central point that is like its "navel." Thus, according to the *Rig Veda* (X, 149), the universe is born and evolves; it starts from a nucleus, from a central point. Jewish tradition is even more explicit: "The Holy One created the world like an embryo. As the embryo proceeds from the navel onwards, so God began to create the world from its navel onwards and from there it was spread out in different directions."[3]

Imitation of the divine model is a third common theme of religion. One of the classic writings from the end of the Middle Ages is called the *Imitation of Christ*. It has also been translated under the title, *The Following of Christ*. We often hear of saintly persons desiring to be "Christlike," "assimilated to Christ" and

[3] Mircea Eliade, "The Prestige of the Cosmogonic Myth," *Diogenes* No. 23 (Autumn 1958). This translation by E. P. Halperin is quoted from *The Divinity School News,* the Divinity School of the University of Chicago, February 1, 1959, pp. 7 f.

the like. Some exceptional individuals have been reported to have the stigmata, an imitation of the wounds of the crucified Christ. A favorite phrase of the apostle Paul refers to his "dying with Christ" and rising with him to a new life (dying to the old self, rising to the new self). The Anabaptists thought of themselves as the "re-pristination of the early Church" of the apostles, repeating in their time the reality of the New Testament model. These are all instances of the standard religious concept that the most sacred and religiously most meaningful act imitates the divine model. The classic case of this is the worship service in the Roman Catholic and Eastern Orthodox churches, where the body and blood of Christ is sacrificed each time the liturgy is served, imitating not just the original sacrifice of the cross as if in commemoration, but actually repeating the act as a present event. The sacrament of Holy Communion or the Lord's Supper imitates the last supper of Jesus and his disciples. Other acts of Christ such as the washing of the disciples' feet, the appearance before the Roman governor who signed the death warrant, and the carrying of the cross have all been imitated by Christian churches.

Mircea Eliade assures us that this is a universal pattern in all religions: "The archaic man acknowledges no act which has not been previously posited and lived by someone else, some other being who was not a man. What he does has been done before. His life is the ceaseless repetition of gestures initiated by others."[4]

The original act of the god or divine hero is referred to as the "primordial act." These acts may offer the justification or explanation for holy days: the biblical story of Creation says that God rested on the seventh day from all his work. It seems appropriate that man should rest, too. These acts offer explanations for various institutions, as men imitate the creativity of God in their art and dance, the justice of God in their legal system, and even marriage has its heavenly prototype. In the Hindu Upanishads the marriage

[4] Mircea Eliade, *Cosmos and History: The Myth of the Eternal Return,* Harper & Row, 1959, p. 5.

rites are an imitation of the union of heaven and earth. Most world faiths have both a masculine and feminine deity or deities. Both are necessary to bring forth crops for the nourishment of man's body and a saviour to redeem man's soul. Further, men in their struggles re-enact the universal battle of the gods against the devils. "For the traditional societies, all the important acts of life were revealed *ab origine* by gods or heroes. Men only repeat these exemplary and paradigmatic gestures *ad infinitum*."[5]

Similar "universal features" common to all known religions can be documented in some length by students of comparative religion and by anthropologists. We are familiar with much folklore that accompanies the end of a year, the beginning of a new year, or the time of festivals marking the beginning of a new harvest that guarantees the continued life of the community. The purifications, fastings, confessions of sins, expulsions of demons, and return of the dead on earth survive either as religious beliefs and practices or as folklore whose original meaning is now largely lost. Professor Eliade discusses these as signs of the almost universal phenomenon of the creation of the world reproduced every year anew with the destruction of the old, as the eternal repetition of the cosmogonic act and the regeneration of time.

Finally, it may be of interest to note that the psychological phenomenon of "guilt-feeling" and the various explanations of the category of sin have rather universal religious association. It has always been assumed that guilt must be expiated. Fasts, oblutions, sacrifices, and penances are characteristic in most religious patterns. Some will lay their sins on an animal and drive it into the desert or place it in a boat and let it drift to sea. Days of atonement are common. So is the insistence that the gods punish sin, from the Code of Hammurabi to the Egyptian weighing of souls and the Persian and Christian images of punishment in hell. These are basic and common experiences as men struggle to find salvation. The themes in any one culture are woven together into a comprehensive pattern that forms the core of a particular religion.

[5] *Ibid.*, p. 32.

The world's major religious faiths are reservoirs of accepted truths concerning the ultimate questions of life. The themes that permeate all religions find expression in historical faiths. They are crystallized in the literature of the sacred books, taught through the educational programs of religious institutions; and manifested in the organized worship and ethical life of the community.

Some prehistoric and historically early religious patterns continue to be characteristic of religion and some do not. All religions assume some sort of force behind the activity of the universe. Sometimes it is conceived as an impersonal power, *mana,* which flows and ebbs through the universe like the tides and currents of the sea. When this energy is given an animate or spirit form it is called animism. Early men attributed such powers to streams, rocks, trees, and animals. Animals with such designated power were often considered ancestors of the tribe or clan and this practice is called totemism. As ideas about spirits became more sophisticated, they became more like the divinities of theistic religions today.

The worship of such power sometimes involved sacrifice and forms similar to contemporary patterns of worship. It also involved practices less common today, magic and tabu. Magic is the belief that by certain incantations or actions one can coerce the powers of the universe to behave in the manner that man wills. Tabu is a system of restrictions on behavior or contact with various objects, implying a belief that inevitable punishments will follow. Elements of these early phenomena are distinguishable in religious practice today.

The history of ancient religions in the East, particularly in India where several of them originated, is very difficult to trace. Archaeological and historical evidences are very sparse. Contemporary Indian historians assume that their culture is essentially the same as it was in ancient times. Hinduism and Buddhism do have ancient roots and we know little of religion in the East before these faiths.

In the West, Egypt, Mesopotamia, and Greece surrounded and penetrated the area which gave birth to contemporary Western religion. Although none of these ancient religious cultures continues to exist, their influence is sometimes apparent.

The religion of ancient Greece was formulated in two traditions. The older, with its anthropomorphic deities, was systematized by Homer out of a plethora of local cults. Each of the gods was given a distinctive personality and assumed residence on Mount Olympus. Sacrifice and prayer were offered to them and a professional clergy evolved to mediate between the gods and men. From the seventh century onward the mystery religions emerged into prominence. The rites of Dionysus, the Eleusinian mysteries of Demeter, and the Orphic mystery cult superceded the Olympian cults. Participating in a system of rites of initiation and communion, the worshipper believed he would gain salvation through his personal saviour. The extent of influence that these cults had on Paul as he developed a Christian theology has been a central debate among Christian scholars.

Egypt had no Homer to systematize its multitude of divinities, so, although her religion represented a syncretism of various local cults, it was unsystematic and filled with contradictory themes. The reliability of the inundations of the Nile allowed a man a control over his natural environment that was reflected in positive attitudes toward man and his accomplishments. The Isis-Osiris-Horus triad became the chief divinities of Egypt and temples in their honor were built. An elaborate sacrificial form of worship was maintained. Ultimate salvation was referred to an afterlife for which elaborate preparation was made.

The physical and climatic conditions of Mesopotamia are in sharp contrast to those of Egypt. The Tigris and Euphrates rivers, fed by snow-covered mountains, flood erratically. Scorching winds drive blasts of sand, rain, and warm air across the fields. In Egypt the engineer can guarantee when the floods will occur and be certain that the crops will come up. The Mesopotamian farmer felt himself to be at the mercy of the whims of the deity. Consequently the religions of the Tigris-Euphrates Valley are more pessimistic about man and seek effective ways to appeal to the gods to assist them with the productivity of their fields. In this context a rich fertility cult arose. Astarte became the chief female deity, with many manifestations. The mythology emphasized the sacred marriage opening the way for the fertility of the land, the dying-rising god who sustained the crops from spring until fall, and the enthronement of the king who assured that the demonic powers were under control. The myth was enacted and fulfilled in the sacrificial ceremonies. Some of the myths, like that of a primeval flood story, may have made their way into early Hebrew thought along with many cultic practices.

Although historically there have been a great variety of different religions in different parts of the world, contemporary world faiths spring almost exclusively from two major sources: Judaism in the Middle East and Hinduism in Central Asia. The roots of Christianity and Islam can be traced to Judaism and these three religions prevail in Russia, Europe, North, Central, and South America, Africa, Pakistan, and Indonesia, involving about 50 percent of the world population. The roots of Jainism and Buddhism can be traced to Hinduism and together these three faiths comprehend India, China, Japan and Southeast Asia, a total of about 30 percent of world population. Confucianism and Shintoism are the only major faiths that belong to neither of these traditions. Hinduism makes up about 10 percent of the world's population, Jainism less than a tenth of 1 percent, Buddhism 5 percent, Confucianism 10 percent, Shintoism a little less than 1 percent, Judaism a little less than 1 percent, Islam 17 percent, and Christianity 33 percent.

There are distinctive emphases that distinguish the East from the West. Western thought views history as a consecutive series of events which lead ultimately and finally to salvation. In the East, history is a continuous repetition of events related only negatively to salvation. One escapes history to find salvation. In general the East understands this world as a prison from which man tries to escape. The West affirms the goodness of this world as a creation of God and seeks salvation, in part, within the context of history. Eastern thought is more introspective and mystical. Consequently, religion is an individual experience exemplified by the monk, the ascetic, and the worshipper at his individual prayers in his home, out of doors, or occasionally in the temple. Westerners are activistic, practical, and ethical in their emphasis. This encourages and facilitates corporate worship.

It is difficult and dangerous to extend any generalizations. The major world faiths contain great diversity and there is as much difference in practice, attitude, and belief within any one of them as there is between East and West. Distinctive emphases and similarities can only be generalized.

From the very beginning Christianity has been a faith with great missionary zeal and has, therefore, been in active and continuous contact with other faiths. According to tradition, Thomas had brought the gospel to India and China at the same time that Paul was preaching in Asia Minor, Greece, and Rome. Surely by the fourth century, Christian churches had been established in the south of India and in China. The missionary movement in the East became particularly active from the fifteenth century onward. Roman Catholic efforts were effective as evidenced, for example, in the work of Francis Xavier in India and China. By the seventeenth century European trading companies had opened the way for Protestant missions and one of the best known of the early Protestant missionaries was a Baptist, William Carey, whose work centered near Calcutta. In the last three centuries an extensive program of Christian missions has been at work in almost every part of the world.

But the twentieth century is witness to a radical change in the relationship of Christianity to the non-Christian world. Participants in the World Missionary Conference held in Edinburgh in 1910 could still affirm their conviction that the East would be absorbed by the West.[6] Eighteen years later when the Interna-

---

[6] Hendrik Kraemer, *The Christian Message in a Non-Christian World,* International Missionary Council, 1947, p. 36.

tional Missionary Council was held at Jerusalem, a new attitude was expressed. Spiritual imperialism was disavowed.[7] Secularism, rather than non-Christian faith, was declared the real enemy. A new era of understanding between Christian and non-Christian faiths was inaugurated when a council called the Laymen's Inquiry met in 1932 and, under the influence of William Hocking, declared, ". . . missionaries will look forward, not to the destruction of these religions around it, but to the continued coexistence with Christianity, even stimulating the other in growth toward the ultimate goal, unity in the completest religious truth."[8]

Several factors had contributed to this change in attitude. Missionaries found themselves unwelcome in many countries newly released from colonialism. Internal reforms often eliminated unsatisfactory characteristics in some non-Christian faiths and the slow progress of the missionary movement led many to doubt that any substantial number of non-Christians would ever be converted.

Indeed, there has been a growing countermissionary activity among the world faiths. Islam has a long history of aggressive evangelism and has been extremely successful in the Orient and Africa. Judaism, which has seldom shown signs of missionary zeal, is actively at work among Christians. Hinduism is represented in major cities throughout the world by the Vedanta Society and the Ramakrishna movement. Buddhism, particularly in its Zen form is enjoying tremendous popularity in the West.

Some few missionaries still go out with hopes of converting non-Christians. But many now go to serve Christian communities in non-Christian lands or to bring educational and technical services to needy people with no explicit plans for conversion. In order to perform such services many must serve in countries where they are forbidden to teach or preach Christianity.

Dialogue rather than evangelism marks most of the encounters between Christians and non-Christians today and the dialogue is

[7] *Ibid.*
[8] Edmund D. Soper, *The Philosophy of Christian World Missions,* Abingdon Press, 1943, p. 217.

becoming institutionalized. There has been for many years a National Conference of Christians and Jews whose purpose is, "To promote justice, amity, understanding and cooperation among Protestants, Catholics, and Jews and to analyze, moderate and finally eliminate intergroup prejudices. . . ." There is also in the making a World Fellowship of Muslims and Christians whose provisional organization, the Continuing Committee on Muslim-Christian Cooperation "seeks to manifest publicly that Islam and Christianity have many beliefs and aims in common; develop and encourage plans to promote better understanding between Muslims and Christians on a world level and in local communities; encourage study and fair presentation and interpretation of the Qur'an and the Bible." For the present the integrity of each of the major world faiths seems mutually respected and assured.

DEFINITION OF CHRISTIANITY

There is a certain futility in trying to define any of the great world religions. All of them encompass such a wide variety of beliefs, practices, and individuals that exceptions will be found to every descriptive proposition. Each individual and each generation brings new interpretations. New interpretations lead often to apparent heresy, but religions are tolerant of all but the most extreme heretics and tend to live with them rather than to expel them. Perhaps the genius of the world faiths is their ability to accommodate even the widest diversity of human belief and practice.

On the other hand, the most radical interpretations of any given faith are by definition held by a minority and some meaningful generalizations can be made about the majority assumptions. The concern of this book is the definition and explication of Christianity. It must begin with an assumption about what is distinctive in the Christian faith. Geographically and historically the boundary of Christianity is marked by the church, doctrinally its source is the Bible and the church traditions, and theologically it is focused on a monotheistic understanding of God with central emphasis in his revelation through Jesus the Christ.

The church as the focal point of community worship and the means of transmitting the Christian heritage is integral to Christianity. Christians from the beginning worshipped as a community in the manner of the Jew. Hinduism, by contrast, has until recent years been practiced in the home rather than in the community. Even temple worship is practiced individually in Eastern religions. Moslems, too, although they center their worship at the mosque, pray individually except at Friday noons when they are led by officiating clergy. Christianity has been much more explicit in community centered worship led by a specially trained clergy. As a result it has a tradition of community hymns and a form of architecture that accommodates a body of worshippers and focuses their attention on a worship center where the sacramental and preaching ministry takes place. All Christians participate in the sacraments of communion and baptism.

Whatever authority is given to the individual, church, or tradition, doctrine in Christianity is ultimately derived from the Bible. This is generally understood to include both the Old and New Testaments. At times the validity of the Old Testament has been challenged, most notably by Marcion in the second century. But this position is held by a very small minority. On the other hand, a sizeable minority would add to these two Testaments the apocryphal writings produced between the beginning of the fourth and the end of the first century B.C. Christians share veneration of the Old Testament with the Jew and traditions of both Testaments are later found in the sacred book of the Moslems, the Koran. The New Testament is uniquely Christian, though contemporary Christianity is unanimous in prefacing it with the Old Testament.

Like Judaism and Islam, Christianity is strictly monotheistic. This means that all believe there is only one God and most

Christians would say that God is personal. Mahayana Buddhism and most forms of Hinduism emphasize the diversity of divine forces in a practical polytheism. In contrast Christianity has emphasized the unity of the divine. Likewise, Hinayana Buddhism and philosophical Hinduism point toward an impersonal ultimate force in the universe in contrast to the Christian assumption of a divine personality.

Some Hindus include Jesus in their roster of saints and Moslem scripture incorporates much of the tradition about Jesus, but recognition of Jesus as the Christ is unique to Christianity. Great debate within the faith has centered on the nature of Jesus and the Christ concept and some Christians would exclude other Christians on the basis of their Christology, but all Christians avow a unique committal to Jesus.

Each of these particular items of the Christian faith will be examined in the following chapters. In addition it will be necessary to consider man, who is the subject rather than the content of religion, and the whole discussion is followed with an evaluation of the relationship of Christianity to the society in which it grew.

CHRISTIAN SCHOOLS OF THOUGHT

Within the spectrum of beliefs held by the many churches there are lines of demarcation which do not divide just one church from another, but form divisions within the same church in such a way that the orthodox members of one church feel closer to those of another church than they do to the liberal members with whom they worship under one roof.

The term *orthodox* (from the Greek meaning correct faith) usually refers to the beliefs supported by the majority of Christians, hallowed by old historic usage and expressed in such formal documents as the ancient creeds. Belief in one God in three persons is an example of an orthodox Christian belief. The term *liberal* used in the context of religion is not identical with the term liberal used in the context of politics. The chief feature common to these two concepts is that they feel free to depart from past traditions, as compared with the conservative who tends to preserve them. Both the political and the religious liberal may also be greatly concerned with freedom, tolerance, and the right of the individual to think and believe for himself. But the religious liberal is most clearly distinguished by his attitudes on religious doctrines on such matters as the Bible, God, and man.

The orthodox believer is likely to take the Bible as the inspired word of God, at times literally. It is the standard of faith and life for his church. The liberal church member feels that human fallibility is apparent in the sacred book and the reasoning powers of the individual are necessary to distinguish what is divine or revealed and what is human.

The orthodox usually begins his thinking with God and stresses God's activity in everything. For example, in the sacrament of Baptism, God forgives sin and gives grace. The liberal tends to be more preoccupied with the problem of man. He has faith in man's basic goodness and free will. Baptism is understood as a pledge or an acceptance of an infant by the group. Human reason and ethical responsibility are the key to salvation.

Several contemporary theologians are identified as *existentialists*. Existentialism is a modern movement with ancient ancestry. Generally it is not interested in abstract ideas by themselves, but rather in relating the thoughts to the life-orientation of the man who thinks them. Similarly, in existentialist plays or novels, the reaction of the audience or reader is equally considered part of the play. This characteristic of involvement of the human life in a play, novel, thought, or religion is a prime characteristic of the existential attitude. The personal involvement is focused upon the concrete, definite individual. To talk about marriage in the abstract is one thing. To face marriage in one's own particular life is another. "All men are mortal," is one piece of general informa-

tion; "I must die," spoken by a particular person fully aware of the inevitability of his own death is a very different piece of information.

Modern existentialism of the humanistic brand is associated with Sartre, Camus, and others. The Christian existentialism of our time begins particularly with Kierkegaard and finds expression in Bultmann, Tillich, Unamuno, Berdyaev, and Marcel. It is full of terms such as "absurdity," "paradox," "despair," "anxiety," "decision," and "leap of faith." These suggest the irrationality of existence, or at least a condition of human life that cannot be encompassed in a neat, straightforward formula or system of thought. In religion this may mean that God's understanding of what human life ought to be and man's understanding of the same may run in opposite directions. Man's weakness before God may be his strength, and his strength his weakness. "It appeared to Kierkegaard as comical that a man should try to take an 'objective' view, i.e., a view which leaves the individual out of account, towards moral and religious questions, when these questions have as their central meaning the life of the very individual considering them. This emphasis upon the involvement of the self forms the most important link between existential philosophy and religion."[9]

CHRISTIAN TERMS AND METHODOLOGY

Theologians, like other academicians, have their own special vocabulary. In the following chapters, the most significant terms will be defined. But a number of key theological concepts have to do with the methodology or way that a theologian approaches his subject. Since it is a methodology uncharacteristic of our technologically oriented culture, the terms that define it seem strange to us and warrant special comment.

The theologian says that God *reveals* himself to man. We are

[9] John E. Smith, "Existential Philosophy," in *The Handbook of Christian Theology,* Meridian, 1958, p. 123.

inclined to think of speech or writing as the obvious ways of communicating and since we have not heard God talk or seen anything in his handwriting, we are suspicious of anyone who has received a revelation. The picture of God sweeping into a room for a conversation in fluent English, or of writing mysteriously appearing on a wall, or a muffled, solemn whisper are unbelievable images. But revelation is better understood as akin to intuition, a phenomenon with which we do have experience. We can frankly admit that we often have acted on the basis of intuition. Revelation may be thought of as a specialized form of intuition: spontaneous insight regarding the basic questions of meaning in life.

In a society that puts so high a premium on reason many individuals may feel that they want something more secure to act upon than an intuition, however specialized. As a matter of fact there may be no more secure way of knowing. The philosopher, Descartes, decided that he would admit no proposition of knowledge unless it was absolutely demonstrable. He began with the proposition: I think, therefore, I am. To that proposition he came with the full assent of all men. But from that proposition he moves to others with varying degrees of support. We know with absolute certainty far less than we often realize. The ultimate paradox is that our commitment to reason cannot itself be based on reason; it is an intuitive commitment.

The individual is not left completely adrift in verifying a revelation. The church passes on a heritage of conscious and unconscious judgment of revelations from the past. These are formulated in the Scriptures, the creeds and the traditions of the church. They constitute a body of general revelations.

The individual has also the certainty of his intuition. The revelation is self-authenticating. He need only respond with *faith*. Faith is the response of commitment to an intuition. Faith is belief in something that is beyond the possibility of proof or disproof. It is not belief in something that is known to be false. It is a total commitment of the individual's rational and emotive being to what he believes to be a truth.

There is a long history within the church of the struggle between advocates of the priority of faith and the advocates of the priority of reason. The most extreme position in defense of faith was classically expressed by the third century theologian, Tertullian: "I believe because it is absurd!" By this he meant that ultimate truths may be incomprehensible to the limited minds of men and must be accepted by faith alone. Several existential theologians hold similar views about the priority of faith. They see reason as an extension of man's proud attempt to control his environment. It is riddled with the same self-centeredness that permeates all humanly initiated activity. Therefore, reason can never be used as a means of discovering ultimate truth. Revelation alone is the medium by which ultimate truth is communicated to man. This means that God must take the initiative in every encounter with man, and man, for his part, ought to respond in faith.

A less extreme position has been put forth arguing for the priority of faith, but allowing that reason can give supportive evidence. Augustine argued such a position. Paradoxically, his own experience suggests a third alternative. He was intellectually committed to Christianity for many years before his conversion. This would suggest that reason is prior to faith and prepares the ground in which revelation and the concomitant faith can take place. The most extreme defense of reason is made by those rationalists who feel that any reference to intuition or faith can and should be avoided.

The language of revelation must necessarily employ a different vocabulary than that of reason. Reason speaks in literal propositions. Revelation speaks through *myth* and *symbol*. Although myth is sometimes used with reference to political and economic ideologies, its most common referents are religious. The West is now so deeply steeped in rationalism that myth seems an anachronistic concept. Commitment to the unrestricted operation of natural causes is so strong that the possibility of other media of truth is excluded. The easy abandonment of myth is further facilitated by the fact that myth is usually associated with specific historical religions like the Olympian religion of Greece and along with other elements of antiquity, myth is relegated to the past.

Anthropological studies encourage such an interpretation of mythology. Myth is understood as the philosophy of ancient or primitive man. With the passage of time our symbols have become more sophisticated and myth may be dismissed as a naïve understanding of the universe. From this conclusion it is not a long step to think of myth as misconception of reality.

The anthropological approach to myth assumes that there is an element of conscious effort in the production of myth. This assumption is modified by various psychologists, notably Jung, who have worked with the idea of myth. Jung understands myth to originate in dream and fantasy rather than in any conscious, deliberate effort to explain the universe. Myth is understood as a spontaneous, unconscious process by which men comprehend the world. Such an assumption implies that myth-making is a continuing process in history and, although any given myth may become antiquated, the process of myth-making itself goes on. It further implies that the ideologies of today are as much myth as the ideologies of other times and implicitly chides those who use the term in a subtly derisive way to apply to ideologies they do not hold.

Theologians and literary people suggest another dimension to myth. It ". . . can never disappear till language becomes entirely commensurate with thought, which it never will."[10] This statement implies both a function of myth and its indispensability. Myth becomes necessary when language cannot express an idea or feeling. Myth arises out of the limitations of language. Often in time of grief, love, or exhilaration, for example, we are at a loss for words. At such times, myth can express what words cannot. Likewise it can convey truths about cosmic realities that cannot be reduced to ordinary language. Since it is likely that certain kinds of experiences are forever out of the grasp of literal concrete lan-

[10] Ernst Cassirer, *Language and Myth*, Dover, 1946, p. 5.

guage, it is likely that myth will always play a part in man's thinking and communication.

Discussion of myth is necessary because so much of contemporary theology is self-conscious about the need and value of myth. However, it should be recognized that many Christians give it little or no place in theology. A number of conservatives deny that there is myth in Christian thought. They assume that the so-called myths are literally true. And some liberal Christians deny both the literal truth of myth and its current value and wish to reinterpret old myths in current jargon. Much of this debate will be apparent in the discussion of the Bible and theology.

A myth is made up of *symbols* and, at the risk of giving disproportionate space to this discussion, something should be said about symbols and their distinction from signs and the usual use of language. The risk is worth taking because the entire discussion of this book is involved with a process of thinking that is unfamiliar to most of us. As a matter of fact, we use words on many different levels, mythological, symbolical, and literal, every day, but we are not conscious of it. Since most of the symbols in which a religion is expressed are other than literal it is necessary to develop some sophistication in the use of religious language.

Meaning can be associated arbitrarily with any sign.[11] There may be no connection between the sign and the meaning except that convention or regulation has specified that a given sign implies a given meaning. Symbols, too, are associated with meaning, but unlike signs they cannot be arbitrarily assigned or changed. They grow into their place as symbols and are integral to the reality they express. They cannot be invented and they cannot be intentionally destroyed. Attempts to create artifical religious symbols fail.

The value of the symbol is that, like the myth of which it is a part, it can reveal dimensions of reality that cannot be conveyed by simple signs or language. Myth parallels in function the arts where

[11] This paragraph is indebted to Paul Tillich's *Dynamics of Faith,* Harper & Row, 1958, chap. III.

poetry or form are created to reveal dimensions of ourselves and our universe that are otherwise inaccessible.

THE PROCEDURE OF THE TEXT

This introduction to Christianity begins with a discussion of the church. In it the breadth and variety of Christianity may be seen. The church is Christianity in concrete form. It embodies the creeds and practices that define the faith. The third chapter focuses on the Bible as the chief source of Christian doctrine and worship. It presents both the analytical scholarly approaches that have brought depth to our understanding of the biblical message and the schools of synthetic interpretation that communicate that understanding. Thus enclosed within the boundaries of the faith as determined by the church and the ground of the faith as conserved in the Bible, the text moves on to consider the traditional threefold questions of doctrine that have grown up in this framework. These questions are comprised under the topics of Man, God, and Jesus Christ. Man searches to bridge the gulf that separates himself from God. Successful crossing of this gap is salvation which in Christianity is mediated and symbolized by Jesus Christ. Finally the text describes something of the impact that Christianity has had on Western civilization.

SUGGESTED READINGS

DeWolf, L. Harold, *The Religious Revolt Against Reason,* Harper & Row, 1949.

Eliade, Mircea, *Cosmos and History: The Myth of the Eternal Return,* Harper & Row, 1959.

Eliot, Charles, *Hinduism and Buddhism,* Longmans, Green, 1921.

Halverson, Marvin (ed.), *A Handbook of Christian Theology,* Meridian, 1958.

Hooke, S. H., *Myth and Ritual,* Oxford, 1933.

Howells, William, *Heathens: Primitive Man and His Religions,* Doubleday, 1948.

Morgan, Kenneth (ed.), *Islam: The Straight Path,* Ronald, 1958.

Richardson, Alan (ed.), *Theological Word Book of the Bible,* Macmillan, 1950.

Rosten, Leo (ed.), *A Guide to the Religions of America,* Simon and Schuster, 1955.

II

The Church

*INTRODUCTION: THE ONE CHURCH
AND THE MANY CHURCHES*

We tend to associate churches with certain geographical areas, and so they have been through most of their history: the Greek Orthodox Church with Greece, the Swedish Lutheran with Sweden, the Anglican with England and the British Commonwealth, the Roman Catholic Church with the Mediterranean countries, Ireland, and Latin America. Consequently, we have supplemented our image of each church with the traditions peculiar to its location, its concepts of life, its festivals, even its folklore.

In the United States the situation is basically different. To be sure, there once were dominant churches in certain parts, such as the Anglican Church in Virginia, the Puritans in Massachusetts, the Quakers in Pennsylvania, and the more "radical" groups (known by such leaders as Roger Williams and Ann Hutchinson) in Rhode Island. But none of the "established" churches has ever been dominant, or established, in the whole country. There is no church in the United States that can claim truly national character either by government support, by the predominance of its numbers, or by its historical importance in America's national history. Pluralism has always prevailed.

Our image of "the church" has been formed by characteristic influences.[1] The First Amendment to the Constitution says that "Congress shall make no law respecting an establishment of religion." Congress did not intend by this language to take an antireligious attitude; it probably meant to leave to the states jurisdiction in religious matters. Yet the First Amendment laid the basis for the tradition of separation of church and state. In the eyes of the law, the churches became *voluntary societies,* and people began to think of them as such. The frontier tradition encouraged loyalty to a local church rather than to a national or universal church, and people began to think in terms of *churches* rather than *the church.* In addition, in our country there is greater social mobility than in Europe, and also greater church mobility. People change more readily from one church to another, without necessarily thinking of the religious and theological implications of such a step.

Allied with this is the proliferation of branches and offshoots from the older churches. Perhaps there is some significance in the statistics that show nearly the same number of churches and denominations in this country as there are of fraternal organizations: upward of 250 of each. Sociologically speaking, one might argue that American denominationalism is an expression of American individualism. In Europe, individualism has traditionally expressed itself in the great numbers of political parties; here, in religious bodies.

[1] See W. A. Visser't Hooft and J. H. Oldham, *The Church and Its Function in Society,* Allen and Unwin, 1937.

On the other hand, Christians have always recognized that there is only *One Church*. This church, in its true religious existence can be fully apprehended and known only by an act of faith. "I believe in one, holy, universal, apostolic church" is a standard profession of historic Christian churches just as much as "I believe in God, the creator of heaven and earth." The image of the one church, held from the earliest times, tends to be obscured, if not dissolved, by pluralism, variety, competition of churches for membership, and by identification of Christian ideals with the social, economic, and even political ideals of certain modern countries.

In this chapter we shall pay attention to the classic model and the ideal of the one church as understood by the great historic churches of the past and present. We shall proceed by this sequence:

1. What the church is not
2. The origin of the church
3. Historic patterns and divisions
4. The functions of the church
5. Worship
6. The ecumenical ideal and some problems in its way
7. Conclusion: The measure of the vitality of the churches

WHAT THE CHURCH IS NOT

Not a mystery religion. The church from the beginning has been distinguished from the mystical gathering of devotees who separate themselves from the world in exclusive, secret societies, in order to purify themselves from the sensory, visible world, and by meditation and secret practices rise to the presence of the immovable, unchangeable, eternal Being. It turns its attention to this world, transforming it, healing its wounds, coming to work in the midst of its poverty and toil.

Not a debating society.   The church from the beginning has been something else than a discussion group of people of philosophical inclination who exchange opinions and arguments on the nature of the world or on high ideals of life. It had its origin in the circle of those who followed Jesus as the Messiah (Christ), as the God acting in history who made it possible for men to live in communion with Himself. The Christian Church is based on faith in the crucified and risen Christ, which to the Greek logician in St. Paul's day was nonsense. Even today, its foundation and its purpose cannot be explained or justified purely on naturalistic principles, or by any idealistic philosophy.

Not seekers, but those who have been found.   The church is also more than a group of people who are looking for some ideal, or seeking for some God to believe in. In its own image it is a communion of people who have been found by God and called by him for a certain task in this world.

The word "church."   The word "church" derives from two separate Greek roots: *ecclesia*—group of those who have been "called out" of the rest of mankind to carry out God's special task. From this, we derive the English word "ecclesiastic" and the French word for the church, *l'église.* The other Greek root is *kyrios,* the Lord. The church then means "those who belong to the Lord." This is the basis of English, German, Slavic, and other words designating church, such as *kirk, kirche, church, cirkev,* etc.

THE ORIGIN OF THE CHURCH

We know virtually nothing about the history of the earliest church outside the New Testament records. Emperor Nero denounced the early Christians as the "enemies of the human race" but such remarks are of little help. According to the biblical sources, the roots of the church are found (1) in Hebrew history, and (2) in the story of the New Testament.

THE PEOPLE OF GOD

To the Christian, as to the Jew, the Old Testament is the record of the acts of God in the lives of his people, as it developed in real history. By the covenant—"if you obey my voice indeed, and keep my covenant, then you shall be a peculiar (special) treasure unto me above all people"—desert tribes became the "people of God." To their God they attributed their very existence, their successful escape from Egypt, the arrival in their new homeland and their history in it. They were not selected because of their special merits or unique goodness, but because of the sheer unaccountable decision of God. They became the means through which their God would become known to other people. Such a role required the rejection of all national messianisms as idolatry. The people of Israel were not a nation, not a tribe, not a race; in the strict biblical sense their identity is that of the "people of God."

But the people "ran after other gods," thus broke the trust of the covenant. God exercised patience with them, warned them through the prophets, even used the neighboring empires as a "scourge" to make Israel repent. They again lapsed into rebellion. God taught them to obey through suffering. Finally—and here we embark upon the exclusively Christian reading of the story—God began to work only through a minority, the so-called "faithful remnant of Israel." The church identified itself with this faithful remnant of Israel. Therefore, it fell heir to the promises made by God to Abraham and Isaac, to Moses, and to the people of Israel. As the "true Israel," the church, too, has its covenant. It is the "new covenant" sealed through Jesus Christ. The church, too, does not live by its own merit and by its own strength, but by the "acts of God in history," particularly those relating to Jesus the Christ; and it, too, rejects all national messianisms. One of the rare accounts of the first-century Christians reports that they refused to sacrifice before the statue of the emperor (a kind of loyalty oath of

the citizens, which was compatible with most ancient religions).
The persecution of early Christians appears to be based primarily
on this fact.

The Pentecost

The second root of the church is described in the story of the
Pentecost (Acts of the Apostles 2). If the church as the true Israel
began to exist by the new covenant—the initiative taken by God in
the crucified Christ—it received its first open manifestation in the
world on the fiftieth day after Easter. Then the disciples of Christ
were gathered together and an unusual, powerful experience crystallized their faith and transformed them into a missionary body.
The New Testament describes it in colorful language and attributes the experience of Pentacost to the Holy Spirit. The imagery is
suggestive: great wind; tongues of flame. . . . The disciples then
went out, testified to the mighty acts of God in Christ, and began
converting many (the ancient account says that on that day 3000
souls were added to them). Of course they were challenged, and
ran into opposition. The story of the stoning of Stephen is a
classic.

On a mountain in France, atop the great divide from which the
rivers flow west, north, and south, stands an old Romanesque
pilgrimage church, the Church of Mary Magdalen at Vezelay. Its
tympanum (the decorative arch above the inner entrance) is often
reproduced in art books for its wonderfully medieval representa-
tion. What it tells is the story of Pentecost, the descent of the Holy
Spirit upon the apostles. (But the masonry rays that radiate from
the hands of the glorified Christ to the heads of the apostles have
also been interpreted as the mission to the church which Christ
gave the apostles immediately before his ascension. It may very
well combine the two events into one image, one idea.) On the
tympanum are depicted various people of the world, with fine
medieval imagination and symbolism. Besides the Greeks, Italians,

and Assyrians, there are the African pygmies, and the dogheaded people supposed to have lived in India, etc. But the gospel is not only to be carried to all nations. It goes out to people of all classes of humanity: fishermen, peasants, hunters, savages, priests, soldiers, etc. The effects of the Spirit are also shown in healing miracles. In the masonry we find the blind, the deaf, the mute, the lame, and those possessed by the devil. Salvation is truly cosmic in scope. The signs of the zodiac and the occupations of the 12 months ring the outer limits of the archivolt. The task of the church is to bring Christ to the whole world, to all peoples of all classes everywhere. No wonder that the Crusades began here: St. Bernard preached the Second Crusade here in 1146; Richard the Lion-Hearted took the cross here in 1190. The original idea of the Crusades was the spread of the gospel: "go into the world, preach the gospel to all nations. . . ." But the fuller meaning included more than preaching, of course: the submission of the world to the rule of Christ.

Missionary zeal has been one of the hallmarks of the church from the beginning. Among Roman Catholic missionary orders, the Franciscans and the Jesuits are especially well known. Among historic Protestant bodies, particularly the Anabaptists (Brethren) considered the *great commission* as their outstanding commitment. To them, every Christian was a missionary. To the present day one of the signs of the vitality of a church is often considered to be its missionary work. This is the spirit of Pentecost.

HISTORIC PATTERNS AND DIVISIONS

All Christian churches consider themselves derived from the early church which is described in the New Testament. An Anglican does not think of his church as beginning with Henry VIII any more than a Lutheran believes that Luther founded his. But the separation of the great churches took place in the course of history.

Of these divisions, two are of paramount importance: the separation between Rome and Constantinople in 1054, and the Protestant Reformation of the sixteenth century. There were of course divisions before 1054; their results survive to the present day, e.g., in the existence of the Coptic Church in Egypt and Ethiopia. There were also divisions between 1054 and the sixteenth century, of which the Church of Czech Brethren in Czechoslovakia, or the Waldensian Church of northern Italy are present witnesses. And there have been innumerable branches and separations also since the Reformation, to which witness dozens of churches such as the Disciples of Christ, the Methodist churches, the Lutheran Synods, or the Polish National Catholic Church. But in all the complexity and divisiveness of Christendom, the major breaks remain 1054 and 1517.

Both of these occasions of major separation had a complexity of causes; some national and cultural, other religious. Of the two, the Protestant Reformation went much deeper in religious and theological differences than the Great Schism. Therefore, even today, when the spirit of understanding and brotherly conversation among the churches is returning, real prospects of union between the Greek Orthodox and Roman Catholic Christians are much brighter than those of Protestant Christians with either of the two.

A brief survey of the two crucial divisions in church history follows. In A.D. 451 the Church Council of Chalcedon divided the organized church into five patriarchates: Rome, Constantinople, Alexandria, Antioch, and Jerusalem. As the Arabs submerged the last three in Moslem lands, leadership of Christian churches was divided between the two remaining centers, Constantinople and Rome. These had the added prestige of being the old capitals of the Eastern and Western Roman Empires. The history of these two parts of Christendom moved in different directions. The West absorbed waves upon waves of barbarian invaders and passed into a period of political chaos. The Eastern Empire continued to uphold its standards of civilization. Contact between the two regions became difficult; understanding was impeded by use of different languages (Greek and Latin). Against this background of differences, the churches, too, drifted apart. The first great dispute occurred over the use of religious images (ikons). Then the primacy of the Pope over other patriarchs became an issue. The Patriarch of Constantinople (Photius) refused to recognize himself subordinate to the Pope; the Pope in turn did not recognize the validity of the patriarch's office. This division lasted till nearly A.D. 900. The final blow came between the proud and ambitious Patriarch Michael Cerularius and Pope Leo IX who affirmed his jurisdiction over the whole church. The Patriarch denied it. The Pope sent his legates to Constantinople but the Patriarch would not accept them. The legates placed in the great church of St. Sophia a papal bull of excommunication of the Patriarch and all his followers. The bull condemned them "along with all heretics, together with the devil and his angels." Today the Roman Catholic Church does not speak of the Greek Orthodox as heretics, but the division has never been healed.

The second great division, the Protestant Reformation, also had its mixture of motives. In its growth as a nation, Germany found Luther the man of the hour. He raised national pride as against foreign slanders and his translation of the Bible was a classic of the German language. He became a national hero. Then the church taxation of various kinds became the focus of discontent of the German masses in the transitional economy. But the real significance of the Protestant movement was religious. It was an outgrowth of 200 years of frustrated clamor for reform. John Hus in Bohemia, John Wyclif in England, the great councils of the fifteenth century, individual preachers of reform, all tried for the reform of the church. From the grass roots, from the government of the kingdom, from the papacy were expected reforms. The councils saw the need for reform "in head and members." The hierarchy was in need of discipline and guidance; there were abuses of office on account of greed; there was the lack of education of the clergy; there was the unbounded growth of popular, unofficial religious practices that bordered on superstition. The reforms did not come. In this atmosphere, Martin Luther came on the stage of history, not as an outsider to the church. He had been a Catholic priest, a doctor trained by the church, a man of long experience in strict monastic discipline. His personal struggles for the assurance of salvation were resolved when he found for himself the biblical meaning of "justification by faith alone." The personal coincided with the historical condition of the church. He provided a forceful leadership to the German movement which led to the establishment of an independent church. Other Protestant leaders followed. They generally acknowledged their debt and their gratitude to Luther. (This is eminently true of Calvin, even though his environment in Geneva, his personality, and his leadership differed from those of Luther.) The Catholic Church then reacted to the shock by its own extensive reforms symbolized by the work of the Council of Trent and of the Society of Jesus. These came too late to save the formal unity of the Western Church.

There were periods of good will and there were hopes of union, but only in our time can we see the coming of a large-scale mutual appreciation, or at least understanding. In the meantime the differences of religious outlook have been encrusted with cultural traditions and self-identities that make close cooperation more difficult.

The historic distinctions among the churches are many, e.g., did this church develop in a strict organizational pattern or a loose one? What emphasis does it have in its self-image: is it mainly the place where God's word of forgiveness and justification is proclaimed? Is it primarily the body that mediates grace through liturgy and the sacraments? Or does it see its principal task as the pastoral one, and as the implementation of divine rule on earth? These are just a few guiding lines along which the historic churches could be characterized. But before we sketch some examples of such churches, we should be mindful of their common ideal and their common profession of unity.

The unity of the churches is given by the commonly quoted definition of the church as *one, holy, catholic,* and *apostolic.* As Christ is one, so the church, which is his "body" and the continuation of his life on earth, is one. Its holiness does not consist in moral perfection of all its members, not even of the hierarchy, but in its origin from Christ and its life through the Holy Spirit. The catholicity described its image in time and space: it includes all Christians who from the beginning of the world to its end shall have existed, anywhere in the world. But it also refers to the universality of appeal: the church's capacity to meet the spiritual needs of all the varied kinds of people from different cultures of the world. Finally, it is said to be apostolic, i.e., standing in uninterrupted continuity of its teachers and pastors with the apostles.

These four marks of the church were specified in the Confession of Faith at the Council of Constantinople in A.D. 381. The Council is considered valid, and these marks true, by all the traditional churches, Eastern Orthodox, Roman Catholic, and Protestant.

Eastern Orthodox churches have a hierarchy continuous with the apostles ("apostolic succession") whose main function is to offer the "divine liturgy." In the liturgy is realized the mystical communion of love on the part of all members of Christ's body. Only in this union of the whole mystical body can the Christian Truth be perceived and salvation attained. Insofar as emphasis is concerned, Eastern Orthodox bishops and priests are not the pastors and rulers in the sense of the Roman Catholic bishops, nor the preachers on the pattern of the Protestant minister. The sacramental and liturgical function expresses their task best. In harmony with the belief that in Christ God became man in order that men may become divine, the liturgy may contain such statements as this: "As we stand in the house of Thy glory, it is as though we stood in heaven itself."

The Orthodox churches have a rich body of Christian theology and teachings, and recognize the first seven ecumenical councils as particularly binding. But they have no single teaching authority which would interpret past tradition to the living generation with the decisiveness of papal proclamation. The truth is contained in the church as a whole, hierarchy and laity together. For practical purposes, of course, catechisms are used, and in controversial matters the hierarchy—particularly the Patriarch—has authority within the region; the Patriarch of Constantinople makes decisions for Greece and the Patriarch of Moscow for Russia.

The Orthodox churches regard themselves as the true church, the one, holy, catholic, and apostolic church that is professed in the creed. They do work with other churches on common tasks, and have sent delegates to various worldwide (ecumenical) Christian conferences and councils.

The Anglican Communion in some respects is similar to the Orthodox churches. It too relies heavily on the rich traditions of the past, and it has no single supreme teaching office similar to the papacy. The churches of the Anglican Communion, like the Orthodox churches, are national churches, not bound together by any central legislative or executive authority. They do share mutual loyalty, and look for direction to Bishops in Conference. The Archbishop of Canterbury traditionally enjoys special prestige and a representative role. These churches, too, pride themselves in holding the catholic and apostolic faith. Their standards are contained in the Book of Common Prayer.

Due to the historical circumstances under which the Anglican Church came into being, these churches share a special distinguishing feature. They have much in common with both the Catholic and the Protestant churches. Their worship is akin to the Eastern Orthodox and the Roman Catholic, and their teachings, especially as they are set forth in the Thirty-Nine Articles, have close affinity to the Reformation churches. Therefore we find here a comprehensive view of the Christian tradition which includes very different types of church concepts and practices, each useful in its own way, none to be excluded, as long as they stand on biblical and apostolic foundations. These features have made the Anglican Communion eminently suitable to stand, as it indeed has stood, in the midst of the movement for mutual understanding of the many Christian churches. It has provided active and vigorous leadership in the ecumenical movement of the twentieth century.

The Roman Catholic Church, which for a long time represented Western Europe's religion and much of its culture, fully accepts for itself the definition "one, holy, catholic, apostolic, Roman church." Later in this chapter we shall have occasion to elaborate on its self-image as the "mystical body of Christ." As the two natures, the divine and the human, were united in Christ, so in the church is effected the union of the sacred and the secular, the divine and the human. It refers to the militant (fighting) church on earth, the suffering church in purgatory, and the victorious (triumphant) church in heaven. The Roman Catholic Church has a strong sense of organization, hierarchy, law and order, defined in its voluminous "canon law." It is very emphatic in its religious instruction, both through parochial schools and through its code of ethics, rules of conduct, marriage, and so forth. Its teaching office (doctrine and ethics) is concentrated in the hands of the Pope.

One of the outstanding features of the Roman Catholic Church is its worldwide unified organization. Centered in the office of the Pope, whose work is prepared by committees of cardinals, the church keeps international relations through papal nuncios, representatives of the church at various governments, and through close relations of the papacy with the bishops of the various parts of the globe. Its unity of liturgical language—Latin—is an aspect of its unified government and worship. It is only in our time that the Second Vatican Council has aimed at a degree of decentralization: the government of the church is to be shared between the Pope and the bishops, and the various languages of the people may be used in the worship next to Latin.

Traditionally, by characteristic emphasis, the Roman Catholic Church has assumed its functions to be to carry saving grace to the world through the priestly powers, to teach the true doctrine, and, not the least, to rule and govern. It believes that Christ himself established on earth this society, the "perfect society" to continue for all ages to come, governed by the bishops and especially by the Pope as the chief and unerring teacher of truth to whom Christ gave the keys of the Kingdom of Heaven.

Protestant churches, too, like to refer to themselves as members of the one universal church. Since their variety is very great (some distinguish churches, denominations, and sects), it is not surprising that an old historic Protestant church may feel that it has more in common with the Roman Catholic Church than with another, quite different, Protestant church. The aim here, therefore, is not to survey all the varieties, but rather to give some basic statement which will serve as orientation and a point of reference.[2]

Some of the special characteristics and emphases that distinguish the Protestant churches from the Orthodox, Roman Catholic, and Anglican patterns are these:

1. The measure of all important matters relating to salvation and basic doctrine is the Bible. Tradition, even local tradition, does develop in practice in almost all churches, but it should not be equal in importance to the biblical authority. In fact, tradition is frequently suspected as arbitrary, and such Roman Catholic dogmas as papal infallibility or the assumption of Virgin Mary have come under much criticism from Protestants on the ground that they are purely an outgrowth of tradition.

2. Form of church organization and administration of a Protestant church is not of its religious essence. "Church polity," as it is often called, may be historically firmly established, and even sometimes gives the church its name (e.g., the Congregational, the

---

[2] Surveys of varieties and characteristics of the many Protestant churches are available in church histories, encyclopaedias, and such works as Frank Mead's *Handbook of Denominations of the United States,* Abingdon Press, 1951.

Presbyterian churches). There are indeed instances when a Protestant church speaks of "the order which our Lord Jesus Christ has established" (The Gallican Confession), but most Protestant churches tend to agree that the Roman Catholic insistence on the exclusive divine origin of its particular hierarchical institution and of the papacy is hindrance to Protestant-Catholic conversations, because it sets up a particular order as of the essence of the church.

3. Apostolic succession, which was of the essential nature of the churches discussed above, and was generally applied to the bishops, carries much less weight with Protestant churches. Some will argue that it applies to all the faithful, and not just to the bishops; some churches will not bother with the term. And even where—as in some Lutheran churches—there are bishops with "valid orders" in the apostolic succession, the episcopal order is not stressed as being an essential mark of the church.

4. Protestant churches use the word "minister" rather than "priest," and with a reason. They tend to agree that the primary function of the church is not to mediate sacramental grace, but to make known God's acts and promises in Christ, and to kindle vital belief. Consequently, preaching is the focal point of the service, and the preaching is done by one whom Luther referred to as *minister verbi divini,* or "servant of the word of God." Priests, on the other hand, from ancient times have been associated with the temple and with the act of sacrifice, and therefore are more appropriate to churches that celebrate divine liturgy or the Mass. One favorite Lutheran definition of the church is: "the congregation of saints in which the Gospel is purely taught and the sacraments are rightly administered" (The Formula of Concord).

In the broad spectrum of the Protestant churches, the Lutherans have preserved most of the old, traditional liturgy, vestments, and continuity with the medieval church. One may say in this sense that they are the most conservative. The "Reformed" churches, which generally follow the Calvinist pattern originating in Geneva, have been freer to break with medieval traditions. They are also known for their *discipline* of the lives of their members, their way of showing Christ's rule in the church, and the need to keep high standards of purity in the church. Both the Lutheran and the Reformed churches go back to that type of reformation in the sixteenth century which was supported by established governments (kings, princes, or city councils). Therefore that reformation was dubbed "magisterial." But there is another pattern of Protestantism, in which each local congregation is a completely self-governing body, in organization, and sometimes also in doctrine and practice. This pattern derives originally from the so-called "radical reformation" of the sixteenth century.

These Anabaptists, or Brethren, as they preferred to call themselves, were called "re-baptizers" on account of their common insistence on believers' baptism. In their conviction, one must first hear the Gospel, then accept it in faith, and only then be baptized. The stress on personal conviction and individual experience made for *free association of believers*. To them, the customary state churches were anomalies and contradictions, since they assumed that all citizens automatically, by infant baptism, were Christians. Even worse, these state churches made use of government power to persecute other Christians and to put them to death, just because of some doctrinal or practical difference. The Brethren attributed this "fall of the church" to the compromise the church made in the time of Emperor Constantine, when it emerged from persecution into the favor of and support by the Roman state. They envisaged themselves as the restorers of the original, "primitive" church that stood apart from the "world." In their desire for perfection and in their earnest devotion, they also saw themselves as the "church of the martyrs." Indeed, most of the early leaders of the Anabaptists were killed because of their convictions and their way of life.[3]

[3] For a good study of this important subject, see Franklin Littell, *Anabaptist View of the Church*, The American Society of Church History, 1952; or the comprehensive work of George Huntston Williams, *The Radical Reformation*, Westminster, 1962. Among the many early documents now available, e.g., Peter Rideman's *Account of Our Religion*, Hodder and Stoughton, 1950.

Modern free churches do not always follow the martyr ideal, and some have assimilated themselves fully to modern society. But they still lay emphasis on the free association of believers, personal conviction, and congregational autonomy. The Congregational, Baptist, Methodist, Quaker, and other churches, are not as directly in historical line of the Anabaptists as are Mennonites or Hutterites, but they have cultivated the same ideal, have defended religious liberty, and in their various individual ways have influenced American life. Some, like the Quakers, became pioneers in international understanding and in social justice. They have in common with the Brethren the ideal of nonviolence and religious pacifism. Other churches have stressed freedom, separation of church and state, or the special mark of sixteenth-century Anabaptists, the very strong sense of missions.

THE FUNCTIONS OF THE CHURCH

The early church expected Christ's return in the immediate future. Its proper task then was to prepare for His triumphal coming that would signify His victory over the evil age and usher in a new era of relation between men and their God. The urgency of the apostles at Pentecost, or of St. Paul in his missions, was great. As the immediate return of Christ was postponed, the church began to concentrate on the slow task of long-range preparation in the effort to subdue the world to Christ and to make Him known to all corners of the world. It became truly the "church militant," waging a war on the powers of evil that dominated this world, and missions have been part of its vital function.

Another important example of the church's functions is the establishment in the world of a nucleus of a new society in which Christ already rules. In practice it is not a perfect society, insofar as in it are the strong and the weak, those who live by their faith, those who are learning to, and those who just manage to hang by the fringes. But it is a society different from all other human societies by its origin, by its motivations, and by its aims. Human relations within it, too, are different. "The church should be the place where barriers of race, nationality, class, sex, and education are done away; where the underprivileged, the down-trodden, the outcast, and the despised find a welcome and feel themselves at home; a meeting-ground where those who are divided in questions of politics and economics can realize afresh their unity in loyalty to a common Lord."[4]

This close community of spiritual sharing has often expressed itself in history through economic sharing as well. The New Testament briefly records that the first church engaged in some distributive sharing of goods. This did not mean a system of economic planning or production but simply indicated that where the community was motivated by divine love, and all things belonged to God, selfishness and greed were overcome and no one went hungry. Again in the second century, Justin Martyr wrote: "The rich among us come to the aid of the poor, and we always stay together. . . . Those who are prosperous, if they wish, contribute what each one deems appropriate; and the collection is deposited with the president; and he takes care of the orphans and widows, and those who are needy because of sickness or other cause, and the captives, and the strangers who sojourn amongst us."[5]

The monasteries of the Middle Ages and up to the present have tried to imitate the early church in this feature, and sometimes have gone much further, into productive community of planned labor where all private property is eliminated. Some important theologians, on the other hand, have stated that private property was intended for men by God. Regardless of this issue, the social

[4] W. A. Visser't Hooft and J. H. Oldham, *The Church and its Function in Society,* Allen and Unwin, 1937, chap. VII, p. 161.

[5] *The First Apology of Justin Martyr,* 65, as translated in *Liturgies of the Western Church,* selected and introduced by Bard Thompson, Living Age Books, World Publishing, 1961, p. 9.

responsibility of the church has always been one of its strong characteristics, and its extensive social work further testimony to its inner life. One might venture to argue that much of the social progress of the Western civilization has been inspired by this sense of social responsibility.

WORSHIP

There is little doubt that in addition to the church's mission to the world, and in addition to its common life, its common worship is one of its oldest and most important characteristics.

All Christian churches claim to derive their forms of worship from the Bible. Indeed, it is possible to reconstruct some fragmentary picture of the earliest church and its worship from biblical records. But the very fact that such a wide variety of historic churches has claimed the same origin and authority testifies to the incompleteness of that image and to the possibility of many interpretations.

The churches, whether they are said to have begun with the Incarnation, the Crucifixion, or the Pentecost—gradually developed their forms of worship in the languages of the people of the region. These forms of worship, or liturgies, in time assumed different variations in different areas. For instance, there came into being the Roman liturgy, the Gallic liturgy, and the Mozarabic liturgy.

The churches of the eastern Mediterranean provinces tended to develop wonderfully rich, long liturgies that were changeless, celebrated as if in the very presence of heaven. The Western liturgies introduced more of the variable elements, in order to exhibit in their worship the appropriate season of the so-called "church year." The church year, or the liturgical year, divided the calendar year into holy cycles and seasons marking the life of Jesus Christ in his incarnation, birth, passion (suffering), death, resurrection, and the descent of the Holy Spirit on the apostles gathered at Pentecost. It also integrated the feasts or holy days celebrated by the church.[6]

An example of a very early order of Christian worship comes to us from about A.D. 155. It is described in the *First Apology of Justin Martyr*. Justin tells how on Sunday the members of the church gathered in one place, and listened to a reading from the memoirs of the apostles and the writings of the prophets, and to an admonition by the leader (president) of the church, which amounted to something like a sermon or a moral exhortation. Then all stood up together to pray.

Our prayers being ended, we greet one another with a kiss. Then bread and a cup of water mingled with wine are presented to the president of the brethren. Taking them he sends up praise and glory to the Father of all through the name of the Son and Holy Spirit, and offers thanksgiving at some length that we have been deemed worthy to receive these things at His hand. When he has finished the prayers and the thanksgiving, all the people present shout their assent, saying "Amen." When the president has given thanks, and all the people have assented, those whom we call deacons give to each one present a portion of the "eucharistized" bread and wine-with-water; and they carry it also to those who are absent.

We call this food the Eucharist, of which no one is allowed to partake except he is convinced of the truth of our teaching and has received the washing for the forgiveness of his sins and for his regeneration, and so lives as Christ has taught us.[7]

Historical growth of liturgies tended to widely separate the churches. Each would take what was closest to its own heart. From such a document as Justin's account, the Catholic is likely to stress

[6] The study of liturgies is the subject of a separate science, the liturgics. The student will find it helpful to become acquainted with some of the forms of worship, perhaps by acquaintance with local churches and their worship, or by study of examples. One handy collection of various historic liturgies, Catholic and Protestant, with excellent introductions, is available in the paperback book, Thompson, *op. cit.*

[7] Justin Martyr, *op. cit.*, p. 8.

the emerging form of the Mass, underline the difference in the early church between the liturgy of the catechumens (those who were preparing to become Christians) and the liturgy of the faithful (the baptized, who alone would be present at the Eucharist). He would also stress the consecration of the elements of bread and wine, and such symbolic and traditional practice as the mixing of wine with water. On the other hand, the Protestant would be mindful of the fact that the early church gave both bread and wine to all communicants, that "the ministry of the Word," and particularly the sermon, was a very ancient form of the liturgy, that the worship was in the language of the people, that the early church's discipline excluded the unworthy members from communion, and perhaps, comparing the later Protestant service such as John Wesley's, would be reminded that the early church used a free, extemporaneous prayer (Justin wrote that the president of the brethren prayed "according to his ability").

The Catholic Mass, the name applied to the Eucharist by the fifth century A.D., will tend to become formalized, will be celebrated in Latin throughout the world, and will focus upon the sacrifice of the altar, "the sacrifice of the true body and blood of Christ." The Protestant worship services, too, will retain definite historic sequences of the order of worship. (The similarity between the Roman Catholic Mass and the Lutheran liturgy has often been noted.) This may be ascribed to the fact that Luther, Zwingli, and Bucer (from whom Calvin learned in Strasbourg) were Catholic priests before becoming Protestant reformers. On the other hand, Protestant services showed radical differences. They abolished the concept of sacrifice of Christ on the altar by the priest, centered the whole worship around the sermon (the preaching of the "Word of God"), and used the language of the people throughout. Calvin, who had no priestly ordination, was freest in denunciation of the Mass with such epithets as "magic" and "idolatrous." The Anabaptists went even further in their complete disassociation from the Catholic liturgical tradition by such pointed barbs as "Christ didn't say to his disciples: go forth and celebrate the Mass, but go forth and preach the Gospel."

All this points to the twentieth-century problems of the divided churches which nevertheless profess their belief in only one church. Can the churches come back together? We have witnessed some signs in that direction. In our time, the Catholic Church has made possible the use of the vernacular in worship, next to Latin. Also, it has furthered more active participation of laymen in the worship service (a matter of historic pride among Protestants). The Protestant churches again have become aware of liturgical tradition and of the meaning of symbolism as they had not been since the days of Luther. In such a large movement as the liturgical revival, there are of course less successful explorations side by side with the genuine ones, and we sometimes find liturgical trimmings motivated only by a vague desire for "something beautiful," or simply liturgical antiquarianism, without any real significance for the life of the congregation. But the approach from both sides has been in the direction of mutual appreciation. Nevertheless, the roots of liturgical separation run very deep, concern basic doctrines, and the whole image of the church.

Before we exemplify some deep liturgical differences, a note on an interesting phenomenon of our day: one place where all the churches seem to vie to outdo each other in the same effort, is the architecture of the churches within which their worship takes place. In the twentieth century, the Eastern Orthodox, Roman Catholic, and Protestant churches have all provided us with examples of freely creative, radically modern designs, and, curiously, they have often employed architects of quite different religious backgrounds than their own. To mind come such examples as Frank Lloyd Wright's Orthodox Church in Milwaukee, Wisconsin, Le Corbusier's pilgrimage chapel at Ronchamp (eastern France), Eero Saarinen's interfaith chapel at M.I.T., and Aalto's Lutheran church at Imatra.

What does this mean? How does the outward shell relate to the spirit, tradition, and worship of the congregations within? There is no easy answer, but it is one of the interesting subjects for the student to investigate.

THE SACRAMENTS

Finally, no discussion of the functions of the church would do without a word about sacraments, which are among its most intimate religious practices. Therefore, they have been the most jealously guarded. By the same token, the teaching of the sacraments has divided the churches, often by hairline distinctions, with the resulting bitter feuds over subjects that should have unified all Christians. The history of sacramental controversies sadly exhibits too much zeal and too little charity. The Catholics rejected the Protestant sacramental doctrines, the Lutherans rejected the Zwinglians, and everybody burned or drowned the Anabaptists for their practice of baptizing adults who had been baptized in infancy (the so-called "re-baptizing").

We shall not attempt any complete survey of the various positions of the churches, or all their definitions of the sacraments. A general introduction and a few examples will have to suffice.

The Latin word *sacramentum* referred to a sacred oath, such as the oath of allegiance required of an army. The churches disagree on the question of how many sacraments Christ actually instituted. Therefore the number, too, has been in question. St. Augustine applied the term to the Creed, among other things. Hugh of St. Victor, a medieval theologian, enumerated as many as 30 sacraments. The tradition of seven sacraments does appear in earlier writers, but came to be uniformly taught from the time of Peter Lombard in the twelfth century. The Eastern Orthodox churches, the Roman Catholic Church, and a few others recognize seven sacraments. A standard feature of most Protestant churches is their acceptance of only two, the Lord's Supper and Baptism.

Definitions of a sacrament by theologians take such forms as these: "visible form of invisible grace," "visible sign of a sacred thing that sanctifies men," or "testimony of the grace of God toward us, confirmed by an outward sign, with a reciprocal testimony of our piety toward him." More liberal Christians will refer to them primarily as symbols of human devout intention or resolution. Orthodox Christians will stress that aspect of the sacrament which *does something*. What does it do? It conveys grace (sacraments have been referred to as the "channels of grace"). Grace again is understood as the power that makes men grow more Godlike, and makes their will conform freely to God's will.

One of the classic summaries of the Catholic meaning of the seven sacraments comes from the Council of Florence of the fifteenth century:

There are seven sacraments under the new law: that is to say, baptism, confirmation, the Mass, penance, extreme unction, ordination, and matrimony. . . . The first five sacraments are intended to secure the spiritual perfection of every man individually; the two last are ordained for the governance and increase of the Church. For through baptism we are born again of the spirit; through confirmation we grow in grace and are strengthened in the faith; and when we have been born again and strengthened we are fed by the divine food of the Mass; but if, through sin, we bring sickness upon our souls, we are made spiritually whole by penance; and by extreme unction we are healed, both spiritually and corporeally, according as our souls have need; by ordination the Church is governed and multiplied spiritually; by matrimony it is materially increased.

Beyond this, the Council's statement becomes more technical, specifying which sacraments may be administered only by the bishop, which by the priest, and which, if necessary, even by a layman. It insists on mixing the wine of the holy communion with water, not only by reason of biblical quotations, but also because of mystical symbolism, because "the mixing of water with the wine fitly signifies the efficacy of this sacrament, namely, the union of Christian people with Christ. . . ."[8]

Typical of some Protestant positions would be such statement as Calvin's: "Baptism is a sign of initiation, by which we are admitted into the society of the Church, in order that, being incorporated into Christ, we may be numbered among the children of God." And on the Lord's Supper: God "undertakes to sustain and nourish us as long as we live. . . . For this purpose, therefore, by the hand of His only begotten Son, He has favoured His Church with another sacrament, a spiritual banquet, in which Christ testifies Himself to be the bread of life, to feed our souls for a true and blessed immortality."[9]

Since Protestantism traditionally stresses the preaching and the biblical message as a corrective to any possible abuse of sacraments, the following quotation from Samuel Terrien is quite characteristic of the Protestant heritage:

The sacrament of the Word assumes a dual form: the celebration of the Eucharist and the reading of Scripture. Without God's presence sacramentally offered in the Eucharist, the Bible contains only the word of an absent God. Without the Bible, the Eucharist offers a Word-less presence that soon risks degenerating into the well-known perversions of Christendom: pantheistic mysticism, sentimental quietism, merit ritualism, spiritual mercantilism, social-club activism.[10]

If the togetherness of the Word and the Sacrament in this statement is typically Protestant, so are the warnings against abuse and "spiritual mercantilism." On the other hand, the use of the term "Eucharist" in place of the more common "Lord's Supper"

[8] James Harvey Robinson, *Readings in European History,* Ginn, 1904, Vol. I, pp. 348 f.

[9] John Calvin, *Institutes of the Christian Religion,* translated by John Allen, Presbyterian Board of Christian Education, Seventh American Edition (no date), Vol. II, pp. 583, 641.

[10] Samuel Terrien, *The Bible and the Church, An Approach to Scripture,* The Westminster Press, 1962, p. 80. Copyright by W. L. Jenkins.

shows that this well-known minister and teacher has bowed in the direction of ecumenical understanding.

It is worthwhile to emphasize the social significance of the sacraments. Sacraments clearly exhibit the power of religion to transform the mundane, everyday life of man into a life of dignity and noble purpose. From birth to death, through marriage, work, sickness, sadness, and joy, it may be either a life on the level of animal existence that one lives, or a life transformed by a glow of holiness.

In the highly sacramental churches, new significance is given to human life at infancy by the sacrament of Baptism, which is accompanied by ceremonial blessings, exorcisms, and anointings. This significance continues by the additional sacraments which will attend the crucial stages and events of man's life. Marriage, for instance, is a contract made by the man and the woman. But the church, through its ritual (the priest's blessing of the ring, the mass for the bride and groom, etc.) lifts the occasion out of mere animal and economic coexistence into the realm of the dignified and the holy. Holy Unction is performed to heal body and soul, while the sacrament of Penance is here to reunite the sinner with his God and to incorporate him again into the communion of his fellowmen. For the lonely moments of dying the churches have always had their consolation and their strong assurance of spiritual communion in heaven as on earth. A whole literature has grown since the Middle Ages on counselling at the deathbed. This, together with the funeral rites, again lift the occasion from its purely biological, statistical, or psychological significance into a situation of sharing within the larger scope of supernatural life. In addition to the major sacraments, for these churches also minor religious acts known as sacramentals, and the various "aids to piety" endow the round of daily life with a light of holiness.

In Protestant churches, the limitation on the number of sacraments, and also the absence of sacramentals, would seem to limit the extent of supernatural participation. In reality, Protestant churches express it just as strongly, if less formally, in their own ways. Their emphasis on lay participation in the church's active life, their doctrine of priesthood of all believers, and their concept of vocation (the belief that all decent human occupations may be performed as tasks given by God, and for the service of men), all tend toward the same end.

Elton Trueblood, in his book *The Common Ventures of Life,* has shown well the sacramental sense of life that is often acknowledged by a Protestant Christian. He suggests that the material can become the vehicle of the spiritual, and the two levels are intertwined, just as "the Word became flesh," and man is both body and spirit.

A vigorous religion will deal more with the home than with the church and more with the workbench than with the altar. . . . The opening of a new home may be glorified by a special ceremony appropriate to the occasion. The dreams and efforts of a family, long anticipating its own home, deserve such recognition. A deed is often a sacred document representing countless hours of toil and saving. There is no worthy phase of human conduct that could not, with equal appropriateness, be brought under the canopy of the spiritual fellowship, for all real achievements of men deserve to be celebrated as occasions for thanksgiving.[11]

As people are born, love, marry, found their homes, engage in their various occupations, lose their loved ones, and generally go through life's trials, triumphs, and tragedies, their community is interested in them as its members. They are a source of its strength or its burden, its shame or glory. And all these acts and moments of life are given sacramental significance when they are brought into the perspective of the grace of God working in human lives.

[11] Elton Trueblood, *The Common Ventures of Life,* Harper & Row, 1949, pp. 26, 30.

THE ECUMENICAL IDEAL AND
SOME PROBLEMS IN ITS WAY

The word "ecumenical" comes from the Greek work *oikumene* which means *the inhabited earth,* and it refers to the worldwide unity of the Christian Church. The ancient councils of the Christian Church, beginning with Nicaea in 325, which are honored as authoritative by all the old historic churches, are called ecumenical councils. In our time, the Roman Catholic Church has its Second Vatican Council which it calls ecumenical. It is therefore good to specify what we mean when we use the designation. Here we shall deal with the ecumenical movement of the twentieth century, organized by a number of Protestant churches and the Anglican Communion, with some participation of Eastern Orthodox churches.

This ecumenical movement began with the conferences on world missions (Edinburgh 1910) and continued under the sponsorship of the International Missionary Council in numerous meetings. The mission field is the logical place for the cooperation of various churches to start. The shame of divided Christendom, to which at home we have become accustomed, is felt afresh when the churches come before non-Christian people, competing with each other and criticizing each other abroad. There had been conferences on Christian life and work (Stockholm, Sweden, 1925, and Oxford, England, 1937) and conferences on faith and order (Lausanne, Switzerland, 1927, Edinburgh, Scotland, and 1937, Lund, Sweden, 1952). The more recent leadership of the World Council of Churches has brought together representatives of many churches at Amsterdam in the Netherlands (1948), at Evanston, Illinois, in 1954 and at New Delhi, India, in 1961. Delegates to the New Delhi meetings represented 197 churches in 60 nations.

The ecumenical ideal, as formulated by its active proponents, is the one holy universal church, the fellowship of Christians who acknowledge one Lord. It also relates to the task of the whole church to bring the gospel to the whole world.

The ecumenical movement has had a realistic perspective. We had seen earlier that the diversity of beliefs, constitutions, and practices of the various churches is so great that any movement demanding formal union of even a fair number of the churches in our time would be Utopian. Visser't Hooft, the longtime general secretary of the World Council of Churches, has written:

It is a grave mistake to suppose that the ultimate goal of ecumenism is a monolithic centralized church structure for the whole world. The churches in the World Council have expressly repudiated such a conception. Manifest unity is perfectly compatible with variety, independence, and decentralization. The New Testament Church had remarkable variety and was in no sense a super-church, but it manifested to all who had eyes to see that the People of God were one single family.[12]

The first practical step, as in other divisions among men, is to bring the parties together into serious conversation. If the churches can get to know each other, explain each other's point of view, and listen to each other's objections, an important step has been made. The problem is not primarily one of compromise. The differences that are really important must stand out clearly and be seen. But the common ground and common loyalty to Jesus Christ also must be affirmed.

There are Protestant churches that for their own reasons would not participate in such a movement. Some are sharply critical of the World Council of Churches. The Roman Catholic Church has not officially participated, but has sometimes sent observers to the ecumenical conferences. We are again hitting at interchurch problems, and they are very real. Let us examine a few selected problems in the concept of the church, which make Protestant-Catholic

[12] Quoted in Marvin Halverson (ed.), *Handbook of Christian Theology,* Meridian, 1958, pp. 94 f.

understanding difficult even in these days marked by the spirit of appeasement.

The first of these examples deals with the concept of the priest. The problem goes back to the Reformation, and a fighting document from the hand of Martin Luther. In 1520, in his *Appeal to the Ruling Class of German Nationality* . . . Luther wrote:

To call popes, bishops, priests, monks, and nuns, the religious class, but princes, lords, artizans, and farm-workers the secular class, is a specious device invented by certain timeservers. . . . All Christians whatsoever really and truly belong to the religious class, and there is no difference among them except in so far as they do different work.

Suppose a small group of earnest Christian laymen were taken prisoner and settled in the middle of a desert without any episcopally ordained priest among them; and they then agreed to choose one of themselves, whether married or not, and endow him with the office of baptizing, administering the sacrament, pronouncing absolution, and preaching; that man would be as truly a priest as if he had been ordained by all the bishops and the popes.

When a bishop consecrates, he simply acts on behalf of the entire congregation, all of whom have the same authority.

The fact is that our baptism consecrates us all without exception, and makes us all priests. . . . The status of a priest among Christians is merely that of an office-bearer. . . . Yet the Romanists have devised the claim to *characteres indelebiles* and assert that a priest, even if deposed, is different from a mere layman. They even hold the illusion that a priest can never be anything else than a priest, and therefore never a layman again. All these are human inventions and regulations.[13]

Luther had been a Catholic priest and a monk for many years when he made this proclamation of the priesthood of all believers. In those days it appeared to strike at the very root of the concept of the church, which had a very special privileged status in all European states, legally and socially. The idea was taken for granted by everyone that the church was sharply divided between

[13] "An Appeal to the Ruling Class of German Nationality," in *The Reformation Writings of Martin Luther,* Vol. I, *The Basis of the Protestant Reformation,* translated and edited by Bertram Lee Woolf, Lutterworth Press, 1953, pp. 109ff.

the hierarchy and the laymen, and that priests had a special quality of holiness given to them by the sacrament of Holy Orders. When Luther charged that all the claims of the clergy to special status were not theologically valid and were a hoax invented to protect their worldly power and interests, it seemed indeed a revolutionary move.

Catholic theologians readily recognized the severity of the issue and its radical consequences. The Council of Trent, which began its meetings at the end of Luther's life, was unmistakable in its answer: "If anyone shall say that the New Testament does not provide for a distinct, visible priesthood, let him be anathema. If anyone says that all Christians have power to administer the word and all the sacraments, let him be anathema. And if anyone affirms that all Christians indiscriminately are priests of the New Testament, he clearly does nothing but confound the ecclesiastical hierarchy."[14] To the present day this rather technical issue is a difficult barrier to tear down. The Protestant minister has no separate sacredness on his person, no indelible character, no unique sacramental powers. He is one of the members of the congregation set aside by ordination for his special task and trained for the function of interpreting to the congregation its own faith, and of performing such functions as the church requires.

Another example of a difficult issue, and one that is bound to come up in every bull session of people discussing Protestant-Catholic issues, is the papacy. Protestants have always felt negatively on this subject for various historical reasons. Popularly, the myth still persists that Protestantism originated because the popes were immoral and greedy. Theologically, the main problem is the biblical authority for such an office. The key passage on the subject is in the Gospel according to Matthew, chapter 16. Jesus asks Peter who he thinks that he is, and Peter professes: "You are Christ, son of the living God." Upon which Jesus says: "You are Peter, and on this rock I shall build my church. . . ." Some Protestants have argued that Jesus never said it, that it was a later addition to the

[14] *Canons of the Council of Trent,* 23rd Session, chap. IV, Canons I and X.

text. But this is inconclusive. Others interpret the words of Jesus as meaning: On this profession of faith—namely, that I am the Christ—I will build my church. Thus they bypass Peter. There are other arguments, all aiming to undercut the opinion that Peter was "the prince of the apostles." Part of the title of the Pope is "successor of blessed Peter, prince of the apostles." Protestant thinking has always rejected the thought that Christ granted the successors of Peter any special office or authority over the others. Most Protestants are inclined to feel that all Christians are the successors of the apostles and of the original church, so that no special claim can be made by the hierarchy, and none by the popes.

Priestly office, the hierarchy, and the papacy are of the essence of the Roman Catholic Church, and therefore are not negotiable. But in the valiant effort at meeting the Protestant churches as far as possible, the Second Vatican Council has changed the emphasis. Not domination, rule, or power, but service is the featured characteristic of priestly, episcopal, and papal ministry. Under the leadership of Belgium's Cardinal Suenens, there has been prominent discussion of the whole church, the laymen together with the hierarchy, as "the people of God," and one receives the distinct impression that the role of the laymen is being spotlighted.

If it is true that the hierarchy, in certain respects, takes precedence over the faithful, since the faithful are brought by it to faith and to supernatural life, it remains no less true that pastors and faithful alike belong to the one people of God. The thought of God is directed to His people and its salvation; in regard to this end, the hierarchy is but a means . . . What now first catches our eye is this community of those who are baptized, who are all made one by the same baptism . . . The mission of giving Christ to the world falls on the entire Christian people, at every level. The Holy Spirit is not given only to the pastors of the flock but to all Christians without exception. In baptism, the sacrament of faith, all Christians receive the Holy Spirit.[15]

[15] Leon-Joseph Cardinal Suenens, "The Council and Church Unity," in *Criterion*, a publication of the Divinity School of the University of Chicago, Vol. 3, No. 2 (Spring 1964).

The attitude here expressed, the unprecedented honors and recognition given to Protestant churchmen invited to the Second Vatican Council, the solicitation of their opinions and reactions, and practical cooperation of the churches in the mission field make it plain that ecumenical conversations are serious and the concept of the hierarchy is not keeping the churches from engaging in a sincere encounter.

On the other hand, no amount of politeness and good will is going to erase the fundamental differences out of existence. Among the barriers which still divide these churches, in the opinion of this writer there are none which are as difficult as the following one. This will be our last example.

Ecclesia—Maria

In June of 1943, Pope Piux XII affixed his signature to an encyclical letter *On the Mystical Body of Christ*. In it he stressed the corporate image of the church: "When one member suffers, all other members share its pain, and the healthy members come to the assistance of those ailing; so in the Church the individual members do not live for themselves alone, but also help their fellows, and all work in mutual collaboration for their common comfort and for the more perfect building up of the whole Body." This image presupposes more than an organizational and a moral union. Beyond the association of individuals for a common purpose, it is of supernatural order, is inspired by the Spirit of Christ and held together by "a distinct internal principle which exists effectively in the whole and in each of its parts."

This corporate image is further strengthened by the image of the church as mother of Christians. "The loving Mother is spotless in the Sacraments, by which she gives birth to her children and nourishes them, who is spotless in the faith, which she has preserved inviolate always, in her sacred laws imposed on all, in the evangelical counsels which she recommends, in those heavenly gifts and extraordinary graces through which, with inexhaustible fecundity, she generates hosts of martyrs, virgins and confessors."

The organic image of the church as a body is biblical, and is often expanded by further similes, e.g., the vine and the branches, which provides one of the oldest visual representations in Christian art. The concept of the church as mother is also very old and very standard. (Luther and Calvin both used it meaningfully, in line with many Catholic and Orthodox theologians.)

But the papal encyclical labors this image of the glorious mother church who "came forth from the side of the second Adam in His sleep on the Cross . . . like a new Eve, mother of all the living," until the church in the papal letter flowers out into the image of the Virgin Mother of God who "in the name of the whole human race gave her consent for a spiritual marriage between the Son of God and human nature." In this superimposition of the two images, that of the church and that of Mary, the encyclical works towards its conclusion: "Free from all sin, original and personal, always most intimately united with her Son, as another Eve she offered Him on Golgotha to the Eternal Father for all the children of Adam. . . . Thus she who corporally was the mother of our Head, . . . became spiritually the mother of all His members. She it was who through her powerful prayers obtained the grace that the Spirit of our divine Redeemer, already given to the Church on the Cross, should be bestowed through miraculous gifts on the newly founded Hierarchy on Pentecost." Thus Mary not only sacrificed Christ on Golgotha, but also was responsible for the Pentecost, and thus for the coming of the church into the world.

Protestants, who have by traditional suspicion of Catholic Marian devotion hardened themselves on this subject, have great difficulty appreciating this kind of language. The question remains whether perhaps there is something fundamentally wrong here. The brilliant Jesuit writer Father Walter J. Ong is one of those who say that the fault is with the Protestant churches. In 1951 he wrote an article in which he argued that all Protestant difficulties in grasping the nature of the church go back to the refusal to accept the feminine principle in religion. He described the Protestant religious attitude on the subject as "unsexed."

Mary is inextricably involved in the notion of the Mystical Body and thereby in the structure of the Church itself. Attitudes toward her become attitudes toward the Church and toward all reality. . . . Anti-Marianism tends to generate separatism and separatism anti-Marianism.

It is a strange psychological fact that, when he has agreed with the Church on all points of doctrine, even on all points regarding Mary, there persists for the non-Catholic a curious uneasiness regarding his personal relationship and that of others to Mary, a psychological block which may even keep him from praying to her as his Mother and which at least warns him to tread somewhat warily here. The state of affairs is quite different from what obtains within the Catholic Church where complete lack of inhibition regarding adulation of Mary is one of the characteristic attitudes which Catholics . . . bear about in the deepest depths of their being.[16]

Ong goes so far as to write of sentimentality and momism as endemic in America today. It may be true that such a phenomenon as *"Oh Dad, Poor Dad . . ."* had a long run in New York, or that some psychiatrists have found with Rollo May that many Americans suffer from overbearing mothers, or that Liberace and his momism was an American phenomenon. But what happens to be true occasionally in America is not necessarily Protestant either in its origin or in its characteristic. But when all has been said, the fact remains that much of Protestant criticism of Roman Catholic piety has had to do with the subject of the Virgin Mary, especially the dogmas associated with her, with the celibacy of the priests, the vows of the monks and nuns, the burning of candles, and all the aspects of liturgy which are psychologically associated with the feminine and the mystical elements of religion. This forms a barrier of misunderstanding, or of simple lack of mutual understanding, which makes any discussion of the concept of the church between the two parties extremely difficult. The more

16 *The Month* magazine; quoted from its reprint in the *Cross Currents,* Vol. II, No. 3 (Spring 1952), p. 25.

Protestant churches accept the self-image of religious individualism for their own, the more difficult it becomes.

CONCLUSION: THE MEASURE OF THE VITALITY OF THE CHURCHES

Rigidity is a sign of old age and of weakness. Self-renewal implies self-criticism, vitality, and strength. Both Protestant and Catholic churches have exhibited a great deal of vitality in the twentieth century, both in their practice of religion under international strains and stresses, and in their self-criticism. The best example of the Catholic spirit of self-renewal is probably the work of Pope John XXIII, and the whole stirring out of which came such books as Hans Küng's excellent *Council, Reform and Reunion*. The Protestant churches have the heritage of continuous self-reform from the Reformation slogan: *ecclesia semper reformanda*—the church is always to be reformed. During World War II, Visser't Hooft wrote a little book entitled *The Wretchedness and Greatness of the Church*. In it he wrote: "The 'vacuum,' the great spiritual void of the masses has become more and more intolerable. The Church does very little to fill it. It has only a private message to offer the multitudes who need to be reintegrated in an order greater than themselves. It has only religious ideas to offer to men who are hungering and thirsting to be confronted with a reality that is powerful and dynamic. This is not really the Church—the people of God—conscious of belonging to the new creation, and manifesting in its life the unshakable certainty that the world is already vanquished."[17]

One may observe that adversity has always brought out the strength of the churches. In face of the great wars, dictatorships, and the challenge of the "shrinking world" (with other peoples of other religions), the churches have been stimulated to review

[17] SCM (Student Christian Movement) Press, 1944.

themselves and to seek again their own true image, so as to be true to themselves.

Most churches know well that they are not social clubs, that the "bohemians" do not represent their main purpose of existence. Most people who go to church do not go there to be dazzled by a masterpiece of oratory or entertained by the eloquence of the preacher. Not even young people go to church primarily to find a mate of whom parents will approve. Most people probably go to church because of a spiritual need. This is answered by common worship, prayers, and the common life.

This chapter dealt with basic images and models of the church. A later chapter will relate the church to the social and ethical life of the individual, the community, and the nation.

SUGGESTED READINGS

Cross, Frank L. (ed.), *Oxford Dictionary of the Christian Church,* Oxford, 1957.

Hughes, Phillip, *A Popular History of the Catholic Church,* Macmillan, 1949.

Küng, Hans, *Council, Reform, and Reunion,* Sheed and Ward, 1962.

Littell, Franklin, *The Anabaptist View of the Church,* The American Society of Church History, 1952.

Man's Disorder and God's Design, The Amsterdam Assembly Series, Harper & Row, n.d.

Mead, Frank, *Handbook of Denominations of the United States,* Abingdon Press, 1951.

Rosten, Leo (ed.), *A Guide to the Religions of America,* Simon and Schuster, 1955.

Thompson, Bard (ed.), *Liturgies of the Western World,* Living Age, 1961.

Underhill, Evelyn, *Worship,* Harper & Row, 1936.

Walker, Williston, *A History of the Christian Church,* rev. ed., Scribner, 1959.

III

The Bible

Christianity is a religion of the book and for Christianity the book is the Bible. It is regarded as a unique revelation of God to inspired and perceptive men of many ages and it is the chief source of church polity, devotional material, doctrine, and ethics for all Christians. The importance of the Bible in Christian thought is seen in all of the subsequent chapters on theology and ethics.

Despite the common central importance given to the Bible, there is considerable lack of unanimity as to what it says or even as to the authority that ought to be attributed to it. There is a significant difference between the theologian who says that the Bible is the sole authority on religious questions and the one who says that the Bible is a helpful guide for moral conduct. Likewise, the man who believes that every word of the Bible comes to us just as God intended has a genuine disagreement with the man who believes that the divine inspiration has in many places been altered and even contradicted by the human fallibility of the writers. There is, however, unanimity among Christians in believing that the Bible is the norm that judges all thought and action and is, therefore, an imperative consideration for all Christians. The primary aim of this chapter is to relate how the Bible came into being, how it has been carried down to us, and what it contains. Various interpretations of the Bible will be outlined.

A professor of anatomy at Harvard set an example that has something to say for all study. He believed that one learned the anatomy of a fish by looking at a fish rather than a textbook about fish. Accordingly, for several days, each member of his class was sent home with a fish and a scalpel rather than a reading assignment. An application may be made to biblical study. The Bible is not known until it is read. For an understanding of the Bible the following pages should not be read in place of the Bible, but along with it.[1]

ORIGIN AND TRANSMISSION OF THE TEXTS

The Old Testament did not reach its present formulation until at least the second century B.C. and was not officially accepted by any Christian group until the sixteenth century A.D. The books were composed during the thousand-year period preceding the second century. Oral traditions, poetry, historical accounts, law codes, and other narratives were passed down from generation to generation beginning probably in prehistoric times. It is not clear at what point these materials became written rather than orally transmitted. The earliest portion of the Old Testament to become canonized (i.e., officially recognized) was part of the book of

[1] A suggested sampling would include: Genesis 1–3; Exodus 1–15; Amos; Isaiah 40, 52:13–53:12; Proverbs 8:1–36, 20–22; Psalms 8, 13, 23, 42, 137, and 148; Mark; Matthew 5–7; and Romans.

Deuteronomy which became an official code under the religious reform of King Josiah of Judah in 621 B.C. By the end of the next century it is commonly agreed that the Pentateuch, or first five books, had reached its final formulation as the captive Israelite priests in Babylon worked to form a rallying point for the people of Israel who no longer had a nation. From this time until the second century B.C. new materials were added to official books and the Old Testament as we know it today was first defined and accepted by the Jewish Council of Jamnia in A.D. 90.

An interesting group of 14 documents was produced in the 200-year period between the concluding writings of the Old Testament and the first New Testament books. Some of these works are of real literary and religious value (e.g., Ecclesiasticus). Some, like Maccabees, are of particular historical interest because they supply information for an otherwise unknown period. Some are relatively worthless (e.g., Susanna and the Elders). The Council of Jamnia did not include these works, which came to be known as the Apocrypha, in the canon of the Old Testament, partly because so many of them survived only in Greek and partly because they had been written after the fourth century B.C. when the Jews believed all prophecy had ceased. Protestants have not officially accepted the Apocrypha, although they are sometimes included in Protestant translations of the Bible. Roman Catholics at the Council of Trent (opened in A.D. 1546) followed the tradition of the Greek Old Testament rather than the Hebrew and accepted these works in the canon of the Old Testament. Anglicans have given them a "deutero-canonical" status. They include them in their list of the Old Testament books, but they do not consider them to be as valuable as the rest of the Bible.

Across the bridge of the Apocrypha we move from the Old Testament into the New Testament period. Like the church today, the early church was also a religion of the book. Their book was the Old Testament alone, but they were soon to add the writings that became the New Testament. The first written materials of the

New Testament were Paul's letters. Fortunately many of them were saved by the communities that received them. After Paul's death these letters were collected to inform and inspire the communicants of the new faith. In a similar way, the Gospels were formulated as men who could no longer know Jesus personally sought to learn who he was. The needs of the emerging church elicited other documents concerning church polity, heresy, and encouragement in the face of persecution. Samples of these were added to the growing body of literature that was being copied and distributed among the churches. In the early years different collections of these books circulated in different areas, but by the fourth century, at least, there was a consensus on the collection of New Testament books as they are today. They were not officially canonized until the sixteenth century.

In these paragraphs it has been seen how the biblical documents emerged and were joined one to another until they formed the complete Bible. None of the original manuscripts still exist. The following paragraphs tell the story of the transmission of the texts from the time they left the author's hands until they appear in modern versions of the Bible.

Both the Old Testament and the New Testament manuscripts have been preserved for us because generation after generation of scribes from the time of the original writing down to the time of the printing press copied them. With the invention of the printing press, transmission of the texts was no longer a problem. Since most of the Old Testament was written in Hebrew (a very few sections are written in Aramaic), the Hebrew manuscripts of the Old Testament are most important. However, many copies of the Old Testament were translated into Greek for the sake of the Jews who had left Palestine through the centuries and came to speak only the Greek of their new homelands. The New Testament was originally written in Greek, although, along with the Old Testament, it was soon translated into Syriac and Latin and a number of other languages as Christianity spread into new areas.

A discussion of the Hebrew manuscripts is simplified by the fact that the earliest and only complete Hebrew Old Testament that we have is from the tenth century A.D. It is the product of a group of scholars known as the Massoretes who were responsible for the transmission of the Old Testament from about the sixth to the tenth century A.D. They made the final decisions when various copies disagreed and they inserted vowel signs to help pronunciation. How well did the Old Testament survive from the time it was written until it was transcribed under the hands of the Massoretes? Something of an answer to that question was provided when a group of scrolls and pieces of scrolls were found in caves near the Dead Sea in 1947. These manuscripts turned out to be parts of the Old Testament and other documents written sometime between 105 B.C. and A.D. 70. This is a thousand years earlier than any previous text of the Old Testament. Comparison of these texts demonstrates that the Old Testament was transmitted over a thousand-year period with great accuracy. Beside these texts in Hebrew, there are manuscripts of the Old Testament in Syriac, Greek, and Latin. These texts date from the fourth century A.D. onward and help in the attempt to reconstruct the original Old Testament. The latter manuscripts are not as valuable as those in the original languages because the skill and reliability of the translator cannot be known.

For the New Testament, the picture is quite different. There is an abundance of manuscripts: about 5,000 in Greek, the original language, and several thousand each in Latin and Syriac. They date anywhere from the third century to the time of the printing press in the fifteenth century. Since the original books were written in Greek, the Greek manuscripts are the most important. By comparing the more than 5,000 Greek manuscripts, the biblical scholar tries to reconstruct what the original said. This is not easy. There are more than 500,000 variations among the Greek manuscripts. Most of them are inconsequential spelling variations or easily detected omissions or errors, but there still remain a substantial number of differences that are not easily resolved. Newly found manuscripts and increasing knowledge of the language continually improve our ability to determine what the original books said.

Since we inherit primarily the traditions of the Western church, the Latin manuscripts have more significance for us than the Syriac, although both are important to biblical scholars. The Latin versions known as Old Latin were probably written in the second century A.D. However, the best known Latin version is the *Vulgate* translated by Jerome in the latter part of the fourth century A.D. It was a copy of the *Vulgate* that Gutenberg printed in 1456 and the *Vulgate* remains the authoritative Bible of the Roman Catholic Church.

John Wyclif produced the first complete English version of the Bible in 1382. It is an example of the dependence of the early English translations on the *Vulgate*. Exactly two centuries later an English version, also based on the *Vulgate,* was translated at Douai, Flanders, for Roman Catholics and, although there are now modern English versions, the Douai Bible is still in use. Shortly thereafter, in 1611, the Authorized Version of the Bible in English was finished under the sponsorship of King James of England. This version was highly dependent upon previous English translations, but it did also reflect some reconsideration of the Hebrew and Greek. Although later authorized versions appeared in 1901 and 1952 (The Revised Standard Version), the King James Version is still preferred by many Protestants. In addition to the authorized versions, there are a number of independent modern versions that offer fresh, readable translations.[2] The labor of a multitude of scholars over many centuries places in our hands a rare collection of ancient documents in contemporary English idiom.

[2] Three of the most important are *The Bible: A New Translation,* translated by James Moffatt, Harper & Row, 1955; Edgar J. Goodspeed and J. M. Powis Smith, *The Complete Bible: An American Translation,* Chicago, 1939; and *The New English Bible,* Oxford and Cambridge, 1961 (New Testament only).

THE OLD TESTAMENT

No book or collection of books is more widely known than the Old Testament. It is revered by Jews, Moslems, and Christians. It is sacred scripture for Jews and Christians and is quoted extensively in the Koran and almost every New Testament book. It was a basic document in Calvin's community at Geneva, the Puritan colony in New England, and among German Christians alienated by the Nazis during World War II. Artists and authors have drawn heavily from Old Testament motifs. The work itself consists of 39 books begun about the twelfth century B.C. and completed before the time of Jesus. Judaism has traditionally divided these books into three groupings: the Law, the Prophets, and the Writings. This division will be adopted for the following survey of the Old Testament.

The Law, *torah* in Hebrew, consists of the first five books of the Old Testament: Genesis, Exodus, Leviticus, Numbers, and Deuteronomy. The term, Pentateuch, which in Greek means "five scrolls," is more commonly used by Christian scholars. The question of the authorship of the Pentateuch points to one of the basic differences of biblical interpretation among Christian scholars and provides a good example of what is meant by textual criticism.

Tradition has assigned these works to Moses and many Bibles insert a subheading, "The Five Books of Moses." Some scholars continue to believe that Moses is the author of the major part, if not all, of the Law. Other scholars find this a difficult position to support. Very early questions were raised as to how Moses could write his own obituary and burial account (Deuteronomy 34:1–12). Conservative scholars have either conceded that this small portion was a later addition or that Moses must have been informed by God. But beginning in the seventeenth century, more far-reaching questions were being asked.

There are apparent duplicate stories in the text and sometimes the duplicates do not agree with each other (e.g., the first account of creation in Genesis 1:1–2:3 which says that man was created last and Genesis 2:4–25 which says that man was created first). The question was also raised whether laws regarding and reflecting an agricultural, settled situation, e.g., regarding harvests (Deuteronomy 23:24–25) and cereal offerings (Leviticus 2:1ff.) could or would have been written while the Israelites were nomadic, desert herdsmen under Moses. Discrepancies were also noted in the style of various sections of the Pentateuch. While conservatives offered explanations of the apparent inconsistencies, others began to search out the various authors that they felt the discrepancies indicated. By the end of the nineteenth century, under the leadership of Julius Wellhausen, this school of Old Testament interpretation had formulated what is known as the documentary hypothesis.[3] This hypothesis supposes that there are in the Law four major documents representing the works of various authors or groups of authors. With the exception of the D document, which is limited almost exclusively to Deuteronomy, the documents have been woven together by a later editor.

The earliest document is called the J document because it consistently uses God's personal name, Jehovah (Hebrew: Yahweh). It is believed to have been written in the tenth century B.C., perhaps as a text to train the heir to the throne of Israel (Solomon) in the traditions of the nation. It is a patriotic, nationalistic document outlining Israel's divine commission in history. The heroes and places that it idealizes suggest that it was written or developed in southern Palestine. An example of the J writer's work is seen in the second account of creation (Genesis 2:4–2:25).

The second document is identified as the E document because it uses the term Elohim when referring to the deity. This is the Hebrew term "god" and contains the basic Semitic root *el,* still in

[3] Julius Wellhausen, *Prolegomena to the History of Ancient Israel,* Meridian, 1957 (originally published in 1878), pp. 6ff.

use today in the Arabic word "Allah." The E document was formulated a century later than the J document and reflects much of the same spirit and many of the same stories, but from a northern, rather than a southern, perspective. The story of Abraham's sacrifice of Isaac in Genesis 22 is the work of the Elohist.

The last two documents are D and P. D is limited to parts of the book of Deuteronomy, so named because it is the second (*deuteros*) stating of the Law (*nomos*). According to tradition, Moses presented the Law during the Sinai experience, but during certain periods of subsequent history part of it was lost or forgotten. It was rediscovered in the seventh century B.C. and became the basis of a reform movement under King Josiah of Judah. The P document is the work of a priestly writer or school of writers of the sixth century B.C. as evidenced by its concern for the regulations of the ritual and sacrifice of the Temple. The book of Leviticus is attributed exclusively to P.

The only other major theory on the authorship of the Pentateuch is a variation of the documentary hypothesis. There is a group of scholars, for the most part associated with Scandinavian universities,[4] that believe that the traditions symbolized by J, E, D, and P were transmitted orally from generation to generation and were not written until the fifth century B.C. In some ways this represents a compromise between the traditional view on the authorship of the Pentateuch and the documentary hypothesis. Although it agrees with the latter that written documents were late, it places greater emphasis on the existence of oral traditions from the Mosaic period where the traditionalists' view would date the earliest written material. It differs from both traditionalists and documentary theorists in its lack of concern for dating specific materials. Instead, the oral traditionalists try to evaluate the Bible in its final composition. Contemporary biblical scholarship is divided among these theories.

[4] For example, Eduard Nielson, *Oral Tradition,* SCM (Student Christian Movement), 1954.

The materials covered in the Law break down conveniently into three sections: the prehistoric narratives, the patriarchal narratives, and the stories associated with Moses. The prehistoric materials are found in the first 11 chapters of Genesis and include the creation accounts, the stories of Adam and Eve, Cain and Abel, the Tower of Babel, the marriage of the sons of God and the daughters of men, and Noah. They answer questions about such matters as the origin of the earth, man, woman, pain, giants, the rainbow, the names of animals, fear of snakes, and the many languages. Some Christians accept these accounts as literal history, others as mythical accounts of early phenomena that could not otherwise be explained. The implications of these interpretations will be discussed later in this chapter.

The patriarchal narratives were also written in response to a question of origins, but rather than concern for such universal phenomena as pain and the natural world, these stories tell of the origins of Israel. They trace her genealogy back to Terah and then forward through Abraham, Isaac, Jacob and his 12 sons, the founders of the 12 tribes of Israel. In the past, many biblical scholars looked upon these narratives as symbolic legends saying, for example, that Abraham was not a man, but a symbol of a tribe or pure fiction. However, in recent years clay tablets found at Mari and Nuzi, cities in areas through which the patriarchs passed, have revealed a cultural environment in many ways identical with that described in Genesis, so that most scholars today believe there is a historical basis for the narratives.

The remaining four books of the Pentateuch describe the deliverance of the Israelites under Moses from bondage in Egypt. These books are of great importance because this was the most important event in Israel's history. It was through this event that God demonstrated his unique commission to Israel and united them as a people in the Sinai covenant. The books of Deuteronomy and Leviticus define the moral and ritual responsibilities that the Israelites are to assume as their obligation according to the Sinai covenant. These laws became the norm for Old Testament religion and Judaism and gave their name to this part of the Old Testament.

As may be imagined, any attempt to classify a group of books as extensive and diverse as the Old Testament into three comprehensive categories will be arbitrary. The Law contains law, but it also contains history, poetry, and myth. Likewise, the division known as the Prophets includes works about a variety of men called prophets as well as historical works. The historical works included in the Prophets are Joshua, Judges, I and II Samuel, and I and II Kings. These books continue a narration of the history of Israel from the entry into Palestine, through the period of the judges and the rise of the monarchy under Saul, David, and Solomon down to the division of Israel into the northern and southern kingdoms and their subsequent fall. Apparently the justification for including these historical works with the prophets is that they express a prophetic bias in their interpretation of history. Israel's military and economic failures are interpreted as a divine judgment against her sin. Her success is seen as dependent upon leaders sent by God.

The remainder of the prophetic books are divided between the "major" and "minor" prophets, a division that refers to the length of the book rather than the status of the prophet. Among the former are Isaiah, Jeremiah, Ezekiel, and Daniel. The latter are Hosea, Joel, Amos, Obadiah, Jonah, Micah, Nahum, Habbakuk, Zephaniah, Haggai, Zechariah, and Malachi. The word "prophet" has come to connote primarily a foreteller of the future. This was a part of the prophet's function. But particularly with the prophets mentioned above this should not be understood as a supernatural perception in a class with reading tea leaves or a crystal ball. It is rather an ability to predict the future because of a sensitivity to the consequences of given acts. Thus, when they predict the fall of Israel, it is not an insight out of nowhere, but a statement of the inevitable consequences of the behaviour of the people of Israel.

Unlike the priest or wise man or other men to whom Israel looked for knowledge, the prophet did not rationally choose or automatically inherit his role. An overwhelming compulsion which he believed to be from God forced him to become a prophet. Amos says, "The lion has roared; who will not fear? The LORD GOD has spoken; who can but prophesy?" (Amos 3:8). Jeremiah exclaims, "If I say, 'I will not mention him or speak any more in his name,' there is in my heart as it were a burning fire shut up in my bones, and I am weary with holding it in, and I cannot" (Jeremiah 20:9). The fire in the bones of the prophets that forced them to prophesy was the lack of ethical responsibility in the lives of the Israelites and their attempt to compensate for it with a hypocritical religious life. They condemn those who "sell the needy for a pair of shoes" (Amos 2:6) and "they do not defend the fatherless, and widow's cause does not come to them" (Isaiah 2:23). They condemn the elaborate sacrifices that allow the Israelites to feel that they are filling their responsibility to God. "For I desire steadfast love and not sacrifice, the knowledge of God, rather than burnt offerings," says the Lord (Hosea 6:6). A unique feature of prophecy was the application of abstract concepts like justice and righteousness to specific situations in the life of the Israelites.

Beyond their emphasis on ethical responsibility and directly related to this emphasis, the prophets enunciated two other concepts that are basic in the Judeo-Christian tradition: monotheism and universalism. Normative Mosaic faith had already demanded that Israel worship only one God, but until the time of the prophets the position that Israel held toward the gods of other peoples was ambiguous. Some would maintain that from the time of Moses, Israel did not recognize other gods, but there are many indications that, while Israel did not recognize other gods for herself, she did recognize the existence of the gods of other peoples. The Israelites were probably henotheists rather than monotheists—henotheism being the belief in one god for a particular nation or tribe along with recognition of other gods for other peoples. However, after the prophet had spoken, the ideal position of Israel was clear: "I am the LORD, and there is no other, besides me there is no God; I gird you, though you do not know me, that men may know, from the rising of the sun and from the west, that there is none besides me; I am the LORD, and there is no other. I form light and create darkness, I make weal and create woe, I am the LORD, who do all these things (Isaiah 45:5–7). And if there is one God, he must be the God of all people, not Israel alone. This was the implication of Isaiah when he declared that Yahweh could use Assyria to punish Israel (Isaiah 10:5–6) and it was stated even more specifically by Amos: "Are you not like the Ethiopians to me, O people of Israel? says the LORD. Did I not bring up Israel from the land of Egypt, and the Philistines from Caphtor and the Syrians from Kir?" (Amos 9:7).

One other insight that emerged in the work of the prophets is of particular importance. Christians have sometimes felt that "justice," "power," and "wrath," are the key words to associate with the Old Testament while "compassion," "forgiveness," and "suffering" are exclusively New Testament concepts. Such a position can be sustained only by overlooking the persistent compassion and forgiveness of Yahweh in delivering Israel first from Egypt and then from a number of oppressors during the subsequent period of the judges. Further, such a generalization overlooks two of the great prophetic books, Hosea and Isaiah.[5]

Hosea is commanded by the Lord to marry a woman who either was or became a prostitute and was unfaithful to him. Simple justice demanded that an adulteress be stoned to death. But Hosea buys her back and hopes to reform her. From this experience he gains insight into the relationship between God and Israel. God is

[5] Most scholars distinguish between Isaiah ben Amoz, the eighth-century B.C. prophet and an unknown prophet of the sixth century B.C. The work related to the former is found in Isaiah 1–39, to the latter in 40–66. The present remarks relate to the latter.

the faithful husband confronted with his unfaithful wife, Israel. The God of justice and wrath would be expected to punish Israel. The God of Hosea exclaims: "How can I give you up, O Ephraim! How can I hand you over, O Israel! How can I make you like Admah! How can I treat you like Zeboiim! My heart recoils within me, my compassion grows warm and tender. I will not execute my fierce anger, I will not again destroy Ephraim; for I am God and not man, the Holy One in your midst, and I will not come to destroy (Hosea 11:8-9).

Yahweh's unwillingness to destroy his people despite their wickedness is seen again in one of the most profound and enigmatic passages in literature, the Suffering Servant poems of Isaiah. An innocent man takes on the just punishment of other men in order that they might be redeemed. It is not clear whether the passages speak of a man or of Israel herself as the servant.[6] It is clear that Israel saw the servant as one sent by God to accept the consequences of the sin of man so that man would not have to bear them.

> Surely he has borne our griefs
>   and carried our sorrows;
> yet we esteemed him stricken,
>   smitten by God, and afflicted.
> But he was wounded for our transgressions,
>   he was bruised for our iniquities;
> upon him was the chastisement that made us whole,
>   and with his stripes we are healed.
> All we like sheep have gone astray;
>   we have turned everyone to his own way;
> and the LORD has laid on him
>   the iniquity of us all.
>
> Isaiah 53:4-6

[6] See C. R. North, *The Suffering Servant in Deuter-Isaiah,* rev. ed., Oxford, 1956.

> by his knowledge shall the righteous one, my servant
>   make many to be accounted righteous;
> and he shall bear their iniquities.
>
> Isaiah 53:11

The third traditional division of the Old Testament is made up of a miscellaneous collection of works written for the most part between the fifth and second centuries B.C. They may be divided roughly into three categories: short stories, wisdom literature, and poetry.

Ruth, Esther, and Jonah are the short stories. The Book of Ruth relates the story of a young Moabite (Ruth) who marries a Jew. When the husband dies, his mother decides to return to Judah, but Ruth does not want to leave her mother-in-law and in one of the beautiful passages of the Old Testament, begs: "Entreat me not to leave you or to return from following you; for where you go I will go, and where you lodge I will lodge; your people shall be my people, and your God my God; where you die I will die, and there will I be buried. May the LORD do so to me and more also if even death parts me from you" (Ruth 1:16–17). She does go to Judah with Naomi and meets another Jew, Boaz, whom she marries. Whatever the historical basis of the story, it was told to condemn the prevalent Jewish nationalism that was isolating Jews from neighboring people. The story condones Jewish intermarriage with foreigners.

The Book of Esther is the story of a Jewish girl who becomes queen of Persia. She is in a position to speak for her Jewish countrymen when a Persian general, Haman, seeks to persecute the Jews and kill Esther's uncle. Through her intervention, Haman is executed and a slaughter of the Persians follows. It is generally believed that the story evolved as an explanation of the Jewish festival of Purim. Because of its bloodthirstiness and lack of religious ideas (it nowhere mentions God), it was accepted into the official canon with great difficulty. It is interesting to note that the monks who copied the Dead Sea scrolls made no copies of the Book of Esther and the Apocrypha contains a book called *The Rest of the Book of Esther,* which tries to fill in the religious concern lacking in the original.

The story of Jonah (or at least one act in the story) is perhaps one of the best known stories of the Bible. Jonah was commissioned by God to go to the Assyrians at Nineveh. Nineveh was a pagan enemy of Judah and Jonah wanted no part of it. Instead, he headed in the opposite direction by ship. According to the story, he was subsequently swallowed by a whale, returned to Palestine, recommissioned by God, and this time he went to Nineveh. This story, like the Book of Ruth, was officially endorsed to condone and encourage Israel's relations with her non-Jewish neighbors.

Ancient Israel, like many of her neighbors, produced a body of wisdom literature. Three legitimate sources of knowledge were recognized: the priest, the prophet, and the sage. The priest was the conserver of the Law of Moses and could instruct Israel on her ritual and ethical obligations. The prophet received the word of God directly and delivered it to those to whom it was relevant. The sage was a wise man who gained knowledge through experience and common sense. In contrast to the knowledge of both prophet and priest, there was no mysterious or unexplainable quality to the knowledge of the sage. The former could demand attention because it was God's word that should not be questioned. The latter could be challenged by any who believed that what they said did not constitute "good common sense." The currency of such wisdom and the affirmation that Solomon was among the wisest of all is recognized in the Old Testament itself: "And God gave Solomon wisdom and understanding beyond measure, and largeness of mind like the sand on the seashore, so that Solomon's wisdom surpassed the wisdom of all the people of the east, and all the wisdom of Egypt. For he was wiser than all other men, wiser than Ethan the Ezrahite, and Heman, Calcol, and Darda, the sons of Mahol; and his fame was in all the nations round about. He also uttered three thousand proverbs; and his songs were a thousand and five. He spoke of trees, from the cedar that is in Lebanon to the hyssop that grows out of the walls; he spoke also of beasts, and of birds, and of reptiles, and of fish. And men came from all peoples to hear the wisdom of Solomon, and from all the kings of the earth, who had heard of his wisdom" (I Kings 4:29–34).

The book of Proverbs, which with Job and Ecclesiastes makes up the wisdom literature of the Old Testament, is an anthology of maxims whose individual authors are mentioned in the text. Many are attributed to Solomon; considering his reputation, it would be surprising if he had not written many of them. Some, however, are explicitly attributed to other authors in Israel and some reflect the influence of other parts of the Middle East. Chapters 22:17–24:22, for example, has many parallels with the sayings of the Egyptian, Amenope: "See thou these thirty chapters: they entertain; they instruct; they are the foremost of all books; they make the ignorant to know" (Amenope 30:7–10),[7] and "Have I not written for you thirty sayings of admonition and knowledge, to show you what is right and true, that you may give a true answer to those who sent you?" (Proverbs 22:20–21). The book of Proverbs is filled with short, barbed sayings directed against the foolish, the lazy, the drunkard, the intemperate, and those with loose morals: "Wine is a mocker, strong drink a brawler; and whoever is led astray by it is not wise. The dread wrath of a king is like the growling of a lion; he who provokes him to anger forfeits his life. It is an honor for a man to keep aloof from strife; but every fool will be quarreling. The sluggard does not plow in the autumn; he will seek at harvest and have nothing" (Proverbs 20:1–4).

The closest that the Old Testament comes to dramatic literature is the Book of Job. A poet of the sixth century took an old folk tale as a motif for his own poem. The poem is the story of an upright man named Job whom God allows to be despoiled by Satan. There follows a dialogue between Job and his three friends

[7] James B. Pritchard, *Ancient Near Eastern Texts,* Princeton, 1950, p. 424.

as to the reason for Job's disaster. Out of this dialogue there develops a pointed renunciation of the dominant Old Testament theme that sin is the source of all suffering. Job is one who did not sin and now he suffers. The three friends represent the traditional view and insist that whether he knows the sin or not, Job must have committed one or he would not be suffering. The book comes to no simple solution of the problem. When God finally speaks to Job, he does not discuss Job's predicament or the problem of evil. Rather he belittles Job's finitude. The most significant thing that the book says is that there is no simple answer to such questions: ultimate answers are beyond rational comprehension.

The Book of Ecclesiastes, like the Book of Job, takes on a serious question and like Job it arrives at no simple answer. Ecclesiastes is searching for meaning in life. The author experiments with different possibilities: wealth, pleasure, fame, and wisdom, and concludes that all are vanity. This theme is so prevalent in current plays and novels that our society can feel a special kinship with Ecclesiastes. The book at times lapses into deep cynicism and counsels that one may as well "eat, drink and be merry" since death is inevitable for all (Ecclesiastes 8:15). Ecclesiastes ends still affirming life, but without comprehending its purpose.

Although much of the Old Testament is written in poetic form, probably because poetry is easier to memorize than prose, there are some distinctively poetic works that were originally written to be sung. The major works would be the Psalms and the Song of Solomon. Another poem, Lamentations, is also included in the writings. Hebrew poetry usually consisted of a rhyming of ideas rather than a rhyming of words, so most of its nuances may be caught in English as well as in Hebrew.

The Psalms are hymns written and collected over a long period of time. Tradition assigns many of them to David, but others were added to the collection over the years. These hymns were used at worship services in the temple, both by the choirs and worshippers.

They reflect such attitudes as adoration, thanksgiving, penance, and petition.

The Song of Solomon is a love song, pure and simple. The maiden sings:

> As an apple tree among the trees of the wood,
>   so is my beloved among young men.
> With great delight I sat in his shadow,
>   and his fruit was sweet to my taste.
> He brought me to the banqueting house,
>   and his banner over me was love.
> Sustain me with raisins, refresh me with apples;
>   for I am sick with love.
> O that his left hand were under my head,
>   and that his right hand embraced me!
>   Song of Solomon 2:3–6

The young man returns her sentiments:

> Arise, my love, my fair one,
>   and come away;
> for lo, the winter is past, the rain is over and gone.
> The flowers appear on the earth, the time of singing has come,
>   and the voice of the turtledove is heard in our land.
> The fig tree puts forth its figs and the vines are in blossom;
>   they give forth fragrance.
> Arise, my love, my fair one, and come away.
>   Song of Solomon 2:10–13

The poetic love dialogue continues. The imagery is rich, colorful, and sensitive.

It may be well to ask how such a book ever got into the canon of the Bible. Jewish and Christian apologists have commonly considered it an allegory. The Jews looked upon it as an allegory of the love between Yahweh and Israel; Christians have seen it as the love between Christ and his church. However, J. G. Wetzstein has substantiated a more likely explanation in his study of wedding rituals among Syrian villagers.[8] The wedding festival sometimes lasts several days and a number of traditional songs are sung. The Song of Solomon probably represents such a collection of songs from ancient Israel.

The last of the poems in the Writings moves from love to lamentation. This book, called Lamentations, is in five separate poems, each a dirge lamenting the fall of Jerusalem to Nebuchadnezzar of Babylon in 587. Four of these poems are alphabetical acrostics. This means that each line or each set of lines begins with a succeeding letter of the Hebrew alphabet. The poem is a forceful expression of Israel's sorrow at the fall of the great city:

> How lonely sits the city
>   that was full of people!
> How like a widow has she become,
>   she that was great among the nations!
> She that was a princess among the cities
>   has become a vassal.
>
>   Lamentations 1:1

The books of Ezra, Nehemiah, and Chronicles are also included in the Writings. All of them are purportedly historical. Although they are sketchy and quite biased, they do provide the only historical evidences that we have for Israel from the return of the exiles from Babylon in the sixth century B.C. until the New Testament period.

THE UNITY OF THE OLD TESTAMENT

From this sampling of the Old Testament, it is obvious that there are many types of literature representing many periods of Israelite history and many aspects of theology. In the face of such obvious diversity it is difficult to talk about any core or unity. The search for such a core has led scholars to make a number of suggestions.

[8] Cited in *The Abingdon Bible Commentary*, Abingdon Press, 1929, p. 622.

Christians see in the Old Testament a prelude to the New Testament. The New Testament is latent in the Old; the Old Testament is revealed in the New. The Old Testament points forward to a promise; the New Testament marks the fulfillment. Accordingly, the core of the Old Testament is often identified with messianic expectations, particularly those found in such prophets as Isaiah:

> For to us a child is born,
>   to us a son is given;
> and the government will be upon his shoulder,
>   and his name will be called
> "Wonderful Counselor, Mighty God,
>   Everlasting Father, Prince of Peace."
> Of the increase of his government and of peace
>   there will be no end,
> upon the throne of David, and over his kingdom,
>   to establish it, and to uphold it
> with justice and with righteousness
>   from this time forth and for evermore.
> The zeal of the LORD of hosts will do this.
>
> Isaiah 9:6–7

The New Testament Gospel of Matthew illustrates such a view of the relationship of the Old Testament to the New. Matthew is anxious to demonstrate that the events in the life of Jesus were predicted and foreseen in the Old Testament (e.g., Matthew 1:23, 2:5, 2:15, and 2:17).

A second school of thought says that all of the materials of the Old Testament can be brought together around three topics: God, man, and salvation.[9] Since these categories speak to the basic concerns of man, they would point to the most significant portions of the Old Testament. Thus works as different in style and time as the creation narrative and Job are related in their concern to say

---

[9] This was the presupposition of the theologies of the Old Testament produced by scholars like W. Eichrodt, L. Köhler, and H. W. Robinson.

something about God and man, and the tedious legal documentation of Deuteronomy and Leviticus share with the impassioned works of the prophets a concern for man's salvation.

In recent years there has been a noticeable emphasis among biblical scholars on a third possible key to understanding the formulation of the Old Testament.[10] According to this thought, the Israelites considered their history worth recording and reciting because it was in history that their God had revealed himself. The Old Testament is then focused upon the great acts of the drama when God acted in history; for example, the promise to Abraham, the bondage in Egypt, the deliverance under Moses, the covenant at Sinai, and the attainment of the promised land. The drama reaches its conclusion in Christ's crucifixion and Resurrection in the New Testament.

These several interpretations suggest an important consideration: no obvious categories can be imposed upon the Old Testament. The various writings are much like the unrelated and sometimes incomprehensible motions of the performer in charades. No action in itself can be related to any other action, but each represents a desperate attempt to convey to the audience a truth that cannot be communicated by words, in the case of charades because of the rules of the game, in the case of the Old Testament because of the infinite nature of the truth. Perhaps the diverse materials share in common only their attempt to express an ultimate truth.

THE NEW TESTAMENT

The New Testament is a much easier collection of books to survey than the Old. In contrast to the centuries that were necessary to produce the Old Testament, the New Testament was produced

---

[10] Characteristically set forth in G. Ernest Wright and Reginald H. Fuller's *The Book of the Acts of God*, Doubleday, 1957.

within a single century between A.D. 50 and 150. It is only about one fifth as long as the Old Testament and its organization is much more comprehensible.

Despite the present order of the New Testament books, the Pauline letters were the first New Testament documents to be written. They were written by Paul to the various churches he visited during his journeys through Asia Minor, Greece, and Rome. The four most significant are his letters to Rome, Corinth, Thessalonica, and Galatia. The "captivity letters," Ephesians, Colossians, Philemon, and Phillipians, so called because they were written during a time of imprisonment, are usually considered to have been written by Paul, and many scholars believe he also wrote the "pastoral letters," I and II Timothy and Titus.

Paul's life encompassed the three great traditions of Western civilization: Israel, Greece, and Rome. Born in the Greek city of Tarsus under Roman rule, he was sent to Palestine for his education. There he was converted to Christianity (Acts of the Apostles 9) and the rest of his life was spent in an itinerant mission through the cities of Asia Minor, Greece, and finally Rome. There has been considerable difference of opinion in Christian circles as to the part played by Paul in the development of Christianity. There have been some who have felt that he so perverted Christianity that Christians ought to get away from Paul and "back to Jesus." The argument is that the Pauline letters show the influence of the Greek mystery religions on Christianity and that Jesus simply provided a historical figure to fit into a religion that had evolved in another culture. This view was quite popular in the last century, but is no longer prevalent. Much that seemed to be dependent upon Greek culture has been found in Jewish apocalypticism and the basic thought of Paul seems quite congenial to the basic thought of Jesus.

The Thessalonian and Corinthian correspondence represent the most personal Pauline works. Paul is seen actively handling a number of specific problems that have come up in the newly formed Christian communities. The promise that the end of the world was to come at any moment had raised a number of questions. The Thessalonians were troubled because some of their members felt there was no longer any need to work (II Thessalonians 3:11), and some of them were concerned about relatives and friends who would die before the end came (I Thessalonians 4:15). In Corinth men wondered if they ought to marry in view of the short time remaining (I Corinthians 7).

The best systematic and detailed presentation of the Pauline theology is found in Romans. In this letter addressed to a congregation he had not yet visited, Paul worked out his theology in forceful and comprehensive form. Man is a sinner. The Jewish Law demonstrated this by defining sinful behaviour, thereby allowing man to see his desperate condition. If salvation depends upon man's goodness, all men are damned. But God in his mercy has chosen some to be saved, not because they are good, but in spite of the fact that they are sinful. He chose certain men to be saved because of their faith, but even faith is a gift from God. All salvation comes from God; man is impotent to do anything for his own salvation. Jesus was the key figure in the historical act by which God took on the sins of mankind and raised Jesus and, in turn, man to salvation.

Paul, Peter, and possibly other apostles travelled extensively throughout Palestine, Asia Minor, Greece, and Rome founding congregations of Christians. The central theme of their preaching was "Jesus and the Resurrection." It was no small crowd that gathered to hear these men talk about the Jesus they knew. And then, as the end of the century came, there were fewer and fewer people who had ever seen Jesus and if any firsthand accounts of his life were to be preserved they would have to be committed to writing. Communities came to treasure the stories they heard about Jesus and writers began to work them into interpretive biographies answering the question raised throughout the Roman Empire: Who was this man, Jesus?

The historical details that emerge are obscure.[11] After his birth sometime before 4 B.C., we hear almost nothing about Jesus until he is an adult ready to be baptized by John the Baptist. Following a brief period of withdrawal in the Judean wilderness, he began preaching around the Sea of Galilee and gathered a following of hearers and a more intimate group of disciples. Apparently he attracted sufficient attention from the political rulers so that he thought it wise to withdraw to Caesarea Philippi for a time (Luke 9:7–9).[12] Once there he realized that if his message was to reach the heart of his people, it was necessary to go to the political heart of the community, and he made his way down to Jerusalem. There he was arrested and crucified.

The Gospel writers, however, were not so much interested in the historical details as they were in establishing the authority and meaning of the man. The earliest Gospel was probably written in Rome about A.D. 70 as Mark incorporated the reminiscences of Peter into other materials available to him. It is the briefest of the canonical Gospels and states in simple and dramatic form the main features in the life and teachings of Jesus. About 10 years later, two other Gospels were written, both heavily dependent upon the work that Mark had written; Matthew and Luke incorporated about 90 percent of Mark. For this reason, these three Gospels are sometimes referred to as the Synoptic Gospels because they "see together." However, the latter two also have their own emphasis and distinctive contributions. Matthew is particularly interested in showing that Jesus fulfilled the promises of the Old Testament. He quotes frequently from the Old Testament. This suggests that he is writing to Christians of Jewish background, since other Christians would not be familiar with the Old Testament. Luke's Gospel, on the other hand, seems to have been written with non-Jews in mind. He explains Hebrew words (6:15,23:33) and goes

[11] The historical Jesus is presented in greater detail in Chapter VI.

[12] This is followed by the account of Peter's confession which according to Matthew and Mark took place at Caesarea Philippi.

to great pains to imply that the Jews, not the gentiles, were responsible for the crucifixion of Jesus. It is generally recognized as the most literary Gospel and is characterized by its humanitarianism. Both Matthew and Luke are more explicit about the divine origin and nature of Jesus than is Mark. These two Gospels alone contain the story of the virgin birth and they are more reluctant than Mark to attribute human qualities to Jesus. Such well-known stories as the Prodigal Son and the Good Samaritan are found only in Luke. Sometime toward the end of the first century, the last of the four canonical Gospels was written. Unlike the Synoptic Gospels, John makes less pretense at history and dramatically portrays Jesus as the pre-existent "logos" in a highly abstract account of the significance of Jesus as the Christ.

Other gospels were written in the succeeding years and many of them, like the Gospel of Barnabas, the Shepherd of Hermes, and the Gospel of Peter have been preserved. But these were written late and did not gain acceptance in the official canon of the church.

One book in the New Testament bears the title, the Acts of the Apostles. It would seem to imply that the original plan was to have a much broader book than we have at present. Paul is the only apostle who is treated with any thoroughness while Peter and John receive less attention and none of the other apostles are mentioned. Perhaps the work was to have included similar treatment of all the apostles, but either the project was not completed or it was discarded or lost. Luke, the author of the Third Gospel, is also considered the author of this work. It is a lively account of the tribulations of the early church after Jesus' death. Extensive coverage is given to the missionary activity of Paul and the travels that took him through Palestine, Asia Minor, Greece, and Rome.

A number of letters remain in the New Testament that were not written by Paul. These letters, James, I and II Peter, I, II, and III John, and Jude are called the Catholic Epistles. An epistle is distinguished from a letter by the wider audience for which it is intended. The Catholic Epistles were open and formal letters to the whole Christian Church (catholic means universal) and speak of the problems that faced it in the early part of the second century. Two of the great issues were persecution and heresy. Christianity was unwelcome in much of the empire and some of these works (e.g., James 1:1ff.; I Peter 1:6ff.) give encouragement to those who are facing persecution. The absence of a formalized creed allowed much diversity of doctrine and some of these epistles reflect attempts of the early church to deal with heresy and backsliding. Important, but less serious issues were also treated: itinerant preachers who exploited the communities they visited (II John) and the economic disparity between wealthy and lower-class Christians (James 2:1ff.).

Although neither an epistle nor a letter, the book of Hebrews contains much the same message as the Catholic Epistles. In fine literary style it warns against the dangers of wrong doctrine and sin. According to its stern message, there is no remission for sin committed after baptism. Chapters 11 and 12 bring forth the heroes of the past to give courage to those persecuted in the present.

There is one example of apocalyptic literature in the New Testament, the Revelation to John. Apocalyptic literature is literature written during a time of oppression by one of the oppressed to bring comfort to his fellow sufferers. He promises them that the oppressors will be destroyed by God in a massive supernatural intervention in history. The book of Revelation was written during the Roman persecution of the Christians. The message is intentionally cryptic since the author did not want to suffer recrimination at the hands of the oppressor for his remarks. The author used signs that could not be understood by those outside his religious community. We are on the outside and understandably cannot decipher much of this book. We can only guess at the meaning of signs like "the great dragon," and "666," and various groups in all ages have given them a multitude of interpretations. The general outline is fairly clear. Satan will be bound for a thousand years during which Jesus and the martyrs will reign. Satan will return to power briefly only to be thrown into a fiery lake and Jesus and all the faithful will reign forever.

There is some magnificent imagery in the book of Revelation. Consider the description of heaven: "After this I looked, and lo, in heaven an open door! And the first voice, which I had heard speaking to me like a trumpet, said, 'Come up hither, and I will show you what must take place after this.' At once I was in the Spirit, and lo, a throne stood in heaven, with one seated on the throne! And he who sat there appeared like jasper and carnelian, and round the throne was a rainbow that looked like an emerald. Round the throne were twenty-four thrones, and seated on the thrones were twenty-four elders, clad in white garments, with golden crowns upon their heads. From the throne issue flashes of lightening, and voices and peals of thunder, and before the throne burn seven torches of fire, which are the seven spirits of God; and before the throne there is as it were a sea of glass, like crystal" (Revelation 4:1–6). To those suffering under the Roman heel such a vision would express a meaningful hope. But perhaps one of the most significant literary units is the closing prayer. After painting the great picture of the cosmic disaster to come and the glory that awaits the righteous, the book closes with the simple, urgent prayer: "Come Lord Jesus!"

THE UNITY OF THE NEW TESTAMENT

Unlike the Old Testament which is difficult to focus on any single theme, the New Testament is focused on the person of Jesus as the Christ. This focus is somewhat divided between what Jesus said and what was said about Jesus. A synopsis of each of these two divisions can be found in two passages from the New Testament itself. What Jesus said is characterized in the Sermon on the Mount found in the fifth, sixth, and seventh chapters of Matthew and what was said about Jesus is summarized in the seventh and eighth chapters of Romans.

The Sermon on the Mount presents the radical ethic of the New Testament. One should not only love his friends, but also his enemies! One should not only refuse to strike back, but also turn the other cheek! One should not only refrain from killing, but from hating! This is a very radical ethic indeed and Christians have been at great odds to explain how finite man can be expected to live it. Liberal and orthodox theologians have tended to say that the genius of the Christian ethic is that it challenges man to the full extent of his capabilities. Other theologians have felt that, on the contrary, it is an ethic that points out the limitations of such capabilities. These scholars say that the ethic is impossible for man to follow and stands as a clear-cut condemnation of mankind. He cannot do what he ought to do. He ought to love his enemies. He ought to turn the other cheek. He ought to refrain from hate. No man does. Therefore, all men are damned if their salvation depends on their fulfilling their obligation. Other positions present something of a compromise. Albert Schweitzer, for example, believes that man could fulfill such an ethic, but only for a short time. However, this is all Jesus was asking, according to Schweitzer. In a short time the end was coming and the ethic of the Sermon on the Mount was an "interim ethic" until the end of the world. When time proved Jesus wrong, the ethic was no longer relevant. However it is understood, a radical ethic of nonviolence and nonmaterial goals is at the core of what Jesus taught.

The seventh and eighth chapters of Romans reflect the core of what was taught *about* Jesus: he was sent to reconcile sinful man to God. The seventh chapter presents the depth of hopelessness of man if he is dependent upon his own rational, willful choices and actions. He cannot do the good he feels he ought to do and he cannot refrain from doing the evil that he feels he ought not to do. Indeed he is a wretched man without hope. But the eighth chapter says that in spite of man's weakness God sends him salvation through Jesus the Christ. It concludes with the powerful affirmation of hope in the face of despair: ". . . in all these things we are more than conquerors through him who loved us. For I am sure that neither death, nor life, nor angels, nor principalities, nor things present, nor things to come, nor powers, nor height, nor depth, nor anything else in all creation, will be able to separate us from the love of God in Christ Jesus our Lord" (Romans 8:37–39).

INTERPRETING THE BIBLE

No Christian takes the Bible entirely literally. One illustration of this point is sufficient. One verse of the Bible says, "Thou shalt not kill" (Exodus 20:13), yet all Christians kill plants or animals for food and most Christians participate in the killing of other people in time of war and for capital crimes. But they interpret the injunction in such a way that they feel they have not acted contrary to the biblical command. If the Bible is to say anything to particular men today, it must be interpreted. It is sometimes said that you can prove anything by the Bible. If this is true, the biblical injunctions may be so relative that they lose all authority. Most Christians would agree that there are many parts of the Bible that are not explicitly understood by anyone, but most Christians would say (to paraphrase Mark Twain's quip) that it is not what they don't understand in the Bible that concerns them, but what they do understand. There are three general methods of biblical interpretation by which Christians try to determine what the Bible has to say to man. Individual Christians use all three methods, although they may emphasize one more than another.

Fundamentalists in particular believe that the Bible is to be understood literally, word for word, as it stands. It is the literally revealed word of God. All answers to the basic religious questions may be found in relevant passages. The literalist is challenged by other Christians on the basis of apparent biblical contradictions. Can the passage that states that man was the first of God's creations (Genesis 2:4–22) be reconciled with the text that says he was the last (Genesis 1:1–2:4)? Can the morality of II Kings 2:23–24 where Elisha curses some 40 boys for calling him "baldy" be reconciled with the Sermon on the Mount? Can the miracles be reconciled with modern science? Literalists assert that any apparent contradictions or inadequacies must be due to the misunderstanding of the men who read the Bible, not those who wrote it. If the Bible, the word of God, should conflict with science or reason, the Bible must be considered true.

Roman Catholics make a slight modification of this first approach. While they tend to be literalists, they do not insist that the entire Bible is formulated in literal terms. Thus, while some passages have been interpreted finally by the church authorities invested to do this, there remain portions of scripture which are not yet clearly understood. Much of the Bible remains in allegorical or metaphorical language and need not be taken literally. However, there are some portions that have been officially interpreted as literally true.

The second approach, the rationalist, also believes that ultimate truths are expressed in the Bible, but it maintains that they will be meaningful to modern man only if the Bible is stripped of its unreasonable portions. Miracle stories are understood either rationally (for example, the star of Bethlehem was a nova star, the waters of the Reed Sea were parted by a strong wind, and the miracle healings represent psychosomatic healing) or they are dismissed as superfluous legends (the virgin birth and the Resurrection, for example). The rationalists believe that by reason the Bible can be stripped of its legendary accretions and by reason its ultimate message can be deduced. In practice what is usually left after the thorough use of such an approach is an essentially ethical understanding of the Bible. Jesus is seen as a moral teacher and example.

The current emphasis in orthodox Protestantism has given rise to a third position. Unlike the literalist, it is not concerned with defending the literal statements of any part of the Bible, but unlike the rationalist, it is not interested in rationalizing or discarding any parts of the Bible. This approach to biblical interpretation emphasizes acceptance of the Bible, but understands its essential truth to be in symbolic rather than literal terms. The interpretation of symbolic terms is difficult. Terms which were meaningful to men of biblical times may no longer be meaningful today and there are truths that are always difficult to state in literal, rational terms. The latter phenomenon we acknowledge whenever we exclaim, "Words can't tell . . . ," or "I don't know how to say it!" Using religious jargon, it is difficult to express infinite truths in finite terms.

According to this point of view it might be said that chapters one and two of Genesis may conflict, but the ultimate truths which are expressed do not conflict. Thus Genesis 1, when demythologized,[13] may tell us that God created the world, while a demythologized Genesis 2 states that man named the animals and that women are inferior companions of men and that human beings are weak. None of these statements are mutually contradictory. Similarly, the account of the Reed Sea crossing during the Exodus is not concerned with discussing the geological questions involved in the natural behaviour of the Sea, but it is an attempt to reveal the truth that God delivered the Israelites from Egypt.

The Bible must be understood in the context of the society in which it originated. Only in this setting can the message that was given to the biblical community be understood and in turn "remythologized" into meaningful concepts for today. This means of interpreting the Bible has been developed by various scholars, notably Rudolf Bultmann of the University of Marburg. In a sermon based on Peter's miraculous catch of fish (Luke 5:1-11) Bultmann says, for example, "We understand it as a symbol depicting the wondrous power which Jesus can achieve over a

---

[13] A term associated with Rudolf Bultmann. In simple terms it refers to the restatement of biblical myths in contemporary concepts.

human life. The story itself guides us to the necessity of so understanding it. For its central point is not that Peter made a miraculous haul, but that Peter is called to be an apostle, a proclaimer of the Word. When Jesus says to Peter, 'Henceforth you will catch men,' it is apparent that the wonder of his fishing is the symbol for something far greater."[14]

Although the primary function of mythological language may be to express truths that cannot be expressed in finite symbols, myth may also be a means of forcing the individual to realize that the universe cannot be described in perfectly rational terms. The mythological symbols involved in such statements as, "Jesus was man," and "Jesus was God," point up a paradox that permeates the human experience. The synthesis of the finite and the infinite, the ideal and the real, cannot be stated in rational terms; it is suprarational. The myth, both through its symbols and its often paradoxical structure, forces the mind to think beyond the rational level.

The last position differs with the rationalist in one other important respect. The rationalist believes that the truth of the Bible may be deduced rationally. The position we are now describing believes that the truth of the Bible must be received experientially or intuitively. The biblical symbols may say something to man or they may not. If they do not, no other authority can make them say something. If they do, they need no other authority. So the Bible speaks to various men in various ways. To some it says nothing. But it is the classic expression of ultimate questions and answers for men and women of Western civilization.

SUGGESTED READINGS

Anderson Bernhard, *Understanding the Old Testament,* Prentice-Hall, 1957.

[14] Quoted in *The Journal of Bible and Religion* (January 1959), p. 30.

Enslin, Morton Scott, *Christian Beginnings,* Harper & Row, 1938.

Hunter, Archibald M., *Introducing New Testament Theology,* Westminster, 1957.

The Interpreter's Bible, Abingdon Press, 1951.

The Interpreter's Dictionary of the Bible, Abingdon Press, 1962.

Wright, G. Ernest, and Reginald Fuller, *The Book of the Acts of God,* Doubleday, 1957.

IV

Man

INTRODUCTION: THE CONCEPT OF MAN, SECULAR AND SACRED

Popular wisdom, based on experience and prompted by common sense, has made many observations about man which a Christian, too, holds valid. Such "wisdom literature" is included in the Old Testament. Great writers since antiquity have expressed truths which a Christian readily acknowledged. Let us consider these lines from the chorus of Sophocles' *Antigone,* written some 450 years before Christ:

> Wonders are many on earth, and the greatest of these is man. . . .
> He is master of ageless Earth, to his own will bending
> the immortal mother of gods by the sweat of his brow,
> as year succeeds to year, with toil unending
> of mule and plough.

He is lord of all things living; birds of the air,
beasts of the field, all creatures of sea and land . . . .
The use of language, the wind-swift motion of brain
he learnt; found out the laws of living together
in cities, building him shelter against the rain
and wintry weather.
There is nothing beyond his power. His subtlety
meeteth all chance, all danger conquereth.
For every ill he hath found its remedy,
save only death.
O wondrous subtlety of man, that draws
to good or evil ways! Great honour is given
and power to him who upholdeth his country's laws
and the justice of heaven.
But he that, too rashly daring, walks in sin
in solitary pride of his life's end
at door of mine shall never enter in
to call me friend.[1]

The twentieth-century reader realizes, of course, that these lines
were written in a time unlike ours: the secular and the sacred were
not sharply distinguished. The sacred penetrated the secular and
gave it meaning. Sophocles' view was broad: man's toil and
mortality on the one hand, his infinite capacity and greatness on
the other; man's moral quality and goodness, but also his sin and
excessive pride. The opening line of the chorus is of special
interest: "wonders are many on earth, and the greatest of these is
man." The word "wonder" has a different connotation against a
religious background of mystery and awe than it has against a
scientific background of "the unknown" which is about to be
explored, analyzed experimentally, and tested. Today, when the
sacred and the secular are sharply separated, the question arises
whether the scientific study of man is removing that quality
described by Sophocles as "wonder." For the Christian understanding of man, here is the first significant issue.

1 Sophocles, *The Theban Plays,* tr. by E. F. Watling, Penguin Books, 1947,
pp. 135 f.

HUMAN NATURE: MERELY COMPLEX, OR FULL OF MYSTERY?

In the orderly and harmonious images of the world created by the Enlightenment, a French author wrote a book with the characteristic title *Man the Machine*. Today we know that man is not as simple as an engine, not even as an automobile engine or a space missile. The very plan of university curricula testifies to the vast complexity of the concept "man." We study man's biological nature, and set up separate courses to study his social nature. We discuss his historical past and his political present. We admire his cultural creations and wonder at his economic behavior, his personality patterns, and his ways of learning. Obviously, the answer to the question "what is man" is not simple.

The Christian religion clearly stands closer to the humanities, which study man through his literature, philosophy, drama, and arts, than it is to the social or biological sciences that measure man by statistical methods or liken him to experimental animals. Yet the issue is not one for or against sciences. It rather lies in the Christian assertion that man is more than the total of determinate and measurable quantities. Man's nature, in the Christian view, is also indeterminate, capable of infinite variety of responses, creative beyond expectation, and always in part unpredictable. The capacity of an individual and of his social group for good and for evil is of great concern to the Christian, yet it is difficult to study by scientific methods. Sciences do not distinguish between good and evil and other value judgments through either their experimental or their statistical methods. Man as "wonder" is contrary to the purely scientific mind. Jaspers, in his philosophical way, says: the very fact that we do not know what man really is, is an essential feature of being man; Toynbee, in his historical context, assures us that beyond the calculable environmental influences on man, such as climate, diet, or geography, there is in the behavior of past civilization an unknown, an "X." A Christian concept (already present in the Hebrew religion) is "the image of God" in man. To look into this finite, limited, and mortal being that is man, is to look into the image (or mirror) of God. Since God is infinite, and his very nature implies mystery, to look into his image is to find some reflection of this depth and mystery and infinity. Therefore, to destroy or to abuse man is to destroy or abuse something with a quality of sacredness.

The accusation the Christian religion makes against secularism is not that the many scientific methods and measurements are applied to man; it is rather that the attitude of those who use such methods often silently implies that they provide *complete* measurement of man; that they claim to eliminate mystery from the image of man. This attitude has potentially vast consequences. "When man loses the sense of sacred mystery, he sees his neighbor as a thing. The profound personal meeting of self with self gives way to the maneuvering of objects."[2] And this, in the belief of the Christian religion, is intolerably wrong.

TOWARD A DEFINITION OF MAN

Can one define this "wonder"? Aristotle spoke of man as a social animal. Isn't man that? Of course he is; but so are ants and bees, whom man transcends by his power of thought, language, and by his civilization. By another common definition man is a "rational being." Again, it must be admitted that he is that. But modern psychology has thrown some very rational doubts on man's rationality; and if the essence of man is logical thinking, the question intrudes whether an electronic brain (perhaps one that can turn out such a statement as "I think, therefore I am"), is also human? Such objections can be made to all definitions by a single trait, from the "economic man" concerned with production and consumption of goods, to the "organization man" who succeeds in the business world, to the "eucharistic man" of Dom Gregory Dix,

[2] Roger Shinn in *What Is the Nature of Man?* by Kenneth Boulding and others, Christian Education Press, 1959, p. 127.

whose ultimate purpose is the common worship of God. Definitions of man must be more inclusive, to meet his many characteristic activities and features.

An example of a broader concept proposed by a modern philosopher is Ernst Cassirer's "symbolic animal" (animal symbolicum): "Man cannot escape from his own achievement. . . . Language, myth, art, and religion are part of his universe. . . . He has so enveloped himself in linguistic forms, in artistic images, in mythical symbols or religious rites that he cannot see or know anything except by the interposition of this artificial medium."[3] The concept of man in terms of broad cultural activity is certainly less vulnerable to criticism than any of the above definitions.[4]

The Christian definition of man will include man as a creature of God, i.e., a being with affinity to the rest of the world, and man as an image of God, i.e., a being with affinity to the immeasurable, unknown, sacred, to God. It therefore defines man as a being with a very special status in the world, with a very special destiny. We shall return to these characteristics after the preliminary approach to the Christian concept of man.

CHRISTIAN CONCEPT OF MAN

MAN IN RELATION

Having established the Christian view of man in depth, we now consider man as a responsive and responsible being, in relation to God and to his fellowman, and ultimately, to himself. There is

[3] Ernst Cassirer, *An Essay on Man,* Anchor Books, 1953, p. 43.

[4] For the development of this concept that myth, music, and religion have real meaning, and that language is more than semantics, see Susanne K. Langer, *Philosophy in a New Key,* Mentor Books, 1948. For fine discussions of certain "secular" images of man see Boulding and others, *op. cit.,* chaps. 2, 3, 5; and a symposium, "The New View of Man," in *The Centennial Review of Arts and Science,* a quarterly published by Michigan State University, Vol. I, No. 1 (Winter 1957).

again overlapping between the secular and the religious views. It is common sense that man is by nature social, that he can survive neither physically nor mentally in isolation. Nor do individuals create culture in isolation. Human relations are inseparable from man's existence and from healthy growth. In the twentieth century we are especially conscious of this fact. Literature is preoccupied with the solitariness of the individual; psychology is concerned with his "detachment from reality" which is a concomitant of man's isolation from his fellow men; the many clubs, associations, fraternal orders, and activities witness to the attempt to escape aloneness.

The Christian Church, too, is in search of fellowship and communion. But in addition to people's meeting in their social roles, the church believes in their communion as spirits. Most of the social groups join men in their partial community of interests, such as business or professional groups, as well as men of good will. They share only certain things. The ideal of the Christian community is to share completely, even beyond the grave. The early apostles had "all things in common," says the biblical record. And the church *universal* aims at joining those now living with those who had gone before and those yet unborn. It aims at more than "joining" them, in fact, it aims at "incorporating" them in one spiritual "body," so that "they may be one."

This unity of a spiritual body can be achieved by relation of all to the spiritual head of the body, Jesus Christ. In other words, the relation is dual: man to man, and man to God.

The covenant of Sinai is typical of this dual relation. The Ten Commandments (Exodus 20) are divided into two groups. One regulates relations between Israel and God, the other mutual relations among the people.

Israel's relation to God is a matter of both worship and the way of life. The people promise to be faithful to God. Then they break the promise, rebel against him. God makes a new approach to them to win them back. There is a whole series of covenants, made at various times through Noah, Abraham, Moses, through the prophets, and for the Christians, through Jesus Christ. All these are new beginnings, new chances for reconciliation, between men and their God. The covenant is not a commercial contract. Nor is it magic power. It is a voluntary mutual giving of trust, love, and service. Sometimes it is likened to a relation of man and woman in marriage.

True relation of man to man is always a relation of free persons, marked by the voluntary giving of trust, respect, and love.

There are no technical tricks by which we can win from persons that response of love on which our very life depends. They stand equal with us, free centers of fully personal existence, not to be commanded, not to be compelled, not to be manipulated. They are open to us only as they choose to be open, they yield themselves to us only on the initiative of their free and personal will. Here, where our happiness is chiefly at stake, we have to give up all mastery of the situation and become suppliants. As persons we stand on equal terms with other persons, at their mercy as they are at ours. This is the area of contract, of covenant; we can make agreements, but we cannot make slaves without doing violence to their nature and to ours.[5]

To designate these characteristically human relations, modern writers frequently use the terms "discourse" or "dialogue." It has been said that in the Western civilization the *philosophical and moral* discourse began when Socrates guided the passionate concern of minds in pursuit of truth. The *dramatic discourse* was codified when Thespis in Athens of the sixth century B.C. added an actor to the chorus. Interaction plus the spoken dialogue opened up unlimited possibilities to dramatic expression. The *religious discourse* began with the belief that God created man. According to the interpreters of this story, God was not satisfied with the eternal contemplation of the self. Nor was he satisfied with creation of "things," a kind of world of toys or objects to play with. He created man "in his own image," and "a living soul," a responsive and responsible being. One might say, not altogether

[5] Alexander Miller, *The Man in the Mirror,* Doubleday, 1958, p. 181.

blasphemously, that God created for himself a company of persons capable of communing with himself. The Almighty did not stay alone, because of his superabundance of love; and the essence of love is sharing.[6]

According to Genesis, God addressed Adam and Eve, and gave them a choice to make, and thus a responsibility. Adam and Eve share the responsibility. They also carry it for each other. The original religious dialogue, the story of creation and of Adam and Eve and of Christ as the Second Adam, determine for the Christian Church the true human relations at all times. These stories become "divine models" which men copy, reproduce, imitate.

Protestant theologians, while developing the age-old category of "man-in-relation," have been much influenced by the writings of the Jewish philosopher Martin Buber, who in 1923 published his little classic *I and Thou*. Discarding the old Greek way of thinking in terms of subject and object, Buber concentrated on personal encounter. God in himself cannot be described. He can only be worshiped or addressed. This means that God cannot be known in himself, but only in relation with the worshiper. Thus one may further say that God *is* not a person but only *becomes* one as he becomes known and as he knows, as he is loved and as he loves. The same is true of man.

That essence of man which is special to him can be directly known only in a living relation. . . . Consider man with man, and you see human life, dynamic, twofold, the giver and the receiver, he who does and he who endures, the attacking force and the defending force, the nature which investigates and the nature which supplies information, the request begged and granted—and always both together, completing one another in mutual contribution, together showing forth man. . . . We come nearer the answer to the question what man is when we come to see him as the eternal meeting of the One with the Other.[7]

[6] Cf. John of Damascus, *Exposition of the Orthodox Faith*, Salmond, S.D.F. (translator), *Nicene and Post-Nicene Fathers*, Eerdmans, 1955, Series II, Vol. IX, p. 18.

[7] Martin Buber, "What is Man?" (1938), in *Between Man and Man*, Beacon Press, 1955, p. 205. This is an excellent essay on various interpretations of man, from Aristotle to Kant, from Heidegger to Buber.

The distinguished Protestant theologian Emil Brunner enlarges on the same theme in his *Divine-Human Encounter*.[8] He argues that the biblical concept of truth is not a deposit of tradition to be captured once and for all times in a doctrine, but rather that Christian truth *comes into being* in an encounter between God and man and between man and his fellowman.

It is a matter of historical record that the encounter among men, even among Christian men, has not always produced the good and the truth, but often has resulted in perversion and in cruel conflict. This brings us to the concept of *sin,* and to the Christian belief that men are universally inclined to use the good and the true for their own selfish purposes.

THE CONCEPT OF SIN

WHAT SIN IS *Not*

The public sometimes misunderstands what the Christian churches believe about sin. It thinks that the human body, particularly sex, is said to be the chief source of sin.

Theologians never cease to point out that this popular notion misses the mark—in fact that the very first book of the Bible denies it. Genesis speaks of God as creating the universe, then the animals, then man; at the end of each phase of creation "God saw that it was good." If God made it and approved of it, who is man to call the material world evil? Jesus indicated that sin does not come from the body, but from the core of the human personality: "out of the heart come wicked designs, murder, adultery, immorality, stealing, false witness, impious speech" (Matthew 15, 19).

In the history of the Christian Church, sometimes sex has been

[8] Emil Brunner, *Divine-Human Encounter*, Westminster, 1943.

regarded as the particular symbol of sin. This was prevalent in Greek Christianity; the Church Father Origen held such opinion. Even an extreme form of dualism which set the spirit (good) against the body (evil) has made its inroads into Christianity from other religions. Again, medieval Christendom with its cult of virginity and with its celibacy has helped create the impression that the married state is lower than the unmarried state. Even within the institution of marriage, some churchmen in our own day have difficulty deciding whether the organs of reproduction were given man merely for procreation of the race, or also for the satisfaction and pleasure derived from them. Thus it must be admitted that the blame for confusion cannot be placed squarely on the shoulders of laymen and heretics. In spite of the haze hovering over this subject, classical Christian theology has always been clear in the conviction that the body as part of God's creation is good. It can be abused as everything else can, but it is not the primary source of sin. It is not "a prison of the soul," but "a temple of the spirit," and man is responsible to his creator for its care.

What Is Sin?

Sin is transgression of God's will. God's will is the law. This simple statement raises difficult problems as we probe into it. First, God is believed to be perfect, and his will covers all human acts and thoughts. To fulfill such a will, man must be perfect. He is not. He is therefore judged by the law which he cannot fulfill even if he tries. The Christian answer is that man is a sinner incapable to overcome sin by his own moral strength. He needs both help and forgiveness. The second problem arises: man is not even capable of comprehending and knowing fully the wonderful breadth and width of the divine will. Does not his ignorance of God's will excuse him? The Christian believes that man's vision of God's will is indeed dulled, but that God is just, and has given man ways of knowing his will. It is of interest now to examine this problem. According to the Christian religion, how does man know what is asked of him, what is right, what he *ought* to do?

The answer lies in man's social nature, first, with respect to the society in which he lives, the second, with respect to the particular community of faith in which he worships.

Man does not live in a vacuum, but in an historic society of a particular time, place, language, and customs. His society has its own mores, sanctions, do's and don'ts. By interaction with other members of his group, man develops both a conscience (a kind of built-in guide), and a knowledge of the specific set of laws and regulations which forbid, order, or clarify certain particular situations in which he finds himself. The majority Christian assumption is that within these human laws, ordinances, and social consciences, varied and imperfect as they may be, there is considerable guidance toward right living and toward fulfillment of God's will.

In the earlier societies, even in ancient Israel, there was of course no issue between secular and religious standards, since the two were combined. Sanctions of society were backed by God's authority. In modern times, we have seen increasing separation of the sacred and the secular spheres. The question of how much of his secular conscience a Christian can incorporate into his religious conscience (as a member of the church) has become pressing.

The ethics of any particular society differ from Christian ethics at many points, and in some ways the two are diametrically opposed to each other. There have always been "perfectionists" among Christians, such as the Anabaptists of the sixteenth century, who have rejected "the world" as belonging to the devil; they took no part in city administration, in fighting, etc. This led to complete separation of the church from the state. But the majority of the large historic churches have made some compromise with "the world." As Augustine put it, so long as the church lives like a stranger in this Earthly City, "it makes no scruple to obey the laws of the earthly city, by which the things necessary for the maintenance of this mortal life are administered." Some churches have become intertwined with particular states until their policies and their use of power went hand in hand. Within all these situations we usually take it for granted that a Christian ought to be "at least as good" as a non-Christian, that his aims are the same as true humanistic aims of betterment, health, decency, and freedom of society. Whenever Christian morality falls below the standards of society at large, the church fares badly and inevitably comes under criticism. The sharp warning of sixteenth-century humanists who clearly admired the "noble pagan" and despised the ignorant, superstitious, and sloppy Christian, still echoes in our ears.

Beyond the sphere of social traditions and mores lies the second community in which a Christian recognizes God's will. It is the church, and it is more important than the first community, because God's will is here revealed to him in a much clearer way. In its Christ-centered teachings, common worship, and practice of communal living, the church not only finds God but also finds its answer to what it means, in the last analysis, to be human. Seen through Christ, man is not judged primarily by the height of his scientific achievement, nor by his intelligence quotient, nor yet by the depth of his private mystical insight. The criterion of man is his fulfillment or failure in love. Love (or "charity," as the Roman Catholic version of the Bible translates it), is of course more than just private feeling. It is the motivating force that has its origin in God and creates the "community of love."

The early church held its "love feasts," or *agape,* which amounted to something like fellowship-meals with worship included at certain times. The whole New Testament abounds with the exaltation of love. Jesus, asked to name the greatest command of the Law, gave his famous answer that the whole Law is summed up in the Love of God and the love of one's neighbor (Matthew 22, 37–40). In John's Gospel we find Christ saying: "I give you a new command: Love one another. Just as I have loved you, you must love one another. By this they will all know that you are my disciples" (John 13, 34 f.). In the first letter to the Corinthians, chapter 13, St. Paul wrote the oft-quoted ode to divine love. He placed love above sacrifice, above faith, above any Christian act or virtue. It is easy to understand that the church cultivates love in numerous ways. Of these the first is common worship. "The ultimate aim of all expressive worship is the increase of Charity; the pure love of God, for Himself alone."[9] Within this community of worship and life, with its definite way and traditions, a Christian develops something of a new conscience that indicates to him when he is right and when wrong, when he is pleasing or offending God and his fellowman. These matters become internalized and "natural" to him.

In addition to the built-in guide described, most churches provide their members with a more or less formal list of laws and ordinances concerning Christian behavior. Some spell out the virtues and the vices, the do's and don'ts in a systematic and detailed way. For example, Roman Catholic teaching, with the help of certain medieval terminology, classifies sins in a number of categories. There is the original sin, and the actual sin. There are mortal (or great) sins and venial (or lesser) sins. There are sins committed and sins of omission. There are material sins (committed without thought or consent of the individual) and there are formal sins. The chief sources of sin are enumerated explicitly as pride, covetousness, lust, anger, gluttony, envy, and sloth. To these are opposed the virtues of humility, generosity, chastity, meekness, temperance, brotherly love, and diligence. Most Protestant churches do not have as complete and formal a classification as this, and they tend to rely more on the guidance of the Christian conscience, nourished by the Bible, the sermon, childhood instruc-

[9] Evelyn Underhill, *Worship*, Harper Torchbooks, p. 45. Anders Nygren in his famous book, *Agape and Eros*, Westminster, 1953, develops the theological centrality of divine love; contrasted with this are more humanistic views such as that of Erich Fromm, *The Art of Loving*, Harper & Row, 1956, which considers the "brotherly love" to be the most fundamental and the one which underlies all other types of love.

tions, and common sense. Some stress particular offenses of behavior, but none pretend to be exhaustive. Even among the Methodists who bind themselves not to smoke or drink there is a
standing joke that "everything else is permitted." Complete listing
of specific sins for all occasions of life would involve casuistry,
which is not only impracticable, but is foreign to the Christian,
spiritual concept of religion.

The actual emphasis upon the gravity of sin in the history of the
Christian Church has somewhat varied in different periods. When
Pelagius placed too much confidence in man, St. Augustine went
to the other extreme, elaborated dramatically the doctrine of
original sin, and referred to mankind as "a mass of perdition."
Again, when late medieval theology, mysticism, and humanism
combined to extoll the goodness of human nature and the dignity
of man, Luther (who was by training an Augustinian monk) did
what Augustine had done before him, viz., he greatly elaborated
the meaning of the profundity of sin, and the accompanying terror
and anxiety of the Christian conscience. Against the humanistic
treatise of Erasmus on the freedom of will he wrote his own
treatise on the "enslaved will" (variously translated into English
as a treatise on "unfree will" or the "bondage of the will").

A classical expression for sin is "pride," or Greek "hubris." It
appears as the key term of offense against the gods in Greek
tragedy, e.g., in Sophocles' Theban plays. Used throughout Christian history, it has been in the twentieth century taken up as a key
concept by Reinhold Niebuhr, who among Protestants has somewhat resumed Luther's cause against easy optimism, this time an
optimism within the Protestant ranks themselves. The most offensive is *spiritual pride,* that is a pretension of assuming divine
authority. Men claim divine sanction for their human standards
and attainments, and thus show their desire to be like God, and to
take the place of their creator. Closely related is *moral pride,* which
is subsumed in the sin of self-righteousness. "The sin of self-
righteousness involves us in the greatest cruelties, injustices, and

defamations against our fellowmen. The whole history of racial, national, religious and other social struggles is a commentary on the objective wickedness and social miseries which result from self-righteousness."[10] Niebuhr's *intellectual pride* is a variation which denotes man's claim of finality for his ideology or for his knowledge. *Pride as lust for power* means that a person is willing to sacrifice others in search for his own security or in the process of asserting his own power.[11] Niebuhr sees great realism in the Christian view of man as sinner. It steers a course between the Scylla of extreme optimism that considers reason a sufficient match for the destructive tendencies and passions in man, and the Charybdis of extreme pessimism, which is blind to man's creative capacities and his true freedom through grace.

ORIGINAL SIN

The Christian Church has assumed that sin is universally present and that it is of the gravest consequences. Without this assumption, it could hardly make a case for the universal plan of salvation of mankind which is its message. The doctrine of original sin (or "inherited sin") expresses this thought. It also throws light on the Christian statement of the paradox of free will versus determinism. Original sin means that man does not become what he is apart from the rest of humanity. As an individual he shares in common humanity, is predisposed by it, and interacts with it. The sin is "Adam's," which to some churches simply means "mankind's." The inclination to evil is inherited from the very beginning by all. On the other hand, this doctrine asserts that each individual man gives consent to every sinful action with his personal will, and thus *original sin* becomes his own *personal sin.* Should then Adam's sin be regarded as natural to all men? The

[10] Reinhold Niebuhr, *Nature and Destiny of Man,* Scribner, 1949, Vol. I, p. 200.
[11] *Ibid.,* pp. 186 ff.

idea of "total depravity" has sometimes given such an impression, yet classic theology cannot admit that sin is of man's essential nature, since man was created good. It is not natural, but it is universal. It is difficult to detail how original sin is transmitted. The answers come dangerously close to confusing religious language with the language of genetics. Suffice it to say that it is clearly believed to be present in all men, with the exception of the "second Adam," Christ (and according to the Catholic tradition, also Mary, Christ's mother). Despite the universality of this inherited sin (or inherited inclination toward sin), man is not freed from responsibility. The individual is not just a bundle of genetic inheritances and cultural bequests. He is able and forced to make decisions with sufficient free will and understanding that he must be held responsible for his actions.

The Christian concept of salvation forms a symmetric counterpart to the doctrine of original sin. Both Adam (Christ) and personal decision are involved in each of them. St. Paul drew a parallel of this kind in his Epistle to the Romans, chapter 5 (and elsewhere). As sin was once introduced into the human race by Adam, its head and first sinner, so through Christ, the "second Adam," a new race of men came into being. This new race, under Christ's headship, is free from original sin. Christian freedom is on the one hand due to Christ and the church in which his life and action are implemented, and on the other hand to one's personal choice, a decision of one's will, free from the action of original sin, and nourished by the community of love.

The preceding pages were in themselves something of a summary of various views of sin, and summary of the summary would not be just. But a concluding paragraph may underline and stress the social nature of sin and salvation.

Love is community-creating and outgoing; self-centeredness is community-destroying, for it assumes the attitude of ultimate self-sufficiency. Ancient Greeks dubbed *idiotes* a fellow-citizen who shunned his public duties and avoided participation in the common good life. The Christian Church sees a *sinner* in a person who by his pride destroys his fellowship with his creator and in consequence also begins to hide some of his true self from his fellowman. It is the imitation of the prototype of sin in Adam and Eve: having desired to be like God, they defied him and began to hide from him. Consequently, they found that they also began to conceal their true selves from each other ("and they saw that they were naked"). Sin separates, isolates, destroys fellowship.

To this classic statement of disturbed and broken fellowship of man with his God and also with his fellowman, twentieth-century writers increasingly tend to add a third separation—that of man from his own true self. To be sure, this is not an invention of our century and one can document such separation in St. Paul, St. Augustine, Pascal, Dostoievski, Kierkegaard, and others. But *the preoccupation with the self* is growing in our day of intensive study of psychology, of the borderline between religion and psychiatry[12] and of philosophical preoccupation of man with the process of his experience. (The popularity of Whitehead in modern Protestant thinking is truly amazing.) It is therefore congenial to our intellectual climate to have Paul Tillich define sin as the estrangement of man from his true self. Perhaps it is time for a turn of the tide, or at least for a corrective, such as the position of Alexander Miller, who writes in his *The Man in the Mirror, Studies in the Christian Understanding of Selfhood:* "Salvation in the Biblical and Christian meaning of the word (in Wycliffe's Bible it is consistently translated *health*) means precisely to be extricated from the self's sinful preoccupation with the self, and to be incorporated into the community which is the fruit of Christ's self-offering."[13]

The many Christian terms for salvation, such as *reconciliation, holiness* (wholeness), *atonement* (at-one-ment), point in the direction of unity after separation. But if the separation of sin is a

[12] Cf. the works of C. G. Jung, Rollo May, Erich Fromm, and others.
[13] *Op. cit.,* p. 133.

separation from one's self, it is certainly at the same time separation of man from his God and from his fellowmen. The self, the church, and God, again cannot be defined completely apart from each other.

DEATH

> I met a Californian who would
> Talk California—a state so blessed,
> He said, in climate, none had ever died there
> A natural death, and Vigilance Committees
> Had had to organize to stock the graveyards
> And vindicate the state's humanity.[14]

Should one substitute the biblical Garden of Eden for California in the above verse, one would very nearly state a belief that is popular among the unlettered as well as widespread among orthodox Christian writers. But for sin, man would not have returned to dust, but would have lived forever. This interpretation, that death is the consequence of sin, has St. Paul's authority to support it, and much later traditional opinion. What is not in harmony with biblical theology is the suggestion that man's creatureliness, inclusive of his perishable body as part of the biological order of nature, is evil. On the contrary, the Bible suggests that creation, body and soul, is good. If God created nature, its "natural" limitations do not make it evil. Therefore there have been attempts to interpret the meaning of death in other ways. Niebuhr writes: "The dominant note in the Biblical view of death is that it illustrates the difference between the majesty of God and the weakness and dependence of man as creature."[15] The dread of death is frequently taken as that of *spiritual* death, i.e., the eternal separation of man from his Creator. The "sting of death" then

[14] From "New Hampshire" from *Complete Poems of Robert Frost.* Copyright 1923 by Holt, Rinehart and Winston, Inc. Copyright 1951 by Robert Frost. Reprinted by permission of Holt, Rinehart and Winston, Inc.

[15] *Op. cit.,* p. 176.

becomes the basic *anxiety* of *separation,* which stems from a wrong attitude toward one's existence. Here we come back to the existential concept of anxiety as the key to man's religious problem.

In any case, physical death is not the last word about man. The primeval pattern of the "eternal return" has very special form in the Christian religion, where each individual "Member of Christ's Body" participates in the change which his Lord over life and death suffered in the Crucifixion and in the Resurrection. Whether taken objectively as hope of immortality, or subjectively, where the old self dies (is crucified) with Christ and the new self rises with Him in everlasting life, death in the Christian religion is only a part of such transformation and is inseparable from the thought of "life eternal."

INTERPRETING GENESIS

For some 1700 years the Christians, and for long centuries before them the Jews, held the book of Genesis to be the authentic history of the origin of the human race. In our universities, we still study Genesis with its vast literary traditions for literary purposes, such as better understanding of Milton.[16] Today few people would quibble over whether Adam was created with 25 ribs, or whether Eve was made from one of his regular 24 ribs, in which instance Adam must later have been given a replacement. Even the problem whether woman has a soul is not urgent today. To the secular public, Genesis has fallen to the level depicted by the French cartoonist Jean Effel who, at the end of a series of 16 pictures on Adam and Eve, drew the Almighty as a benign old man sitting on soft puffs of clouds and telling his rapt angels the end of the story: "and they lived unhappily ever after and had many children."

---

[16] See Arnold Williams, *The Common Expositor,* University of North Carolina Press, 1948, a truly fascinating scholarly account of some patristic, medieval, and Renaissance views of Genesis.

Most of the Christian churches today take the story of the creation of man to be a "religious myth," by which they mean, that whether or not the story has historical accuracy, it expresses truths of profound meaning and universal validity. For instance, Protestant Alan Richardson writes: "Today we do not interpret Genesis myths literally. But nevertheless we assert their amazing insight into the truth about human nature. . . . Adam is everyman. . . . Man is at every moment 'falling.' "[17] Roman Catholic writers are somewhat more restrained, since they are by faith bound to believe that "Adam" is not a reference for "everyman," but rather a definite reference to the first man of history. Even here, the general trend is not to consult the Bible as a scientific treatise. Writes a contributor to the *Twentieth Century Encyclopedia of Catholicism:* "That a serpent spoke is the myth; that the temptation took place . . . is the teaching of revelation which will stand for ever."[18] Interestingly enough, some Jewish scholars have taken the same attitude; writes Maimonides: "The account given in Scripture of the Creation is not, as is generally believed, intended to be in all its parts literal."[19]

At this point the student is advised to read the first chapters of Genesis—the story of the creation and fall of man. In this story, "Adam" appears both as proper name, and as a Hebrew noun meaning simply "man" (or "mankind"). There are those who take the story as representative of the actual origin of man in time, and others who take it in the purely mythical sense. "The time-element in the myth of Creation and Fall (as in all the Biblical myths) must be discounted; it is not that *once* (in 4004 B.C.—or a hundred thousand years ago) God created man perfect, then he fell from grace. God is eternally creator; He is eternally making man and holding him in being. . . . And just as creation is an

[17] Alan Richardson (ed.), *A Theological Word Book of the Bible,* Macmillan, 1962, p. 14 f.

[18] Nicholas Corte, *The Origin of Man,* Faith and Facts Books No. 29, 1959, pp. 94, 121.

[19] Menahem M. Kasher, *Encyclopedia of Biblical Interpretation, a Millennial Anthology,* Genesis, Vol. I, 1953, p. 253. This is a learned commentary which also contains a rich anthology from the sages of the Jewish tradition.

eternal activity, so the 'Fall' is an ingredient of every moment of human life. Man is at every moment 'falling,' putting himself in the centre, rebelling against the will of God."[20]

Some have derived the word "adam" from "adamah," which means "ground." This suggests man's earthly origin, his affinity to the rest of the material world. Such is indeed the thought in the Bible concerning man: made of dust of the earth, he is clearly limited; his life span has its limits. His possibilities have boundaries given by his creatureliness, and by his created environment. His free will is not unlimited like the free will of God. But this thought is only partial truth about man.

The other truth about man the Bible proclaims is his "image of God." No one knows the precise meaning of this expression, and speculation thrives on uncertainty. Common suggestions of the meaning of this phrase are: man has free will and responsibility; man is rational, capable of understanding; man reflects divine glory, perfection, grace; perfection can be seen particularly in his physical, moral, and intellectual endowments.

The book of Genesis gives us little to go on about the state of innocence, i.e., the "time" before Adam and Eve transgressed the will of God. Nor does it offer any opinion on how long Adam might have lived in the Garden of Eden. Karl Barth is of the opinion that "there never was a golden age. There is no point in looking back to one. The first man was immediately the first sinner."[21] The Bible therefore gives no clue to the image of God undisturbed by sin, until we reach the New Testament and the image of God in Christ.

THE PARADOX OF MAN

From the preceding emerges one characteristic of the biblical view of man: man is a composite of varied elements and opposite aspects. Theologians like to use the word "paradox" in expressing

[20] Richardson, *op. cit.,* p. 14.
[21] *Christ and Adam, Man and Humanity in Romans 5,* Harper & Row, 1957, p. 14.

these opposites (both of which are true). Man is *both* the "dust of the earth" *and* the "image of God," both temporal and eternal, both material and spiritual, both good and a sinner. The poetry of the Psalms often corroborates these paradoxes: "As for man, his days are like grass; he flourishes like a flower of the field; for the wind passes over it, and it is gone, and its place knows it no more" (Psalm 103:15f.). "Man is like a breath, his days are like a passing shadow" (Psalm 144:4). On the other side: "Thou hast made him little less than God, and dost crown him with glory and honor. Thou hast given him dominion over the works of thy hands; thou hast put all things under his feet" (Psalm 8:5f.).

There is the duality of man's ethical nature, which also may be brought under this heading. Man was created "very good," but in 10 generations he turned so bad that God was sorry he had ever made him (Genesis 6:5f.).

Man is *conscious* of his own greatness and ability, but also of his depravity and cruelty. Both Protestant and Roman Catholic writers express themselves with relish in terms of paradoxes on the nature of man. "Man is nothing and yet everything; he is brute and yet godly; he is a victim of necessity but genuinely free; he is a creature but yet a creator. Of himself he can do nothing worthwhile and yet he can do anything through Him who strengthens him. He finds his soul by losing it. . . ."[22]

The notion of paradox is useful insofar as it brings to view the extreme complexity of man, and the "mystery of man" described earlier in this chapter. It has more a defensive function than an explanatory one, for it prevents a Christian from accepting any simple explanation of human behavior or of human motivation and leaves room for growth and for investigation. It also guards against demagogical oversimplification of men as "dishonest" (Machiavelli), all good in their "natural state" (Rousseau), superior racially to other men (Nazi ideology), etc. On the other hand, it is true that by the very setting of the words of these paradoxes, a

[22] Gustave Weigel, "The Christian as Humanist," in Boulding and others, *op. cit.*, p. 111.

Christian classifies the problem of man as a religious problem, and his nature as definable correctly in the last analysis only in religious terms, i.e., in relation to God.

EVOLUTION AND CHRISTIAN BELIEFS

Christian attitudes toward evolutionary theories are broadly divided into hostility, coexistence, and cooperation.

Some fundamentalist churches in the United States have been openly hostile to evolutionary theories to the point of excluding them from school curricula. It appears that their objection is founded on a literal interpretation of the Bible. They find no difference of meaning between the language of religion and the language of science. Genesis does not contain a religious myth whose meaning must be freshly rediscovered, but a scientifically accurate and precise piece of information. The dichotomy then is between the truth as known through the Bible and the truth as known through a textbook of biology. The choice is either for God or for Darwin and company, and the choice must be made.

The majority of Christian churches find that such a conflict either need not or cannot exist if we make proper distinction between the spiritual implications of the evolutionary theories and their biological implications. In a Protestant spirit, M. H. Hartshorne writes: "Between the theory of evolution as a scientific hypothesis and Christianity as faith in Christ there could be no real quarrel."[23] And the Roman Catholic priest Nicolas Corte concurs: "Today it is readily accepted that the Bible is not to be consulted as if it were a scientific treatise, and that such seemingly scientific facts as are to be found in it have no other value than to inform us of the ideas current at the different times at which the books composing it were written. Neither Moses nor the anonymous

---

[23] *The Promise of Science and the Power of Faith,* Westminster, 1958, p. 84.

sixth century editor of his work had any concern whatever with science."[24]

It is taken for granted that both Protestant and Catholic scholars have made extensive use of scientific aids, such as archaeology, or historical and literary criticism, in order that they might arrive at better understanding of what the writers of the Scriptures in ancient times had intended.[25]

Use of sciences, and the denial of conflict between the Christian religion and evolutionary theories does not mean that the great churches give their wholehearted support to the latter. They simply make room for them and admit their scientific legality. What the Christian churches in this respect are really interested in is that the unique value of the human being be clearly preserved.

Up to a measure, the scientists could also admit the unique value of the human beings. Man is unique among animals by his brain capacity, by his use of tools and language, and by his creation of civilization. Perhaps it is a difference in degree only, so that man represents the high point of a natural continuum, the peak of evolution. But here the roads part: a Christian insists that man is a person responsible to God and to his fellowman. This a scientist can neither prove nor disprove. Society does act on the *practical assumption* that man has freedom and responsibility. But a *person* cannot be established by quantitative measurements. Moreover, this assertion is based on the *belief* that there is a God. Therefore the Christian statement about man of necessity is an act of faith. This is a specifically religious assertion of the difference of man from all other beings. The traditional terms for this human specific are the "image of God in man" (which has already been discussed) and "the soul." The "soul" also has its support in the Bible, although the term appears in other religions as well. The book of Genesis singles man out: all vegetation was produced by

24 Corte, *op. cit.*, pp. 94, 100.
25 The Papal Encyclical *Divino Afflante* issued by Pius XII in 1947 deems the use of such sciences "absolutely necessary" for this purpose.

the earth (Genesis 1, 11, and 24), but man is a product of God's special act: God breathed a breath of life into man, and he became a "living Soul." Man among all creatures has special relation to God, his "Father." In Roman Catholic theology this distinctiveness is made an important point of doctrine: although the human body may be a product of evolution, each individual *soul* is *especially created* by God. The Protestant tradition leans toward what it believes to be more biblical preference, namely the inseparable unity of man, body and soul.[26] In this tradition, the process of *how* man becomes the unique being (different from animals, yet in evolutionary continuity with them) is usually not elaborated.

The position just described, viz., coexistence of the Christian and the evolutionary viewpoints, has certain stumbling blocks. Consider, for example, the problem of *monogenism* and *polygenism*. It is a question whether mankind has come from *one* human pair only, or from *several* original human pairs which emerged in different places within the same general period. In the absence of evidence, scientists must remain open-minded. Yet there are very good reasons for scientists to support a theory of polygenism. Such theory raises no problem to those Protestants to whom "Adam" simply stands for "mankind" or "everyman." But to the Jewish and the Catholic traditions compelling reasons of doctrine make such opinion unacceptable.

In these two traditions it is a vested doctrinal interest that calls for *one only* ancestor of the human race. In the Hebrew religion, such a doctrine concerns the solidarity of mankind, or brotherhood of all men. An ancient Hebrew comment on the verse of Genesis 1:27 ("and God created man") is: "God created only one man at first. Why? Lest the righteous boast that they are the descendants of a righteous first man, whilst the wicked plead that their first progenitor was evil."[27] The Roman Catholic and Protestant orthodox reason for *one only* ancestor of the human race is the

[26] Cf. Niebuhr, *op. cit.,* chap. VI.
[27] Kasher, *op. cit.,* Vol. I, No. 247, p. 64.

custom of reading the Old Testament through the eyes of the New Testament, which in this instance means to read Genesis through the mind of St. Paul, especially through his Epistle to the Romans. St. Paul here interprets Adam in terms of Christ. "Just as that one man's disobedience made the mass of mankind sinners, so this one's obedience will make the mass of them upright" (Romans 5, 19). One wrecker of the human race, and one restorer, have provided a symmetry to all traditional Christian theology for so long that it seems built in, and would be very hard indeed to change.[28]

This thought has various implications. If it is true that without Adam's fall there would be no need of Christ, it is equally true that without Christ we would not know what the glory of man was. *True humanity is revealed in Christ more fully and clearly than it is in Adam.* Karl Barth, the staunch Swiss representative of new Protestant orthodoxy ("neo-orthodoxy"), and one of the most learned Christian theologians now living, has made this a major point in his voluminous writings.[29] The following statements are excerpted from his study of Romans, chapter 5, called *Christ and Adam:* "Man's essential and original nature is to be found not in Adam but in Christ. Adam can therefore be interpreted only in the light of Christ and not the other way round."[30] "The status of Adam is lower than the status of Christ, the sin of Adam counts for less than the righteousness of Christ."[31] "Adam is only the first among equals. He has no other essential priority of status over men. He cannot be their lord and head; he cannot determine their life and their destiny." Christ, on the other hand "is the true man in an absolute sense, and it is in His humanity

---

28 "There were not several 'wreckers' of the human race, any more than there were several redeemers. The oneness of the new Adam is the necessary counterpart of the oneness of the old Adam." Corte, *op. cit.,* p. 137.

29 Particularly the *Church Dogmatics,* Harper Torchbooks, 1962, and *Christ and Adam, Man and Humanity in Romans 5.*

30 *Christ and Adam,* p. 29.

31 *Christ and Adam,* p. 34.

that we have to recognize true human nature."[32] For the comparative value of Adam and Christ, there is an interesting parallel in Jewish tradition. Kasher[33] quotes this comment on the verse "then the Lord God formed the man": "The Holy One, blessed be He, reasoned: 'I will create Adam first, so that if he sins, Abraham will come and set things right.' Abraham 'deserved to be created before Adam,' and would have been save for this reason, that if he sinned, there would be none to set right his sin."

Through such reasoning the characteristic *monistic* tendency of Christian thought is preserved. The origin of all things is from one God; the origin of all men from one man, and the consummation of history in the one man through whom God entered history, Jesus Christ. He reveals God, but he also reveals man to himself. It would be a matter of speculation whether this preference for monogenism is part of the wider tendency of the Western civilization which is manifested in monogamy, in Aristotle's prime mover, in Einstein's unified field theory, and in a thousand other ways. But here we are obviously in the realm of patterns of thought.

Some notable Christian writers, however, have attempted to *harmonize* evolution and the Christian faith. The elements of such an undertaking go back to the time of Church Fathers. St. Augustine held a theory of "seminal causes," according to which everything that exists develops out of the primeval origins created by God. He gives the analogy of a seed of a tree in which all the characteristics of a tree are already contained, and they simply develop as the tree grows.

A contemporary Roman Catholic palaeontologist, Teilhard de Chardin, believes that evolution indeed takes place, but not by *random* variations or *chance;* it is guided and directed by progressive steps toward its final goal—*a God-oriented evolution.* The "*Omega point,*" as he designates *the end* of all evolution, reminds

[32] *Christ and Adam,* pp. 93, 94.
[33] *Op. cit.,* No. 85, p. 96.

one of Aristotle's belief that the *goal* moves the world by drawing everything to itself as if by the power of evoking love for itself in all things (*hos eromenon*).

E. L. Mascall, an English scholar, again presents us with a combination of Julian Huxley's evolutionary philosophy with the Christian Church's ideal of progress. The progress of course amounts to the progress of the world toward salvation, rather than the secular concept of progress based on the industrial society, science, and the belief in man's natural tendency of self-improvement. Mascall takes up Huxley's thought that in man the evolutionary process has reached a new stage, since it has become conscious of itself, aware of future possibilities, and capable of directing itself. "We can go on to say that the only kind of consciously directed human evolution which we can recognize as fully valid is evolution within the Body of Christ; that is to say, the progressive incorporation of the human race into the sacramental Church, and the development and use of all man's newly won powers under the governing influence of supernatural grace."[34]

In conclusion let us repeat that modern Christians are generally open to the ideas coming from secular investigations of man, from whatever quarter they may arrive. But they would not be true to their religion if in the last analysis their view of man were not Christ-oriented. To them, the Christ of faith is at the same time the historic person, Jesus of Nazareth who spoke of the kingdom of God to the unlettered, blessed the poor, came to bring more abundant life to those troubled in body and in spirit, and who, coming into a tragic conflict with society about him, revealed the true nature of man and the immense love of God for man. His incarnation—the fact of God becoming man—assures human worth and dignity, but also reveals the depth of human sin. All Christian theology centers here; all the doctrines meet in Christ.

---

[34] E. L. Mascall, *The Importance of Being Human*, the Bampton lectures in America, Columbia, 1958, pp. 100 f.

Christ is the true measure of man, and one who gives meaning to being human.

SUGGESTED READINGS

Buber, Martin, *Between Man and Man,* Beacon Press, 1955.

Cassirer, Ernst, *An Essay on Man,* Anchor, 1953.

Corte, Nicolas, *The Origins of Man, 20th Century Encyclopedia of Catholicism,* vol. 29, Daniel-Rops. (ed.), Hawthorn, 1958.

Mascall, Eric Lionel, *The Importance of Being Human,* Columbia, 1958.

Niebuhr, Reinhold, *The Nature and Destiny of Man,* 2 vols., Scribner, 1949.

Tillich, Paul, *The Courage to Be,* Yale, 1952.

V

God

Spiritual and supernatural forces, traced in records of man's life on earth, have played a vital role from the earliest times on through the great civilizations. The image of these forces has progressively changed. There is great distance between the animistic beliefs and the attempt of man to appease the spirits in nature on the one hand, and the sacred law codes of the great ancient civilizations on the other. The Greek trilogy of Aeschylus, the *Oresteia,* spells out for us such a change. And there is again a further distance between the images of gods among the ancient peoples and today's philosophical discussion of God as "ultimate concern," or as the organizing principle that gives continuity to modes of being. Thus, we may speak of an evolution of the concept of God, or simply of changes and transformations.

There are peculiar difficulties for those who wish to be truly modern in the approach to the subject. In our semireligious culture, especially in classroom discussion, God may be a pale reflection of the vital, upsetting, and powerful reality that he was to Moses or to Aeschylus, to Socrates or to John the Baptist. Nowadays we find the "problem of God," the "agonizingly absent God," or simply the "absent God" discussed in literature; Martin Buber has written on "the eclipse of God," Herman Kutter asked "where is God?" and Nietzsche pronounced that "God is dead." *Waiting for Godot,* Samuel Becket's brilliant play, fascinates us because it gives us insight into the human condition. But the Godot who never comes gives no answers, and men are left to their own wisdom, reflecting on their condition. Again, with Lagerkvist's Barabbas, mankind sees itself crucified and gazing into darkness with some vague glimmer of hope in the immense space of its suffering and of its blunders. But giving up one's soul to darkness is not enough to live on. The negation of bread does not satisfy man's hunger, nor does a dramatic effect satisfy his deepest longing. It is guidance for living and the meaning of life that the Christian churches have sought in their worship of God. The present-day discussion of the subject reveals the crisis of our time in its spiritual dimension. At the end of this chapter, we shall return to it. For the present, we begin with (a) two selected examples of ancient concepts of God that are of special interest to us, and (b) basic Christian thoughts concerning God.

THE HINDU CONCEPT OF SUPREME GOD

We often ask: aren't all the gods of major religions about the same? What is the difference? For one point of comparison, here is a statement of a Hindu concept of the supreme god, Brahman, the beginning of beginnings, life of life, all-pervading creator, sustainer, and destroyer—three in one, the source and end of the universe.

Brahman is One, and there is nothing beyond him. Though he pervades *everything in the world, yet the universe is not Brahman.* . . . He is the same towards all existence including the meanest. Being One, He is in them all, just as the moon is reflected in a thousand vessels of water. The taste of salt is the same, though there may be different grains. The quality of sweetness is the same, though there may be thousands of pieces of sugar-cane. Brahman, while pervading everything in this uniform manner, is also *the source of the universe.* As waves come out of the ocean and as the ocean itself is the cause of the waves, *so all life finds its support in Him.* Just as the body is the same, though it passes through the three ages, viz., childhood, manhood, and old age, *so Brahman is one and unbroken through origin, existence, and end.* Just as the sky does not change during the morning, mid-day and evening, so as *creator,* He acquires the name of Brahmadeva, as *supporter* He gets the name of Vishnu, and as *destroyer* He gets the name of Shankar, and *behind these threefold qualities, He remains quality-less.* When the final element disappears and when the threefold qualities disappear, He remains the great negative. He is the final goal of knowledge. This is the supreme doctrine of the Vedas. He is what burns in fire, what cools in the moon, what shines in the sun. He gives light to the stars and He is the lustre of lustre. *He is the beginning of beginnings.* He is the growth of growth, and intelligence of intelligence, and consciousness of consciousness. *He is the life of life.* . . . He holds the earth, He makes water flow, light travel and wind move. He contains the sky in Himself. Everything which is felt and seen, is through Him. He pervades everything perfectly and in Him there is no duality.[1]

THE HEBREW CONCEPT OF GOD

The most closely related to the Christian concept of God among the world religions is the Hebrew. The Hebrew God, too, is one, and all life finds support in him. He as creator of all things is master of creation, from the sky and the loftiest mountains to the

[1] Dnyaneshwar Maharaj, *Gita Explained,* 2nd ed., translated by Subedar, Palli Hill Bandra, 1941, pp. 213–214.

fertility of the earth, and the insects. The major holidays of the ancient Hebrews coincided with agricultural cycles of life such as the beginning of the harvest. Offering of thanksgiving for the fruits of the earth acknowledged the dependence of men on their God. But where the Hindu religion stressed the *all-pervasiveness* of Brahman, the god within and behind all experience, the Hebrew emphasized the *lordship* of the creator, and the lofty control over all things. The Hindu god is more *immanent,* the Hebrew more *transcendent,* over and above the world.

The Hebrew belief in the immense *creativity, power, control,* and *governance* of the universe was expressed in fine religious poetry.

> he who removes mountains, and they know it not,
> when he overturns them in his anger;
> who shakes the earth out of its place,
> and its pillars tremble;
> who commands the sun, and it does not rise;
> who seals up the stars;
> who alone stretched out the heavens,
> and trampled the waves of the sea;
> who made the Bear and Orion,
> the Pleiades and the chambers of the south;
> who does great things beyond understanding,
> and marvelous things without number.

> Job 9:5–10

The Hebrew prophets, who are very much in the bloodstream of the Christian religion, saw the *hand of God* also *in the events of history,* including wars and natural disasters. Consider this passage from Prophet Isaiah.

> Rouse yourself, rouse yourself, stand up, O Jerusalem,
> you who have drunk at the hand of the Lord
> the cup of his wrath,

who have drunk to the dregs the bowl of staggering . . .
These two things have befallen you—
who will condole with you?—
devastation and destruction, famine and sword;
who will comfort you?
Your sons have fainted, they lie at the head of every street
like an antelope in a net;
they are full of the wrath of the Lord,
the rebuke of your God.

Isaiah 51:17, 19–20

Essential to all traditional concepts of god is a *sense of mystery*. Man will never fathom the depth of God's purposes; he cannot question God. This is not to say that God is a rational puzzle which has no solution. The purpose of this characteristic is not, as has been cynically suggested, to muddy the waters in order to better capitalize on people's credulity. It is rather to stress that God is incommensurable with man. There is a basic qualitative difference between the creator and the creation. Man as part of creation has no categories of thought adequate to express God, nor complete knowledge and understanding of God. Man's life passes "like the flowers of the field that wither"—to use a favorite Hebrew phrase—while God spans all the generations of living beings. Since God's will, power, understanding, and eternity are totally out of proportion to those of man, God can be properly approached by man only in an attitude of worship.

In the Hebrew religion, as in most ancient religions, this sense of mystery is part of the essential characteristic of God, viz., *holiness*. Holiness refers to the "numinous" presence, the power over man's life and death, which Rudolf Otto so well described in *The Idea of the Holy*. It includes awe-fulness, overpowering energy, the "mysterium tremendum." The mortal who would come face to face with the Holy One would surely die.

When Moses was ready to engage in the solemn mediation

between God and his people (to bring to them the famous Ten Commandments), he first asked the people to prepare themselves for the holy day. The period of consecration lasted three days. They were ordered to wash their clothes—no doubt symbolic of purification—and to practice abstinence ("approach no woman"). Most of all, they were to have respect for the holy mountain where the Lord would manifest himself:

> whoever touches the mountain shall be put to death;
> no hand shall touch him, but he shall be stoned or shot;
> whether beast or man, he shall not live . . .
> (And, as the people stood at the foot of the mountain)
> Mount Sinai was wrapped in smoke, because the Lord descended
> upon it in fire; and the smoke of it went up like the smoke
> of a kiln, and the whole mountain quaked greatly.
>
> Exodus 19:12, 13, and 18

Reverence for the holy was expressed in various ways: the name of God was not used, but indicated by various substitutes, such as "the presence" or "heaven." The Sabbath was meticulously observed, the laws were carefully kept, because they were the Lord's day, and the laws of the Holy One.

Another characteristic feature of the Hebrew concept of God that transferred into Christianity is the *covenant*. Far from being some vague energy spread throughout the universe, or a speculative philosophical concept of some order of nature, the biblical God is one who acted in the lives of historic people and entered into relation with them. In the Old Testament the covenant is mediated by a patriarch or by Moses. In the New Testament, by Jesus Christ. The covenant is usually not an individual matter, but a collective one: The people of Israel, or the "new Israel," as the Christian Church liked to refer to itself. It is not so much people's choice of a god to suit them, as God's choice of the people that constitutes the covenant. God chooses at the time and place of his own. It is God who is completely free. The controversy over man's freedom of will is of much later date.

DIFFERENT APPROACHES TO THE KNOWLEDGE OF GOD IN THE CHRISTIAN RELIGION

WORSHIP

Great art Thou, O Lord, and greatly to be praised; great is Thy power and of Thy wisdom there is no number. And man desires to praise Thee. He is but a tiny part of all that Thou has created . . . yet this tiny part of all that Thou has created desires to praise Thee.

With these words opens one of the most famous of the classics of Christian literature, the *Confessions* of St. Augustine. The whole book is a great hymn of praise of the Creator by one who was "first created and then re-created" by him. Augustine's praise is an example of the personal, individual, worshipful attitude, very much like the attitude of the writers of the Psalms of the Old Testament:

> Bless the LORD, O my soul;
> and all that is within me,
> bless his holy name!
> Bless the LORD, O my soul,
> and forget not all his benefits,
> who forgives all your iniquity,
> who heals all your diseases,
> who redeems your life from the Pit . . .
>
> Bless the LORD, O you his angels,
> you mighty ones who do his work,
> hearkening to the voice of his word!
> Bless the LORD, all his hosts,
> his ministers that do his will!
> Bless the LORD, all his works,
> in all places of his dominion.
> Bless the LORD, O my soul!
>
> First and last verses of Psalm 103

The same tone of thanksgiving, exultation, and praise is found in many such psalms and prayers (cf. Psalms 113, 148, etc.).

The individuality of the worshipful attitude is deceptive. Usually it will be found that individuals first practiced collective worship, which is the most universal approach to god in all religions.

Something has been said about collective worship in the chapter on the Church. Here we stress the act of worship as a response to the revelation (or self-disclosure) of God; Christian worship is distinguished from other religions particularly by being a response to the self-disclosure of God in a specifically Christian way, that is, in Jesus Christ. Religion generally has been mainly *an act,* or series of acts, of a community: dances, initiations, sacrifices, prayers, etc. Christian worship also is an act in response to the act of God. Dogmas, doctrines, beliefs, and apologetic writings of the Christian religion have full meaning only insofar as they relate to the action and life of the religious community. If in the twentieth century we have had much academic discussion and writing on religion and its private meaning to individuals with some special interest or philosophical bent, we recognize such discussion as culturally valid, and even necessary in our pluralistic and individualistic culture. But we should not confuse such cultural expression with religion. The basic expression of the Christian religion in the world is not an opinion, not even a doctrine, but the fact of a worshiping and living church.

LOGICAL ARGUMENT

Despite the fact that the primary religious expression is an act, the content of the act has repeatedly been conceptualized and verbalized. It has been expressed on various levels as dogma, doctrine, or traditional opinion, and written down in formal summaries of doctrine—the creeds—or in prepared series of questions and answers for the purpose of religious instruction—the catechisms. But much creative writing has been done, too, by those Christians who sought to express to the mind what is obvious to the heart, or to defend their faith against attacks or misrepresentations, or again to elucidate the mysteries of faith by means of rational argument.

There is voluminous literature of the devotional, meditative, expository, theological, apologetic, and other kinds, that would fill a good-sized library. Some of it is of the philosophical type, using the logical argument to prove or disprove a point, pointing out inconsistencies, and generally aiming at philosophical adequacy. For the moment, we shall be concerned with a very small sample of this vast field, the doggedly tenacious "first-cause" argument for the existence of a god, first advanced by the Greeks before the Christian era, and formulated by Aristotle in the form taken over (quite consciously) by St. Thomas Aquinas and other medieval Christian philosophers. The gist of the argument is well known; everything has a cause without which it would not exist, and that cause again has a cause, and that cause again, etc., and finally we must arrive somewhere at the beginning of all these causes and effects, the first cause, which began the whole chain of all there is without itself being caused by any other cause. This first cause then is called god.

It is clear that there is a parallel between the philosophical idea of the first cause which caused everything without itself being caused by anything, and the religious idea of a god who created everything without himself being created. In the Middle Ages, and well into the modern times, these seemed congenial arguments. However, we note that they seemed congenial only while they accompanied religious devotion or conviction. As verbalizations of the secret arguments of the heart, they seemed "obvious" to those who were steeped in the corporate worship.

Taken out of the church, and separated from active religious practice, in a society which is far from uniformly religious, these arguments are now seen in the rarefied and transparent atmosphere of pure logical analysis. Here they become easy targets of the technicians of the mind and of linguistic analysts. Some early critics, like Thomas Hobbes, pointed out that such logical demonstration as the argument from cause really leads to many first causes, not one. Again, it has been said that if we begin with the general assumption that everything has a cause, it is ridiculous to use this method of argument to prove that "that's why God does not have a cause." Bertrand Russell became known as one of the logical sharpshooters at the old arguments. He would even deny that logically everything must have a cause or a beginning. (Some mathematical series do not have any beginning.) And if everything did have a beginning, it would not be necessary to suppose that it must have been such a great beginning as the creative will of God; it could very well have been a more ordinary event, just a little start; (perhaps a chemical reaction?). On the other hand, a religious defender could argue that the "proof" of the existence of God is not primarily a metaphysical or logical matter, but a religious-psychological matter. The first cause is that which satisfies the mind, which gives the mind rest. This effect then provides the true justification for the use of such an argument. It is the thought which gives the mind rest (peace) that is the true idea of the first cause, or God.

Reasons for the existence of God clearly relate to the experience of a civilization in a certain stage of its development. They have thrived particularly in the three periods of grand synthesis in the Western civilization in which all human experience was somehow correlated with a unified view of the universe: The time of Plato and Aristotle in ancient Greece; the time of St. Thomas and Dante in the Middle Ages; and the time of Leibnitz and Newton in our modern times. The Newtonian concept of the universe still pointed toward harmony, toward that "great engineer" who made this wonderful world machine, gave it its scientific laws and its original movement.

But the last period of grand synthesis already had within it the seeds of radical skepticism that point toward the disintegration of the corporate beliefs, and to the breakup of unity into the multiple, and extremely complex, concepts of the world which are characteristic of our own times. To be sure, it is possible even after Newton to conceive of unity. The evolutionary theory which brought about various well-known "conflicts" between science and religion does not defy unity and harmony. Father Teilhard de Chardin contended that all evolution tends toward an "Omega point" which is God.

Again, in the twentieth century, our concepts of energy cross the barriers between the animate and inanimate categories of the past and unite the whole universe in one continuous, new kind of "chain of being." Physicists such as Mr. Pollard have argued that the biblical interpretation of the universe, essentially unified by the concept of God, can be well brought into harmony with astronomical and physical knowledge of the most up-to-date kind. But such attempts are overbalanced by the general complexity of individual research projects and the lack of will toward a truly unified philosophy of life. To many today, pluralism is at least as satisfying intellectually as monism, and most scientists, even if they have private convictions, have been discouraged by the obscurantism of the past debates on the subject of science and religion, and have learned for various reasons to bypass the question of God altogether.

In conclusion, it would be hoped that a class in religion would be stimulated to investigate further some of the arguments for the existence of God; but that it also would keep in mind the historical fact of the origin of Christianity. The Christian religion did not begin with the faith of Aristotle's disciples in his arguments, but with the faith of the disciples of Jesus the Christ in the mighty acts of God in history, in Christ's spiritual and physical healing, and in revelation to his disciples of the possibility and power of a new life. Those who worship as Christians do not do so generally for reasons of logical argument any more than a person entering a marriage does so because of the computer data on his bride.

Today such arguments belong more to the history of philosophy than to the history of religion. One outstanding exception is the Neo-Scholastic philosophy found particularly in some Roman Catholic schools, which naturally look toward St. Thomas for extraordinary source of authority and guidance.

THE THEOLOGY OF THE CROSS: LUTHER

Martin Luther is a good example of a theologian who rejected scholasticism and particularly "Aristotle" in Christian theology. This position is by no means confined to Luther, not even exclusive to Protestantism. But Luther was so vehement and so eloquent in his statement of it, that he will serve well to define a type. Luther assumed that God's metaphysical being cannot be known:

Speculatively they define god by all kinds of similes, such as "god is a center which is everywhere, or a sphere, which is nowhere." But these are mathematical and physical concepts and we leave them to other professors. We are seeking a theological definition, and that is not a definition of divine essence—which is incomprehensible—but of will and affection, that is, what pleases him and what displeases him . . .

God is such a god who in the last analysis does nothing but look upon and love the contrite, the vexed, and the perturbed, and thus is god of the humble and those full of sorrow for their sins. If one can inwardly embrace this definition, he is a theologian.[2]

What was Luther's central concern when he spoke about God? Obviously, the forgiveness of sins, which is to say God as known through Jesus Christ. Why does Luther enlarge on this topic practically to the exclusion of other ways of speaking of God? There is a historical reason for it. The church in sixteenth-century Europe exhibited a marked tendency known as *semi-pelagianism*. This meant in practice great emphasis upon man's share in "co-operating with God" toward his own salvation. Meritorious works were popularly understood to be very nearly stepping-stones to

[2] WA (The Weimar Edition of Luther's Works), XL, sec. 2, p. 458, translated by Peter B. Fischer.

heaven. People expected direct benefits in proportion to the number of prayers said, relics viewed on holy days, etc. Somehow in practice people assumed that the church could assure and control the spiritual benefits in heaven in proportion to their own merits. Luther, as a practicing priest, knew this tendency well, and against it he threw the whole weight of his Augustinian and biblical upbringing. He went to the other extreme, in order to provide the corrective emphasis, and also in accordance with his strong personal experience (his extreme effort to pursue the path of recommended religious works, and his disappointment with their effect upon his personal religious problem). Therefore, the cross of Christ alone, the grace of God alone, are the basis of human salvation.

To be sure, to a mere onlooker, God is hidden even in the Crucifixion. It is by no means obvious that the man hanging on the cross is the incarnation of the Creator of the world. Only faith can apprehend it. The benefit of this act of God is appropriated by a Christian (Luther's favorite phrase was: God *for me*), when man has stopped relying on his own goodness and on the merits of his own works. The cross is God's announcement of forgiveness, of reconciliation, of victory over the powers of the Evil One. Luther's theology is Christocentric. Luther's initial personal question was: "How can I be sure that God is merciful to me?" The answer for him lay in God's act in the crucified Christ.

THE IMMANENT GOD: THE MYSTICS

If Luther's God was one of *personal* relation to man, relation of trust, confidence, forgiveness of sins, and so forth, he nevertheless remained the holy Creator of the world, between whom and man there was an absolute qualitative gulf (*transcendent*). There is however another approach equally based on *personal* experience, in which God is *immanent* (dwelling within). Instead of stressing the difference and distance of the creature from its creator, this approach emphasizes the relatedness, the similarity of the soul to God.

The mystical approach has these primary characteristics: it is universal to practically all religions; it is based upon personal, unmediated experience; the God of the mystic is ineffable, inexpressible, unutterable; a mystic ascends (climbs) to God inwardly, step by step; and, finally, the soul becomes transformed by the proximity and love of God into the likeness of God.

Another quotation from St. Augustine, a man so many-sided that he stimulated monks, mystics, philosophers, and theologians, Protestant and Catholic, alike, will illustrate the first few points.

What art Thou then, my God? . . . Most highest, most good, most potent, most omnipotent; most merciful, yet most just; most hidden, yet most present; most beautiful, yet most strong; stable, yet incomprehensible; unchangeable, yet all-changing; never new, never old; allrenewing, . . . ever working, ever at rest; still gathering, yet nothing lacking; supporting, filling, and overspreading; creating, nourishing, and maturing; seeking, yet having all things . . .[3]

Now compare this with a paragraph from the *Bhagavad-Gita* (chapter XIII). Krishna:

The Para-Brahm, the All, the Uncreated; . . . Glorified by the senses He hath given, yet beyond sense He is; sustaining all, He dwelleth unattached; of formes and modes Master, yet neither form nor mode hath He; He is within all beings—and without—Motionless, yet still moving; not discerned for subtlety of instant presence; close to all, to each, yet measurelessly far! Not manifold, and yet subsisting still in all which lives; for ever to be known as the Sustainer, yet, at the End of Times, He maketh all to end—and re-creates.

In these two fine examples we see the groping for words which simply are not adequate to express the meaning of god who is ineffable. Superlatives will not do. Opposites, paradoxes, come closer to expressing the inexpressible, if words must be used.

[3] *Confessions,* Book I.

Another mystic manner of speaking is that of symbolism: love, fire, flowing water, marriage, etc.

The language, then, is what distinguishes the mystic's writing. Behind this writing is the personal experience of the individual—for mysticism is predominantly individualistic. Insofar as there is some meaningful experience behind most people's religious commitment, it would be correct to say that mysticism is universal. But in the proper sense of the word, as used by the famous mystics of the past, the word does not simply refer to a profound insight of a moment, or an emotional uplift associated with a particular occasion; not even the preconversion convulsions of the revival meetings, such as those described by John Wesley as having taken place at Bristol, fall into the same category.

The hallmark of true mysticism is the ability of man by proper guidance and practice to raise himself spiritually into the near presence of God, and through this presence to become increasingly godlike, transformed by the divine love. The titles of many mystic books indicate this gradual progress of the soul to God: *The Hill of Perfection; The Way to Perfection; The Pilgrimage of Perfection; Ladder of Perfection; Ascent of Mt. Carmel,* etc. On the mystic way, there are certain standard stages, so as to arrange the sequence of progress into (a) the way of purification, in which the individual is freed from attachments to all sensory goals and is purified from sinful will; (b) the way of illumination, where he obtains enlightenment, and the soul is inflamed with the love of God more often and more ardently; and (c) the way of union, in which the soul attaches itself to God and finally surrenders itself to him.

In the popular mind, mysticism is associated with ecstatic phenomena, visions, voices, and emotional utterances. To mind comes usually Bernini's group sculpture of "St. Theresa in Extasis" (or the "transverberation"), in which the angel is said to have pierced her heart with a fiery spear, exciting in her the rapture of intimate union with God.

One of the most important of the great mystics was St. John of the Cross, a sixteenth-century Spanish poet and scholar, whom Pope Pius XI raised to the dignity of a "doctor of the church." Here we shall introduce a few samples, not to present the whole of the systematic progress and the philosophy of St. John, but simply to document the immanent concept of God, and the typical language of mystic symbolism.

In his *Ascent of Mount Carmel,* we find frequent use of such idiom as the mystical "ladder of love, by which the soul ascends, one by one, to God"; again, "an inflowing of God into the soul" and the soul "in union of love with God." Many of the picturesque images have their source in the New Testament book of Revelation, and many more again in the Old Testament Song of Songs (known also as the Song of Solomon, or Canticles). This imagery is passionate indeed; e.g., on the seventh step of the ascent, "the Bride (the soul) grew bold and said: 'I thirst for a kiss from these lips' " (Canticles 1:1). To this the soul could never dare to aspire unless it had first received the inward grace, bestowed upon it "by the sceptre of the King." On the eighth step "the soul is united with the Beloved. . . . On this step of union the longing of the soul is satisfied." The ninth step of love makes the soul "burn with sweet rapture. . . . aflame with the sweet love of God." The tenth and final step may be attained immediately upon the death of the body, when the soul attains to "a clear vision of God" and "perfect likeness to God." (Perhaps it is this kind of imagery that made the old psychological critics proclaim religion an erotic sublimation.)

The realm of mystical knowledge of God is one of direct personal experience, based upon "a certain intimate contact between the soul and the Deity, so that it is God himself who is herein perceived and tasted" (St. John of the Cross). There is no mediation of religion here, by the priest, by the sacraments, the common worship, or by the doctrine. It is so direct that God is "tasted." No wonder that such an experience is claimed to impart to the soul a special knowledge. As the Delphic Oracle learned the mind of Apollo, and the Old Testament prophets saw visions and heard voices imparting to them the message from their God, so John of the Cross lists various types of revelation, or unveiling of hidden secrets, including the knowledge "concerning that which God is in Himself, and therein is included the revelation of the mystery of the Most Holy Trinity and Unity of God."[4]

The above examples have been taken from Roman Catholic devotion (and from Hinduism). Protestantism has its examples of mysticism, but they are few and not typical. Protestantism is characteristically not mystical. It has its emotional and revivalist history, it has its enthusiasm, but systematic, step-by-step practice of the mystical life is an exception rather than a rule. Instead of the soul's ascent, mysticism will rather be defined as introversion, as looking into oneself. Closing one's eyes to the diversity and division of all things and finding in all things unity is also a process similar to the mystic's. The search is for the unconditioned, for that beyond all divisions and distinctions, beyond individuality and temporality. It involves the loss of self as an individual and the merging of the self in the all. Some Protestant critic described a mystic as one "climbing up the ladder and then pulling up the ladder behind him." This is not entirely true of the best-known Catholic mystics; they returned into this world, rolled up their sleeves, and went to work, founding hospitals, ministering to those sick with deadly epidemic diseases, and living among the poor. Their experience confirmed in them the decision to serve God and to give their lives to him. But psychology has applied its labels to the mystics, and due to that, and to our pragmatically minded civilization, mysticism does not often flourish as a legitimate phenomenon.

---

[4] A convenient edition of selections from St. John of the Cross is that of Kurt Reinhardt, *The Dark Night of the Soul,* Ungar series of *Milestones of Thought.* The above quotations come from *The Ascent to Mount Carmel,* chaps. XXVI and XXVII.

THE TRANSCENDENT GOD: CALVIN

Reformed Protestantism has been traditionally suspicious of mysticism, and usually it has leaned in the opposite direction, that of the transcendent God. A God distant in being, transcendent, and yet with definite claims on the lives of his church and of all men, is by no means Calvin's monopoly. It belongs to the common Christian concept. But right or wrong, Calvinism in our society has been built up into an image of austerity, strictness, unbending law, and rigid moral demands. Its corresponding image of God then has the same strictness, austerity, lack of human warmth.

It is true that Calvin, as contrasted with Luther or with St. John of the Cross, gave little attention to man's inner struggles for faith. He was not concerned with religious feelings or with religious consciousness as a basis for religious certainty. To him, the foundation of all Christian religion is clearly the biblical proclamation of the majesty and sovereignty of God. He is quite certain that human salvation is based upon the eternal and immutable counsel of God, his free decision before all ages. Such things as the experience of the unity of the soul with God, or human religiousness, are not sufficient to change the Creator's eternal decree.

Calvin's assertion of divine transcendence was so strong, that he had to defend himself repeatedly against charges of fatalism and of determinism:

The Stoics wove their doctrine of fate out of Gordias' web of complex causes, in which, when they had entangled God Himself, they fabricated certain golden chains to find the very God of heaven, and to make Him *subject to inferior and secondary causes!* The Stoics are imitated by the astrologers of the present day, who make their doctrine of *fated necessity* out of certain positions of the stars. We leave the Stoics, then, to their doctrine of fate, while we acknowledge the will of God to be the ruling cause of all things.[5]

[5] John Calvin, treatise on *The Secret Providence of God*, in *Calvin's Calvinism*, Eerdmans, 1950, p. 234.

Predestination, total control of God over the Creation, and transcendence, go together. What is their religious purpose? Calvin tells us (in his treatise on the *Eternal Predestination of God*): it is intended to lead to better worship of God, induce humility and faith, and stimulate to "admiration of the unbounded goodness of God toward us, while it elevates us to praise this goodness in our highest strains." In spite of Calvin's intentions, posterity has retained the austere, cold image of the distant and watchful God as representative of Calvinism.

This impression was further confirmed by one of the best-known of the confessional statements of Protestantism, the Great Puritan (or Westminster) Confession of Faith. Its definition of God can be read as rather cold, distant, judicial, devoid of the love of Christ or of personal concern:

There is but one only living and true God, who is infinite in being and perfection, a most pure spirit, invisible, without body, parts, or passions, immutable, immense, eternal, incomprehensible, almighty, most wise, most holy, most free, most absolute, working all things according to the counsel of his own immutable and most righteous will, for his own glory; most loving, gracious, merciful, long-suffering, abundant in goodness and truth, forgiving iniquity, transgression, and sin; the rewarder of them that diligently seek him; and withal most just and terrible in his judgments, hating all sin, and who will by no means clear the guilty.

God has all life, glory, goodness, blessedness, in and of himself; and is alone in and unto himself all-sufficient, not standing in need of any creatures which he hath made, nor deriving any glory from them, but only manifesting his own glory in, by, unto, and upon them; he is the alone fountain of all being, of whom, through whom, and to whom, are all things; and hath most sovereign dominion over them, to do by them, for them, and upon them, whatsoever himself pleaseth. . . .

To stress such a complete self-sufficiency of God unto himself, his aloofness, his lack of need of any creature, even of man, this is transcendence with a vengeance. It goes beyond the biblical spirit that combines human understanding and sympathy with the holiness and majesty of the Creator.

An extreme form of the transcendent emphasis developed into a caricature of the Christian viewpoint in the seventeenth and eighteenth centuries in a rationalist movement called Deism. This movement is more positively associated with tolerance and with the concept of natural and universal religion. As to the concept of God, some deists totally separated the Creator from the Creation to the point where God can have nothing to do with man or with the world, and sits immobile and detached in splendid isolation. Deism of course has had great cultural significance. But the view of God associated with it is hardly compatible with church worship and life, and therefore it belongs more to the discussion of philosophy than to religion.

We have summarized and given examples of the several major approaches to the religious concept of God: The Old Testament origins; the act of worship; the logical argument; the personal, Christ-centered approach; the immanent God of the mystical experience; and the transcendent God. It is safe to say that all of these approaches to God, and all of these views, belong properly to the Christian tradition. They have all been valid, and complete omission of any one would unbalance the fullness of Christian faith. It is true that different Christian churches at different times may place strong emphasis on one or the other approach. But the church is not limited to mystics, rationalists, or to any one group exclusively. It is the interaction of all that makes the church.

We are now ready to briefly deal with the most difficult and yet most characteristic traditional Christian concept of God, the doctrine of the Trinity.

THE DOCTRINE OF THE TRINITY

The doctrine of the Trinity, or the "Blessed Trinity," as some Christians refer to it, is barely mentioned in the Bible, and certainly does not provide us with any central biblical imagery or thought. But in Christian history it has played a most prominent role. It has two aspects: the apologetic, defensive, or negative one, and the positive one, which delineates something important about the content of the Christian faith.

In its formative years as a doctrine, the trinitarian formula served as a hedge against various heresies that would have dissolved Christianity into another ancient mystery religion, with a semidivine being at the center; and against such philosophical tendencies that would have made it into a pantheistic philosophy of universal harmony of the world and soul. Augustine's work stands out among the many formative stages of the doctrine (he wrote a large book *On the Trinity*), and the basic summary of the doctrine as accepted by both the Catholic and the Protestant churches is the creed usually called the Symbolum Athanasianum, or, according to its opening word, the "Quicunque." The formula seems somewhat formidable today, and its insistence upon certain distinctions is not always obvious. But it served definite purposes of defending Christian faith against distortions. Here is a sample:

This is the universal faith, that we may venerate one God in the Trinity, and the Trinity in Oneness,
neither mixing the persons together, nor separating the substance;
for one is the person of the Father, another of the Son, and another
again of the Holy Spirit. But the Father and the Son and the Holy Spirit
have one divinity, equal glory, and co-eternal majesty.
Aeternal is Father, aeternal the Son, aeternal also Holy Spirit
and yet these are not three eternal ones, but one eternal one.
Just as not three are un-created, not three immense, but one uncreated,
and one immense, thus there is the Lord Father, Lord Son, Lord Holy Spirit
and yet not three Lords, but one is the Lord

Thus there is one Father, not three Fathers; one Son not three Sons;
one Holy Spirit, not three Holy Spirits; and in this Trinity nothing is
earlier or later, nothing greater or smaller.

The trinitarian doctrine was generally taken by the churches of the Christian Western Europe as a measure of orthodoxy. Protestants did not like philosophical language, and rejected the word *substance* in "trans-substantiation" relating to a sacrament. But they did not object to it in the Athanasian Creed; the Lutheran churches incorporated it in their collection of doctrinal standards, the *Formula of Concord*. Sixteenth-century Geneva, under Calvin's leadership, put to death the outspoken critic of the doctrine of the Trinity, Michael Servetus. No doubt it strengthened Geneva's reputation for orthodoxy.

The philosophical language of the creed was hard on popular imagination, and more homely similes (or models) for the Trinity were coined, from the early Christian centuries on, such as the light of three lamps which combines to light a room, three rivers combining their water into one, the three human faculties of memory, knowledge, and will, or even the shamrock with its three leaves.

Positively, the doctrine of the Trinity brings together the three-fold belief of a Christian, which distinguishes it from all other religions: (1) God as the *Creator,* qualitatively different from his *creation, is related to it as its lord* (not as its universal soul, nor as an abstract monotheistic concept, nor as a universal intelligence dispersed throughout the cosmos). (2) Christian faith is not satisfied with the Hebrew profession "Hear, Israel, the Lord our God, the Lord is one" (Deuteronomy 6:4). The same God who spoke to Moses on Sinai became man, in a historical moment, in a definite place on earth, and lived among men. (3) The same God who is the *creator* of all things, and who became *man in Jesus Christ,* as the *Holy Spirit* makes men's hearts glow with love for himself, seals their common experiences into one faith, and their lives into one church. The church, therefore, is not merely a human institution, but also, and primarily, a society brought into being by the Holy Spirit. The famous passage in the beginning of the Acts of the Apostles vividly speaks of the formative power of the Holy Spirit on the gathered apostles.

How much does the doctrine mean today? In our time, when all values are being reevaluated and all language subject to analysis, there appear doubts as to the usefulness of the ancient formulation of the doctrine. James A. Pike, Bishop of the Episcopal Diocese of Los Angeles, wrote frankly: "The Philosophers, using Greek concepts, did their best, but what they did does not speak very adequately to me now. . . . all the verbiage associated with the Trinity is quite unnecessary."[6] He is even bolder in suggesting that the whole doctrine might better be expressed in the language and concepts of our day: "I see nothing in the Bible, as critically viewed, which supports this particularly weak and unintelligible philosophical organization of the nature of God. I believe all that the early Fathers meant to be saying by the doctrine of the Trinity, but I do not find particularly helpful now their time-bound solution to the problem."[7]

Canon Ian Ramsey, an Oxford professor much concerned with religious language, has rejected the trinitarian doctrine as descriptive of the actual nature of God; the important thing is what it does to us: to lead us in the direction of worship and of behavior.

"Three persons in one substance" may be the better read as: "There are three sorts of logically distinguishable language leading us to God, three sorts of language not to be confounded, each of which can lead us to a disclosure of God's Unity. . . . The Trinitarian formula is a means of specifying in three terms of models for unity the logical relations between those three strands to insure that together they do all that the word 'God' does for the theist or Jew, and much more besides."[8]

It is possible that the language about God in terms of "a model of unity" and "three strands of discourse" will not fill the need of the churches in practical worship, but it leads us directly to the fact that many intellectuals in modern times have had their difficulties with the traditional concept of God.

[6] *How My Mind Has Changed*, Harold E. Fey (ed.), Living Age Books, 1961, p. 177.
[7] *Ibid.*, pp. 177–178.
[8] Lectures delivered at the Chicago Theological Seminary, 1964.

SOME MODERN DOUBTS AND PROBLEMS

One of the sources of perplexity is modern man's historical awareness. It was all right for the medieval mystery plays to present a simple three-decker universe, and to watch the devil, as a fallen angel, tumble down from the upper story (heaven) to the bottom. But what does it mean to the modern man who sends rockets to the moon and is aware of the complexity and speed of the moon's orbits, to say that God is "up there," that "heaven is above"? No wonder that Paul Tillich complains of the loss of the "dimension of depth" out of modern man's religion. We have lost the outward image by which to indicate the spiritual analogy of "up" and "down" in our universe.

Another example of the historical change which makes simple acceptance of traditional expressions difficult is the language of social analogy. In the Middle Ages, as in early Christian times, a staircase society of classes was taken for granted. We therefore expect St. Benedict's language to have been clearly understood: "When we make application to men in high positions, we do not presume to do so without reverence and humility; how much more then are we bound to entreat God, the Lord of all, with all humility." But our society cultivates "healthy aggressiveness" rather than humility as an ideal. And in democracy we stress equality, we do not serve "lords." How can a modern student feel the vitality of the biblical language full of images of "lord, king, slave" when applied to God, to Jesus, or to an apostle? Many a modern student takes it for granted that God must be "fair," i.e., like a good citizen, law-abiding, and a supporter of the basic principles of the American Constitution. This is just as natural to him as the image of a king was to a citizen of an ancient country.

Another type of study modern man brings to the investigation of traditional language is that of mythology. When God is manifested in the Bible as a fiery column, a burning bush, or a voice out of the whirlwind, he will be compared to similar manifestations of god in other religions, and the comparative study of religion, study of mythology, and even psychology of the "collective dream" will attempt to unravel for modern man the mystery of the vitality of such symbols for the ancients.

What did the ancient inhabitants of Palestine mean by words like "messiah," "son of man," or "son of god"? With all the study of the old languages and cultures, can a scholar today translate the old Jewish, Hellenistic, or Gnostic concepts into our modern language so as to preserve their original meaning? Or is it sufficient to simply repeat the phrase "son of man" about Jesus without having any idea of its special significance for those who wrote the Bible? Is it possible to successfully "demythologize" the Bible and translate it into modern thought without pouring out the baby with the bath?[9]

THE CONCEPT OF THE "LIMITED GOD"

In his Adams Memorial Foundation lectures in 1930, Professor Edgar Sheffield Brightman of Boston University developed his philosophical concept of the "limited God." It was his conviction that the concept of God was in need of revision, of updating in keeping with modern thought and scientific knowledge. "In the past few decades there have arisen many doubts and new opinions about God. . . . It is almost self-evident that the advance of knowledge must mean a change in our thought of God."[10] Brightman is serious about this, and is not seeking a painless, sugary view of God. He would like to defend the goodness of God against his detractors. Part of his definition of God is as follows:

[9] It is suggested that the student read Rudolf Bultmann's *Primitive Christianity in its Contemporary Setting*, Meridian, 1956, or his *Kerygma and Myth*, Harper & Row, 1961, and form his own opinion.
[10] E. S. Brightman, *The Problem of God*, Abingdon Press, 1930, Preface, p. 9.

His purpose and his nature (is) gradually attained through effort, difficulty, and suffering. Hence there is in God's very nature something which makes the effort and pain of life necessary. There is within him, in addition to his reason and his active creative will, a passive element which enters into every one of his conscious states, as sensation, instinct, and impulse enter into ours, and constitutes a problem for him. This element we call "The Given."[11]

What are some of the factors that limit God? One is, Brightman argues, the free choice of other persons. If man is truly free, then God cannot foreknow the outcome of his decisions. His omniscience is truly thwarted. Also, if God is supremely rational, he must be confused by the irrational use human beings make of their freedom.

More serious are the limitations within divine nature given by the presence of earthquakes, cyclones, diseases, etc. These give the distinct impression that the divine power "is working under great difficulties." Then again there are the "facts of evolution." They suggest, on the one hand, a design in nature; and on the other hand, a frustration in the achievement of such a design.

"The Given" which constitutes a problem for God reminds one of the work of the great mathematician and philosopher Leibnitz, who in 1710 published his "Essays on the Justice of God and the Freedom of Man in the Origin of Evil." The argument, referred to as "theodicy" (justification of God in the presence of evil) extends the thought that evil is necessary because of the limited (finite) world and because of moral freedom. This world is not the ideal one, but merely the best one of all *possible* worlds (i.e., those compatible with such limiting factors as moral freedom).

While these arguments have unquestionable academic merit, they are far removed from the concept of the Holy God of the people of Israel, with which this chapter began, or from the Christian doctrine of "creation out of nothing." Moreover, a suffering person might find it cold comfort, and a worshiping

11 *Ibid.,* p. 113.

congregation might find it strange, to feel sorry for their God's limitations and inabilities. Nevertheless, our civilization as a whole has semiofficially assumed the mantle of a "Christian civilization." Therefore such problems and doubts crop up in our general culture, and are reflected, for instance, in literature and drama. Justification of God's ways to man has often been stated poetically (Milton, Pope), and the idea of this being the "best of all possible worlds" ("therefore let us keep it such") given a fine corrective treatment in Voltaire's famous *Candide*.

THE PROBLEM OF EVIL

One of the most disturbing thoughts connected with the belief in God in our civilization has been that of suffering of the innocents, and the problem of evil generally. The Book of Job in the Bible, not greatly used by Jewish or Christian congregations, has stirred the imagination of many philosophers, writers, and dramatists, and has often been interpreted as dealing with the suffering of man, particularly the suffering of the innocent.[12]

One of the most famous literary treatments of the suffering of the innocent is in Dostoevski's *Brothers Karamazov* (Book V, chapter 4). Ivan Karamazov has recounted at great length examples of brutal beating of children, their sadistic torture by adults, and awful deaths. Now he sneers: God's plan is to make men happy in the long run, to give them peace and rest; yet he is unable to do so without the most cruel suffering of innocent children.

It's not worth the tears of that one tortured child who beat himself on the breast with its little fist and prayed in its stinking outhouse with an

[12] On the *Book of Job* see such treatments as those collected in R. E. Hone (ed.), *The Voice Out of the Whirlwind: The Book of Job*, Chandler, 1960; Samuel Terrien, *Job, Poet of Existence*, Bobbs-Merrill, 1957; Soren Kierkegaard, *Repetition*, Harper Torchbooks, 1964; and Archibald MacLeish, *J. B.*, Houghton Mifflin, 1956.

unexpiated tear to "dear, kind God"! It's not worth it, because those tears are unatoned for. They must be atoned for, or there can be no harmony. But how? How are you going to atone for them? Is it possible? By their being avenged? But what do I care for avenging them? What do I care for a hell for oppressors? What good can hell do, since those children have already been tortured? And what becomes of harmony, if there is hell? I want to forgive. I want to embrace. I don't want more suffering. And if the sufferings of children go to swell the sum of suffering which was necessary to pay for truth, then I protest that the truth is not worth such a price. . . . And so I hasten to give back my entrance ticket, and if I am an honest man I am bound to give it back as soon as possible. And that I am doing. It's not God that I don't accept, Alyosha, only I most respectfully return Him the ticket.

Twentieth-century novelists and playwrights have dealt seriously with the problem of evil. But their answers often transpose the meaning from religious to humanistic. Read Sartre's *No Exit* and *Lucifer and the Lord,* or the heartrending outcry of protest against the suffering of man in Camus' *The Plague,* which was manifestly inspired by Dostoevski. Many intellectuals today claim to find profound Christian insight in the work of Samuel Beckett, Franz Kafka, and Bertolt Brecht, where God is often distant, absent, or negative. The spotlight is on man who just suffers and to whose hopeless, ageless suffering there is no answer. Here the image of God is either faded, erased, or revitalized.

In theory, the problem of evil probably has no satisfying solution. The logic is awesomely simple. If blame for the existence of evil is to be assigned to anyone, and God is said to be all-powerful, then is he not also involved in the presence of evil? This contradicts his attribute of goodness. Let us then assume that man was created with free will—can we not blame evil on man? Much of it, perhaps, but it is absurd to blame earthquakes, cyclones, and epidemics on man's free will. That leaves a lot of explaining as to why God permits natural disasters to happen. Is he limited in power or in goodness? This does not satisfy a traditional believer, but we have seen a modern attempt to exonerate God by saying that he is limited (Brightman). Or did God punish whole cities for their "wickedness" as the Old Testament prophets had said? When modern churches stress the goodness and the kindness of God, that is a difficult answer to swallow.

One *speculative* solution to the problem of evil has enjoyed long popularity. It originated with the non-Christian, Neo-Platonic philosophy, and goes back to Plato. It defines evil as the non-*being*. Is evil simply absence of good, as darkness is the absence of light? It seems attractive to say that dark areas in a painting are needed to make the light ones stand out better by contrast, and to create the total harmony of the picture. But this is an aesthetic approach, which is basically passive. It has made its appearance in Christian guise, even in the writings of St. Augustine.[13]

The Christian will usually find the speculative answer too weak. For him, evil is something real that must be fought. To him evil belongs among real forces and powers in this world. He is assured of the victory over these powers by the crucifixion and the resurrection of Christ. (When a Christian daily prays "deliver us from evil," in the original Greek sense of his words he is praying: "deliver us from the Evil One.")

Another solution to the problem of evil has made its way to the fringes of Christianity, and it takes evil seriously, as a power: the Persian dualism, which in the semi-Christian form of *the Manichees* has periodically reappeared under different names. Evil is a separate, independent, eternal power. It eternally opposes the power of Good. Thus we find two divine eternal forces: those of good and those of evil. It is easy to blame all disasters and all evil

---

[13] Evil as "non-being" is discussed fluently in Dorothy Sayers' *The Mind of the Maker*, Living Age Books, 1956, chap. 7, "Maker of All Things—Maker of Ill Things." The student will find theological and philosophical discussion of the problem of evil in such studies as Nels Ferre, *Evil and the Christian Faith*, Harper & Row, 1947, and Nelson Pike (ed.), *God and Evil*, in the series *Contemporary Perspectives in Philosophy*, Prentice-Hall, 1964, with an excellent selected bibliography of various classic treatments of the problem, ancient, medieval, and modern.

in man upon the forces of evil, and the good deity remains blameless. This is essentially the answer of fatalistic and environmental explanations of evil such as astrology, which may blame evil in man and nature upon the constellations of stars and planets, moon, and celestial phenomena. The very word *disaster* derives from *dis-astrum,* referring the calamity to the unfavorable disposition of the influences of a *star*. In more recent times, evil has been attributed to such outside powers as physical forces, environment, society, heredity, vitamin deficiency, or psychological determinants. (If a criminal is a victim of such forces, how can he be personally guilty?). If any of these factors can be equated with the traditional concepts of "hell," "devil," or the powers of "the Evil One," is rather doubtful. Yet it has been often stated that the psychic torments of a person in trouble are essentially the same as religious, spiritual torments. If this is so, then the traditional powers of evil are taking on different masks. Modern man's transformations of the problem of evil go hand in hand with his transformations of the problem of God.

The genuine Christian answer to the problem of evil is not theoretical, nor environmentalist. It is the assumption of faith that man must fight evil, and the assurance that the battle in the spiritual realm has already been won. To maintain hope and courage in the face of the many disasters and evils present in the world is the test of faith. The ideal response of the Christian is active: overcome evil by the good. Patience, work, risk, devotion are the ingredients of the best that the Christian Church has offered since its early days when it practiced mutual aid, organized care of refugees and displaced persons in the Roman Empire (and again in modern times). To this one could add the many hospitals and the varied services to the destitute that mark the work of the early, medieval, and modern churches; the work of Dr. Albert Schweitzer in his African mission, the Catholic sisters of the Order of the Missionaries of Charity in the streets of Calcutta, and the thousand other responses to human needs, too numerous to list.

One of the most frequently employed similes in Christian literature is that of *a soldier*. St. Paul used the image of Christian armor. The Church Fathers and the reformers developed it. Baptism is the enlisting in the ranks to become a soldier of Christ. Ordination, in the Roman Catholic Church, is like becoming Christ's officer—the commitment is for life (hence the idea of a permanent imprint on the soul, called "indelible character"). Erasmus wrote a *Handbook of a Christian Soldier*. The "militant" church, the church "victorious," and a whole group of hymns by their terminology suggest that the tenor of the church is active, and ultimately optimistic. The optimism is based on the promises and the acts of God, not on human self-confidence. Solutions of a theoretical nature have been offered. There are many books written by Christian writers on the problem of evil. But they should be read with the consciousness that in their background is Christian faith and the church.

Naturally, the Christian churches also have the reputation of failings, of contributing to human suffering, even of cruelty. These are quickly pointed out by critics, and admitted by the Christians. Our task here has not been to evaluate the total of Christian history but to establish Christian sensitivity to evil and the direction of the Christian answer to the problem of evil.

THEISM AND THE SEARCH FOR THE RELEVANT GOD: PAUL TILLICH

Theism in our day has been under attack from existentialist quarters, and charged with the deterioration of the concept of God. Basically, theism is an aspect of the traditional, even biblical faith. It deals in terms of the person-to-person relationship between man and God. God is understood as a person, whose character is ethical. It does generally omit the mystical experience, and may lose the concept of mystery. Tillich's objection to the theistic concept is that it gives the impression of an encounter of man and God as of two persons "who have a reality independent of each other," as if they were nearly equal partners, bound by the same social code of behavior. People then begin to think of God as a being among other beings, perhaps as a distant star in space, or a cloud image of Santa Claus, simply as part of our world of things and persons, with the same characteristics. This narrows the concept of the Creator into the dimensions of created being. In the face of evil in the world such God then must appear to be an absolute tyrant who disposes of men as objects. This, says Tillich, is "the God Nietzsche said had to be killed because nobody can tolerate being made into a mere object of absolute knowledge and absolute control. This is the deepest root of atheism. It is an atheism which is justified as the reaction against theological theism."[14]

What to put in place of theism? Tillich believes that the theistic concept of God can be transcended by "absolute faith," one that incorporates radical *doubt* into itself, even the doubt about God. The object of absolute faith is the "God above God." Tillich is convinced that this is the God the mystics try to reach in their practice of spiritual life, but they are unrealistic, since they hope to attain the absolute by direct personal experience. Only the church under the cross of Christ can reach the God above God, Tillich believes.

It may here be pointed out that the presence of the element of doubt within faith is a standard ingredient of Protestant thinking. Kierkegaard particularly is noted for his exposition of the dualism of faith and despair. But the basic pattern of it goes back to Luther, in whose experience the triumph of faith and the anxiety of doubt were superimposed. To Luther, a Christian is "sinner and saint at the same time," as God is both hidden and revealed at the same time. It is God who sustains man's faith in the presence of doubt, God in the Christ who cried "why hast thou forsaken me" even while he was giving his life for the sins of men. It would be

14 Paul Tillich, *The Courage to Be*, Yale Paperbounds, pp. 180 ff.

only fair to point out that the great Catholic mystics, too, speak of the Dark Night of the soul, of times of "spiritual aridity, wherein the soul believes itself to be completely lost. . . . being filled with darkness, misery, afflictions, and temptations."[15]

Thus Tillich, in his faith in the God above God, implies tension, personal war, rather than an easy, comfortable faith of emotional consolation. This is an important part of the modern religious problem. In literary form it is pointed up as a challenge in Dostoevski's story of the Grand Inquisitor (in the *Brothers Karamazov*), and boldly blocked out in Unamuno's story *San Manuel, Bueno, Martir* (published in 1933), in which the corporate faith of a Spanish village of ignorant and simple, unquestioning people is likened to a deep sleep, and sharply juxtaposed to the personal faith of the priest who serves the village lovingly and faithfully, but who is torn by doubts up to the edge of despair.[16]

A WORD ABOUT ATHEISM

Here we shall deal with atheism only as a historical epithet in practical use. It frequently arises as an honest protest against cheap theism with a deteriorated concept of God. That is, theism has often been used as a vague affirmation of belief in God to create a reverent mood, because belief in God—like praise of mother and denunciation of sin—has evoked popular approval and an emotional connotation of security. "Politicians, dictators, and other people who wish to use rhetoric to make an impression on their audience like to use the word God in this sense. It produces the feeling in their listeners that the speaker is serious and morally trustworthy. This is especially successful if they can brand their foes as atheistic."[17] This suggests that religion has been used for purposes other than its own, largely to gain selfish advantages.

[15] St. John of the Cross, *The Ascent to Mount Carmel*, Prologue.
[16] English translation by Harriet de Onís in *Spanish Stories and Tales*, Pocket Library, 1956.
[17] Tillich, *op. cit.*, p. 182.

Using religion to demonstrate social conformity and respectability has frequently been combined with use of the invective "atheistic" as a socially defamatory term. Don Cameron Allen in his study of doubt in the Renaissance period offers interesting documentation of this widespread practice: "For the Renaissance an atheist was one who could not accept any religious principle shared by all Christian creeds. A Jew, a Mohammedan, a deist was an atheist, and the definition could be narrower: to many Protestants, the Pope was the chief of Roman Catholic atheists; to many a Roman Catholic, Canterbury was head of the Anglican atheists . . ." Thomas Hobbes, who made very positive statements of belief in God, was dubbed by the divines an atheist, and so were Herbert of Cherbury and John Toland; "yet any one of these men could occupy a modern seminary chair, although he might not be liberal enough for some of his colleagues."[18] The word "atheism" then is relative, depending on the period of time in which it is used, and on the person who uses it. Indeed, self-professed atheists sometimes have a clear antireligious bias. On the other hand, it is possible that by this label is designated a person who simply protests against the form of belief in God that to him is ineffective, obsolete, and dead.

Are the doubts and the disturbances described in the last few pages symptoms of the *sickness* of our civilization? Are they signs of its *maturity?* Are they simply indications of *evolutionary changes* in our categories of thought and our ways of grasping reality? Can such questions as these be answered objectively? If so, how? If not, can each person answer them for himself out of his own life?[19]

[18] Don Cameron Allen, *Doubt's Boundless Sea, Skepticism and Faith in the Renaissance,* Johns Hopkins, 1964, Introduction.

[19] Great publicity in our day has been given to a little book (first published in London in 1963 by the SCM Press [Student Christian Movement]) by John A. T. Robinson, Bishop of Woolwich, called *Honest to God.* The interest was aroused because many people in our day could identify themselves with the problem of Bishop Robinson, representative of a staid, traditional Anglican Communion, who was shaken to the ground of his being by the impact of the

Further questions arising out of the subject matter of this chapter may call for discussion. Is the creativeness of the Western civilization related to the creativeness of its image of God—on the assumption of the imitation of the divine model? Is its social concern an outgrowth of the ethical and social commandments of its God? Is the flexibility of its ideas, and its continued growth and search (as in sciences) related to the fact that its God has no name (an open image of God) as compared to the Gods of most religions who have individual proper names? Such questions are posited on the analogy, that if the father of a family has to do with the family's way of life, and the government of a country with the way of living of its people, then the concept of God shall have some relation to the life of the civilization in which he is acknowledged.

But at the moment we begin to speculate how useful God is to civilization, we already reverse the issues. Traditionally God has been worshiped for his own sake, because he is God, and not because he is useful to people.

Whitehead felt that for the individual, there is no God without experience, nor experience without God. Perhaps we may apply the idea to the church, and even to the whole civilization: the two

radical questioning coming from the continent of Europe, particularly by the thought of Tillich, Bultmann, and Bonhoeffer. The provocative content of the book is suggested by such titles as: "The End of Theism?," "Must Christianity Be 'Supernaturalist'?," "Must Christianity Be 'Mythological'?," "Must Christianity Be Religious'?." Here the bishop gives us summaries and personal interpretations of these twentieth-century outcries for a more relevant and meaningful Christian grasp of God. The student will wish to read the booklet, perhaps together with the answer by the Archbishop of Canterbury, *Image Old and New*, SPCK (Society for Promotion of Christian Knowledge), 1963.

The phrases "religionless Christianity," "the death of God," and "post-Christian era" are often encountered in contemporary discussion such as the works of Thomas Altizer or Gabriel Vahanian, or in the Spring 1964 issue of *The Centennial Review* published at Michigan State University. Their purpose must be evaluated, and measured against the early Christian and Hebrew understanding of God, and also against the principal approach of any Christian church to God, i.e., the practice of worship. But further discussion of these *avant-garde* trends would go beyond the scope of an introduction.

should not be discussed separately, but the civilization and its God belong together in one view.

SUGGESTED READINGS

Aquinas, Thomas, *Providence and Predestination,* Regnery, 1953.

Brightman, Edgar Sheffield, *The Problem of God,* Abingdon Press, 1930.

Kerr, Hugh Thomson, Jr., *A Compend of the Institutes of the Christian Religion by John Calvin,* Presbyterian Board of Christian Education, 1939.

Otto, Rudolf, *The Idea of the Holy,* Oxford, 1923.

Robinson, John A. T., Bishop of Woolwich, *Honest to God,* SCM (Student Christian Movement), 1963.

Sayers, Dorothy, *The Mind of the Maker,* Meridian, 1956.

Smith, G. D. (ed.), *The Teaching of the Catholic Church,* Macmillan, 1949.

Underhill, Evelyn, *Mysticism,* Meridian, 1955.

VI

Jesus the Christ

The central feature that distinguishes Christianity from all other faiths is its attitude toward Jesus. This is not simply a matter of attributing a particular importance to Jesus. Many Hindus appreciate his message and incorporate both his teachings and his person into Hinduism. Moslems accept miraculous stories about Jesus more readily than some Christians and think of him as one of the great prophets preceding the final revelation through Mohammed. Liberal Jews accept Jesus as another prophet of God whose teachings, while not entirely new, are worthy of consideration. Christians distinguish themselves by the fact that they believe that Jesus of Nazareth was a unique incarnation of God in history and they interpret his significance in such manner as to warrant his designation as the Christ, the saviour of mankind. His importance continually directs the attention of Christians toward the historical

facts of his life and the interpretations which subsequent generations of Christians have made regarding his place in the drama of
salvation.

THE HISTORICAL JESUS

In the nineteenth century biblical scholars were engaged in an
exhaustive search for the historical facts about Jesus. This search
was motivated in part by a wave of liberalism that swept all fields
of inquiry urging men to re-examine their disciplines in the light
of the prevailing rationalism. Many biblical scholars, feeling that
Christianity had accumulated an extensive, superfluous theological
coating over the centuries, sought to cut back through that covering
with the new tools of rational methodology and rediscover the
historical Jesus with whom, they assumed, pure Christianity could
be found.

This was an exciting search. In later years Albert Schweitzer was
to collect the many volumes that were produced as a result of this
endeavor and stack them on his living room floor. His description
of these attempts, published in his *Quest of the Historical Jesus*,
defines the breadth and direction of the search. Since all the
writers assumed that church dogma and the gospel writers themselves had beclouded the historical Jesus, none of these modern
"lives" followed traditional interpretations of his life. Some were
openly fictitious accounts because their authors believed that the
essence of the historical figure had been overlooked or intentionally disregarded by the Gospel writers. From various clues in
the New Testament they tried to reconstruct by imagination the
life and personality of Jesus. Others remained closer to the biblical
text, but tried to find rational explanations of events that were
described in supernatural terms. Each volume tried to clarify some
of the questions that seemed ambiguous in the New Testament.
Each scholar made decisions as to whether or not Jesus thought of

himself as the Messiah, whether or not he expected an immediate end of history, and how to resolve the picture of Jesus given in the Synoptic Gospels with that of John. By imagination and critical scholarship they hoped to bring to the attention of Christendom the untouched picture of the historical Jesus.

In the long run the very diversity of apparent facts did much to contribute to doubt that the historical Jesus could in fact be uncovered and in the twentieth century the search was all but abandoned. Although much less could be said with certainty about the historical Jesus, the extensive sifting of materials led to an understanding of the historical problems and their significance.

Utilizing the scholarly efforts of those who sought to construct the life of Jesus, the interpretive biographies of the Gospel writers, and the few scant references to Jesus in contemporary writings of the first two centuries A.D.,[1] it is possible to point out the major problem areas in reconstructing a life of Jesus and perhaps to state a few generally accepted facts.

There can be little doubt that Jesus did exist and that he lived in Palestine during the Greco-Roman period of the early part of the first century. As a Palestinian he suffered with his fellow Jews under the oppressive Roman power that culminated six centuries of subjugation under five great powers: Assyria, Babylon, Persia, Greece, and Rome. Jesus would have known about the Maccabean attempt to end this oppression by armed revolution in the early part of the second century B.C. Although the revolution was briefly successful, the Jews were ultimately overpowered by the Romans. He would have known that the Zealots of his own time hoped to overthrow Roman rule in the same manner. He would have been aware that the Essenes, in contrast to the Zealots, had sought refuge from oppression by retreating to communities which they created in the isolation of the desert wilderness in the lower Jordan

---

[1] These include the work of Josephus which is difficult to evaluate because it contains so many later additions, and the works of Roman historians Tacitus and Suetonius which can do no more than substantiate Jesus' existence, his execution, and the subsequent spread of his movement.

valley. He would have been aware of the great expectation among his countrymen that God would miraculously intervene to lift oppression from his people. Some expected the earthly Messiah whom the Old Testament had promised would re-establish the throne of Israel (e.g., Isaiah 9:7; Amos 9:11). Some expected a supernatural messenger of God, the Son of Man, who would miraculously deliver God's people from political bondage (Daniel 7:13–14).

Along with the Zealots and Essenes two other groups were influential in Jesus' day. Among the aristocrats, particularly those of the priestly class, the party of the Sadducees was popular. They clung strictly to the Law of Moses as found in the Pentateuch and objected to any additions or new interpretations. Since there is no mention of the resurrection of the dead in the Pentateuch, the Sadducees rejected this belief. The other group, the Pharisees, found its major constituency among laymen of the middle classes. The Pharisees added a great written and oral tradition to the scripture in an attempt to apply the injunctions of the Law to more specific life situations. In contrast to the Sadducees, the Pharisees had also embellished Jewish thought with an angelology and belief in a resurrection after death. It is against this background that the birth of Jesus took place.

Ironically, although the Western world dates its calendar from the birth of Jesus, the date of his birth is one of the first perplexing problems facing the New Testament historian. The New Testament, which is essentially our only source for the life of Jesus, places his birth in the reign of Herod the Great (Matthew 2:1). Herod died in 4 B.C. according to the Jewish historian, Josephus, which means that Jesus must have been born sometime before that date. There is little help in finding a more precise year. The tradition that he was born on December twenty-fifth was not crystallized until the fifth century when Christmas was probably substituted for the celebration of the birth of the Greek divinity, Mithra.

It is not impossible that Jesus was born in his hometown of Nazareth. Biblical tradition places Mary and Joseph in Nazareth both before and after the birth and there is some question whether Roman authorities would require a Nazarene carpenter to go to Bethlehem, 70 miles from his home, with a wife who was near the end of her pregnancy. No explicit biblical evidence supports Nazareth as the birthplace, but only two books in the New Testament mention the birthplace at all.

Nevertheless, when the New Testament does state the birthplace, in Matthew and Luke, it agrees that the scene of the Nativity was Bethlehem and not Nazareth; and both agree that a census brought Joseph and Mary to Bethlehem. Old Testament prophecy had foretold that the Messiah would be born in Bethlehem and the overwhelming tradition of the Christian Church affirms that Jesus was born there. One of the earliest churches of Christendom, a fourth-century Greek Orthodox church founded by Constantine, marks the traditional site of his birth.

Only Luke interrupts the long years of silence between Jesus' birth and the beginning of his ministry with the brief interlude concerning Jesus instructing the elders in the Temple at Jerusalem at the age of 12 (Luke 2:41). Otherwise nothing explicit is known of this period of time. Apparently he shared his childhood home with several brothers and sisters (Mark 6:3; Matthew 13:55). With his brothers (possibly half brothers or cousins according to Semitic usage) he probably spent six years of his life at the synagogue learning the Old Testament, the customary education of his time. After finishing this training, he may have become an apprentice to his father in the carpenter shop, and perhaps later was a carpenter himself. Attempts to place Jesus in the Essene monastery at Qumran or into a marriage terminated by his wife's early death are based on no more solid evidence than other fanciful legendary materials that grew up in the later church to fill in our knowledge of this period.

All of the Gospels bring us quickly to the scene of Jesus'

baptism at the hand of John the Baptist. Only the evangelist, John, in the Fourth Gospel, is reluctant to acknowledge that Jesus actually accepted baptism. At this time he was about 30 years old (Luke 3:23) and had an awareness of his special mission which received more specific direction immediately afterward in the "temptation" experience. The relationship of Jesus to John the Baptist is difficult to assess on the basis of the brief texts that are available. There are indications that Jesus' disciples and perhaps Jesus himself recognized John as the leader until John was imprisoned (Matthew 11:11).[2] Many later Christians could not believe that Jesus would ever have been a follower and contend either that he was actually in competition with John for disciples or that he never recognized the leadership of John at all and never consented to baptism at his hands. The synoptic tradition at any rate does accept the fact of Jesus' baptism and does not introduce us to his teaching ministry until after John is arrested.

Very shortly after his baptism, Jesus began his ministry. The gospel record is not clear regarding his image of himself as he began to preach. The earliest Gospel, Mark, records only one instance when Jesus acknowledges himself as the Messiah (14:61f.). This has led some scholars to conclude that Jesus had no messianic consciousness. Surely if he did, he made considerable effort to conceal it, perhaps realizing that such a profession would raise eyebrows rather than save souls. Despite the lack of substantial evidence from the gospel record, most Christians have believed that Jesus did think of himself as the Messiah.

Inspired by his baptism and committed to his ministry, he now experienced the struggle of the temptation (Matthew 4:1–11), a struggle in which he had to define what his ministry meant. Three tempting possibilities presented themselves: he could set himself to improving the economic lot of Israel, he could seek to restore the kingdom of Israel, or he could call upon his power to perform miracles to awe the masses. Each of these he considered and each

[2] The evidence is presented in Maurice Goguel, *The Life of Jesus*, Macmillan, 1945.

he rejected. No concrete description is given of the job he decided he was to undertake and we can only deduce it from his subsequent ministry.

As crowds began to gather and then to follow, Jesus appointed 12 men as special disciples (Matthew 4:18, 21; 10:1–4) whom he trained and sent to preach in his cause. But his ministry as described in the Gospels continued to be centered primarily upon his own preaching and it was not until after his death that the disciples gained distinction on their own.

Jesus' ministry went in two primary directions, preaching and healing. Many of his words are preserved for us in the Gospel accounts. Sometimes he preaches from the Old Testament (Matthew 5:21f., 5:27f.), sometimes he utters simple chastisement (Matthew 6), and sometimes he discusses his plans in conversational narrative (Matthew 12:1–8). But one form of address, the parable, stands out in particular as expressive of Jesus' style.

The parable utilizes symbols or experiences common to everyone and therefore provides a good level of communication. More important, the parable offers a means of expressing concepts that cannot be expressed in simple propositions. It illuminates an ultimate concept by an analogy sufficiently parallel to be meaningful, but sufficiently distinct so that it will not be taken literally. The growth of a mustard seed is latent with imagery that can point toward a truth about the kingdom of God, but there is no danger that the kingdom of God will be mistaken for a mustard seed. To say that the kingdom of God is like a cool drink of water runs little risk of being taken literally, but it has great limitations in what it can express about the kingdom. To say that the kingdom is like the life of a wealthy man in a great castle in the sky may open more dimensions of comparison, but runs the risk of being taken literally. The parables of Jesus stimulated the mind to wrestle with common imagery to come upon infinite truths. Through their use he could talk to the most uneducated peasant about the most complex issues of life.

Jesus was also a healer. In part this was necessitated by the fact that the Israelites thought in terms of the health of the whole man and did not clearly distinguish between physical, spiritual, and mental well-being. In any case Jesus felt a responsibility to heal the bodies of broken men. As a consequence he was pursued by physically sick men and women and the Gospel records many instances of healing which will soon be discussed in more detail.

His early ministry was spent in the vicinity of his home in northern Palestine and particularly in the towns around the Sea of Galilee. It was here that he picked his disciples and it was here that he preached the sermons recorded in Matthew 5–7. The green hills surrounding the beautiful sea provided an idyllic setting for the enthusiastic success of the early months of the ministry.

Jesus' message centers around one main theme: the Kingdom of God. As the ultimate hope for mankind, it was not a simple concept to define and Jesus used his full talent trying to express its meaning. It has generally been understood as a kingdom yet to come. In the thought of many this means an objective change in the world about us, either through an amelioration of social evils or direct intervention of God in history. For others the kingdom is otherworldly, transcending this world either as an attitude of mind or a heavenly place. Those who understand the kingdom as already here (perhaps implied by Luke 17:21) must give it some subjective interpretation. It is a kingdom of self-respect or a reign of love or a spiritual community of those who do God's will. This is the direction of all existential interpretations. It has been suggested that the universal church is the kingdom of God. Some historical churches have thought of themselves as the kingdom. The Roman Catholic Church is the best example. Jesus' hearers understood him to say that the kingdom was good and that they were eligible citizens. To men who had inherited many centuries of political and religious oppression, this was good news.

The constitution of the kingdom of God is the Sermon on the Mount and the radical ethic it espouses. It becomes obvious from any reading of this ethic that the kingdom of God is like no kingdom of man; it has no place for materialism or resistance. The ethic is so radical that it raises the question whether or not it could seriously be proposed as a universal ethic for all men at all times. Men who had been heartened by the promise of citizenship in the kingdom of God may have felt a sense of frustration when they heard its ethical demands. But the great freedom promised in this message drew large crowds of hopeful listeners to Jesus.

Permeating the teaching of Jesus is a tremendous sense of urgency. He sends the disciples out on a tour of villages with the warning that the end will come before they have returned (Matthew 10:23). He warns all to be watchful for the end is at hand (Mark 13). In the letters of Paul the urgency becomes more explicit: ". . . we who are alive, who are left until the coming of the Lord, shall not precede those who have fallen asleep" (I Thessalonians 4:15). It is related to almost everything that Paul says. The expectation continues to be an important part of the New Testament message (e.g., James 5:7ff.; II Peter 3:3ff.; I John 2:18ff.; Revelation 16:15).

The promised intermediary violence and destruction demonstrate the clear distinction that is made between the present age and the age to come. "For nation will rise against nation, and kingdom against kingdom; there will be earthquakes in various places, there will be famines; this is but the beginning of the sufferings" (Mark 13:8). In this respect Jesus' thought is closely parallel to the apocalypticism that permeated Jewish thinking from the fourth century B.C. until the destruction of Jerusalem in A.D. 70. It was an affirmation of hope in the face of apparently hopeless oppression. The present age was so corrupt and chaotic and in the hands of such evil men that the forces for good could not conceivably improve it. The whole scene would have to be destroyed by a power greater than evil, a supernatural power, and then the new age could begin.

Most people in the early church quite literally believed that such a supernatural change would come about. A good many Christians still expect such a cataclysmic divine intervention in history. Many others have demythologized the idea of an objective new age and believe that the new age is something that each individual can experience when the evil is destroyed within him and he is "born again" (John 3:3).

The idea of a "new age" intrigued thousands of oppressed Palestinians and they anxiously followed Jesus to hear more about it. But the idea of a new age stimulated apprehension in those who were satisfied with the present age and they moved to defend it. The Pharisees, for example, felt that Jesus treated too lightly the Law and the traditions that had been passed down from the fathers and they sought to test his orthodoxy. The political leaders, remembering the success of the Maccabees, looked with suspicion on any talk of supplanting the existing administration. Thus an opposition developed and increased in intensity until Jesus and his followers felt it necessary to withdraw from Galilee to the east side of the Jordan for safety.

This stay, centered at Caesarea Philippi, was a determining point in the ministry of Jesus. Whatever he had thought of himself up to this time, he had kept secret from his disciples. Now with the leisure to assess all that had transpired, the disciples were brought to the awareness that the long-sought Messiah of Israel and the master who walked among them were one. Peter crystallized this affirmation for all of them when, in the course of a discussion of Jesus' work, he exclaimed: "Thou art the Christ!" (Matthew 16:16).

While Caesarea Philippi gave them the respite in which to think through the implications of their work and to organize their mission, it did not give them a field in which they could fruitfully serve. They were safe in Caesarea Philippi, but not effective. In Jerusalem they would be effective but not safe. The decision to go to Jerusalem pointed Jesus to the peak of his ministry and also to its end. To Jerusalem Jesus and the disciples came. He preached, he was arrested, and at the bidding of the multitude he was executed.

Fifty days after Jesus' death, the disciples were together again in Jerusalem. In the meantime they had fled to Galilee. There, in some manner that the simple words of the New Testament are at a loss to express, they experienced the continued presence of Jesus[3] and a renewal of their calling to fulfill his mission. Convinced that their leader had been victorious over death, they returned to Jerusalem. As disciples of a dead master they were confronted with a tremendous task if they were to win new followers. They were left to answer two very difficult questions: Who was Jesus, and Why did he die? The explanations that began in the sermons of the original disciples and finally were formalized in the Gospels and the creeds of the church may be understood as definitions of the Christ of Faith. Their concern was not to present a simple biography of the historical Jesus, but to present a statement of his significance to the history of mankind.

OLD TESTAMENT CONCEPTS APPLIED TO JESUS

Since the Jews had been anticipating an ideal leader for several centuries, tradition and scripture provided some ready-made categories and terms by which the disciples could convey the significance of their master whom they took to be the fulfillment of Old Testament hopes. The two most important categories were "Messiah" and "Son of Man." The title, "the Christ," given to Jesus was a Greek word used to translate the Hebrew "Messiah." "Messiah" referred literally to "an anointed one" and was used many times to refer to a king of Israel (e.g., I Samuel 2:35; II Chronicles 6:42), once to refer to Cyrus the Persian (Isaiah 45:1) and occasionally to refer to a high priest (e.g., Leviticus 4:3). All of these men were understood to be commissioned by God. The title "Son of Man" as applied to a divinely appointed messenger,

[3] At times he appears like a ghost capable of passing through walls (John 20:19 ff. and 26 ff.), and yet with a body needing food (Luke 24:41) and capable of being touched (John 20:27 ff.).

has no specific human referent in the Old Testament passage in which it is found.

Despite the variety of uses of the term "Messiah" in the Old Testament, the Israelites came to look forward to a particular kind of Messiah. At the end of the eighth century the northern kingdom of Israel fell to Assyria. The destruction and subjugation of the southern kingdom of Judah followed early in the sixth century. Israel began to look for a great leader who would return her to her former glory or better. The designation for this leader was "Messiah." His coming and its consequences were described in many passages like the following: "But you, O Bethlehem Ephrathah, who are little to be among the clans of Judah, from you shall come forth for me one who is to be ruler in Israel, whose origin is from old, from ancient days" (Micah 5:2). He will be a descendant of David who will reign over Israel with wisdom and justice and restore peace and prosperity for all of the people.

The early Christian Church understood Jesus to be the awaited Messiah. Whether or not Jesus understood himself to be the Messiah is a matter of debate within the church. Most Christians believe that he did, but such New Testament scholars as Wilhelm Wrede, Rudolf Bultmann, and Martin Dibelius claim that Jesus never regarded himself as the Messiah. Jesus did believe he had a unique commission and the early church believed it could be understood in terms of his Messiahship. Matthew in particular went to special pains to show that Jesus was fulfilling a role that had been extensively described in the Old Testament (see, for example, Matthew 1:22, 2:6, 15, 23). His Gospel frequently states that what Jesus did was done "that it might be fulfilled what the prophet had said."

The other term which already had some parlance in Israel and came to be associated with Jesus was the term, "Son of Man." In essence this term is simply the Hebrew idiom for "man," but in practice it had taken on a specialized meaning in some parts of the Old Testament and intertestamental apocalyptic works (particularly Daniel and Enoch) and in other non-Jewish literature from surrounding cultures. The term was often used as an exalted term for man, implying his majestic, divine-like attributes. From this it moved on to imply a kind of superman, more divine than human. A few references in the New Testament seem to use the term only to refer to Jesus' humanity and by the second century the church used the term almost exclusively in this sense. But the Gospel writers seem to be greatly influenced by the second meaning of the term also and found it a ready framework within which to present their master as a cosmic supernatural figure who had come to destroy evil and preside over the final judgment. The New Testament implies various modifications of some sort of supernatural man.

Each of these terms, "Messiah" and "Son of Man" implied a cosmic and central significance that Jesus did fulfill for the Christian community. On the other hand each of these terms implied certain things, a military-political leader in the first case and a catastrophic end of the world in the second; both proved irrelevant to Jesus even though many in his own time may have understood them to be relevant. In part these terms helped the early community understand something about Jesus. But new doctrines also emerged as the early community tried to express its beliefs about him.

UNIQUE CONCEPTS APPLIED TO JESUS

The central affirmation of the Christian faith was that Jesus had risen victoriously above death and still lived among his followers. "If there be no resurrection," cries Paul, "then Christ was not raised; and if Christ was not raised, then our gospel is null and void and so is your faith" (I Corinthians 15:12). Given Paul's understanding of the Resurrection as derived from his Pharisaic background, he was not talking in symbolic terms. The Resurrection was an objective event. However, his use of the term body probably did not have the same connotations that body has in contemporary Western language. Paul explicitly recognized that the Resurrection must imply a different kind of body (I Corinthians 15:35ff.) and a body distinct from the soul would have been an artificial division in Hebrew thought.

The study of comparative religion has raised the question of the origin of many beliefs including resurrection. Paul, who presents us with the most comprehensive statement of Jesus' Resurrection, was heir to two cultural traditions that already had a belief in resurrection. The Pharisees emerged in the second century B.C. as a distinctive group with a belief in the resurrection of the dead and the mystery cults of Greece had such a doctrine. In addition, the mythology of the cultures of the Middle East had a predominant theme of a dying-rising god who controlled the agricultural cycles. These myths may have had some influence on the shape of the Christian doctrine, but this is not likely. The imagery of the good rising victorious over evil forces is a basic myth that must occur in all religions. In Christianity it was expressed in the Resurrection of Jesus.

The historical fact of the Resurrection has wider literary witness than that of the virgin birth. All of the Gospels describe an empty tomb. Although Paul is equally silent about the empty tomb and the virgin birth, he strongly affirms the Resurrection. Many Christians, including Roman Catholics and conservative Protestants, believe that Jesus rose bodily and ascended into heaven. Their belief is based either on their literal acceptance of the Bible or the logical demand that a sinless body could not die since death is the wage of sin. Other Christians strongly endorse the doctrine of the Resurrection and its importance, but cannot accept it as a literal objective event. Karl Barth, a twentieth-century existential theologian, says, "We may believe in [Christ] only if we believe in his corporal resurrection. This is the content of the New Testament. We are always free to reject it, but not to modify it, nor to pretend that the New Testament tells something else. We may accept or refuse the message, but we may not change it."[4] At this point he seems to join more conservative Christians. But the significance of his statement is seen in a different light when he writes:

. . . if the Resurrection be brought within the context of history, it must share in its obscurity and error and essential questionableness. Against the influence which the Resurrection has exerted upon individual souls must then be set the far more obvious distortions and disfigurements of which it has been the cause.

Why do ye set the truth of God on the plane and in the space where historical factors, such as "Christendom," rise and fall, ebb and flow, are great and are little? The conception of resurrection emerges with the conception of death, with the conception of the end of all historical things as such. The bodily resurrection of Christ stands over against His bodily crucifixion—and nowhere else can it be encountered. Only in so far as He has been *put to death in the flesh* is *He quickened in the spirit* (I Peter 3:18), revealed and perceived under a new heaven and a new earth as the new man: that is to say, only in so far as He has, in order to die, abandoned and left behind all concrete, human, historical possibilities—even the possibility of some wonderful super-physical existence. He is the Risen—Crucified One. He is the invisible new man in God. He is the end of the old man as such, for he has put behind Him death and the whole relativity of historical and time-enveloped things.[5]

With these words Barth denies any rendering of an objective literal resurrection as belittling the message of the resurrection experience.

Many liberal Christians have tried to explain away the rationally unpalatable aspects of the Resurrection. The empty tomb has been accounted for by some as the result of thieves who removed the body so that it could not become a focal point for martyr worship. Others suggest that the women may have come upon the wrong tomb. It has also been said that perhaps Jesus was only half dead

[4] From a 1962 press interview.
[5] Karl Barth, *The Epistle to the Romans,* Oxford, 1933.

when placed in the tomb and the cool air revived him. The post-Resurrection appearances have been attributed to hallucination or poetic license. These explanations destroy the inherent significance of the Resurrection and understand its importance mainly as a revitalization of the discouraged disciples. But whatever differences in interpretation may exist, there is agreement that the early followers of Jesus believed that he was still with them in some sense and this faith was the basis of the early church.

That Jesus was an incarnation of God is ultimately demonstrated by the Resurrection, but the early church saw a secondary witness to this truth in his unique birth. Scripture and tradition state that Mary had not had sexual intercourse when she found herself pregnant with Jesus. Thus another historical occurrence confirmed the divine origin of Jesus' mission. But this event plays a secondary role, first because there is less supporting evidence and second because the event is superfluous: the supreme statement of the Incarnation has been made in the Resurrection. The virgin birth is an additional statement "that it pleased God to send."

The creeds, following the biblical text in Matthew 1:20, state that Jesus was conceived by the Holy Spirit. In some parlance it is said that Mary was the mother and God was the father of Jesus. This provides a clear background for the theological position that Jesus was both human and divine. Others are reluctant to use the parental imagery for the divine action and prefer to simply state that God was the power that made it possible for Mary to have a child and remain a virgin.

All of the evidence for the virgin birth is found in the two Gospels, Matthew (1:18) and Luke (1:26ff.). Neither Paul nor the other Gospel writers, nor any other New Testament book makes mention of the birth. Paradoxically, Matthew goes to great lengths to establish the geneology of Jesus through Joseph and then turns around to assert that Joseph was not the father. This has led some to conclude that Joseph was the real father and the virgin birth narratives were later incorporated by Matthew to demonstrate that Jesus fulfilled Old Testament prophecy and by Luke as a poetic expression of the uniqueness of Jesus.

Nevertheless conservative Christians accept the virgin birth as a literal biological fact. Biblical literalists accept it as a necessary conclusion to their primary assumption and they have often used it as a key test of orthodoxy. Catholic Christians accept it because of its scriptural support and, in addition, they feel that it is a logically necessary doctrine. If Jesus was an incarnation of God, some rationale must be given to account for the manner in which he inherited his divinity. The concept of the virgin birth offers such a rationale.

More liberal Christians are divided in their attitude toward the virgin birth. Many of them do not accept it in any literal sense, but do believe that it symbolically makes a basic affirmation of Christianity. Some years ago an Episcopal bishop made the statement, "I don't believe in the Virgin Birth, but I do believe in the doctrine of the virgin birth."[6] By this he meant that symbolically the virgin birth said something to him about the purity and mysterious uniqueness of Jesus and his divine mission in the world. Some liberals are inclined to dismiss both the fact and the significance of the virgin birth. For them it adds nothing to Jesus' message which they see as the essence of Christianity and distracts from the message by its embarrassing unscientific suppositions. They are inclined to think that the doctrine is the product of later Christians anxious to affirm the uniqueness of their leader. The virgin birth of Jesus is seen as a parallel to accounts of virgin births of leaders in other cultures. But for most Christians, it is another way of proclaiming the incarnation manifest in the life of Jesus.

The authority of Jesus was established for the early church by the Resurrection, the virgin birth and one other important group of phenomena, the miracles he performed in the course of his ministry. According to the Gospel writers, for example, Jesus walked on water (Matthew 14:22ff.), calmed the sea (Mark

6 Cited in *The Christian Century,* April 4, 1962, p. 420.

4:35), and healed the sick (e.g., Mark 2:9ff.). Even granting the fact that the first-century population did not have the categories of natural law to distinguish between miracle and nonmiracle, the Gospel writers were surely saying that Jesus accomplished unusual things. The Resurrection, the virgin birth and the miracle stories all point to the fact that Jesus was decidedly different from other men.

The miracle stories are usually divided into two categories, the natural miracles such as changing water to wine (John 2:1ff.), walking on water (Matthew 14:26), and multiplying the loaves and fishes (Mark 6:36ff.); and the healing miracles such as the healing of the hemorrhaging woman (Mark 5:25ff.) and the healing of the lame and blind (Luke 7:21ff.). The healing miracles are the easiest to explain, especially for those who wish to avoid a supernatural explanation. In most cases Jesus does not even claim to have effected the cure; he dismisses the one healed with the words, "Your faith has made you whole" (e.g., Mark 5:34, 2:5). This may be readily understood even in the light of modern medicine which grows increasingly aware of the relationship between mind and body in health. Any physical symptoms can be produced by the mind and medical people give increasing importance to mental health as a requisite to physical health.

But with the nature miracles, no such rational explanation is readily available even to those who would prefer it. They are much more difficult to explain away. There have been Christians who have felt that the miracles do more to embarrass the Christian cause than to enhance it. Thomas Jefferson compiled a New Testament in which he deleted all of the miraculous in order to preserve the integrity of the teachings of Jesus. Many liberal Christians, while not using quite so radical a method, have tried to apologize for the miracles by giving them rational explanations. Thus, they may say, Jesus did not really walk on water, but because of the angle of vision and the haze on the beach, the disciples mistakenly thought he did. The water did not really change into wine, but diluted the little remaining wine and the wedding guests, preoccupied by the festivities, were unconcerned about how great the water content had become. Jesus did not multiply the fish and loaves but shamed the selfish crowd into sharing their lunches and when everyone had pulled his lunch from under his cloak there was more than enough.

Existential theologians insist that the historicity of the miracle events is quite irrelevant to the truths they convey. The miracles must be understood, they say, as a means of communication or a teaching device. Rudolf Bultmann, for example, says that the miraculous haul of fish described in Luke 5:1–11 symbolically tells us of the drawing power of Jesus:

Surely it is permitted us to say of the miracle-stories something similar to what Paul says about eating meat offered to idols: "If we believe them we are no better off, if we do not believe them we are no worse off" (cf. I Corinthians 8:8).

. . . [But now that we have clearly said that], we must just as clearly say: Christian faith is faith in wonder, faith in the wondrous dealing of God, readiness to experience God's wonders in our own lives. Now we must let this story guide us in understanding what that means.

We are not debating whether this story is an actual occurrence or whether it is reverent poetry, a legend.

But lest I be misunderstood, let me say that I do regard it as reverent poetry. But whether it is the report of a historical event or whether it is a poetic creation, in either case it still teaches us what it intends to teach. We must understand it as a symbol depicting the wondrous power which Jesus can achieve over a human life.[7]

This position is characteristic of a great many theologians in the contemporary liberal and existential schools of thought.

Conservative Christians accept the literal fact of the miracle stories and look upon them as evidence of God's power in controlling the natural world. As such they are a proof that Jesus was invested with this power. Assuming an all-powerful God, they argue, why should miraculous occurrences cause any difficulty?

Through these doctrines of the Resurrection, the virgin birth,

[7] Quoted in *The Journal of Bible and Religion* (January 1959), p. 30.

and the miracle stories as set forth in the Gospels and the creeds, the early church expressed its faith in Jesus as the Christ. Each of these doctrines said that Jesus was more than a man. In some sense he was also uniquely related to God. He died for the sins of mankind and had been raised from death to take a special place in heaven.

JESUS AS HUMAN AND DIVINE

The early church very soon found itself in an apologetic stance.[8] Followers of Jesus whose personal experience with him had inspired complete loyalty to his mission faced multitudes who had had no such personal experience. The personal overtones had to be translated into concrete propositions. As the spontaneous faith that had unified the early followers was forced into rational terms, disagreements arose over the terms in which it should be expressed. The greatest difficulty was found in defining the human and divine nature of Jesus.

Even the Gospels reflect this dilemma. Mark portrays the most human Jesus. There is no account of the virgin birth. Jesus appears at his baptism for the first time. He has ordinary human emotions (e.g., Mark 10:14), he is puzzled at times (e.g., Mark 5:30), and he engages in self-depreciation (e.g., Mark 10:18). Supported by Mark various theories of "adoption" have evolved which state that Jesus was an ordinary man who was chosen at his baptism to be a unique messenger of God. As early as the beginning of the second century the adoptionist position had a spokesman of note in Hermas of Rome. In the latter part of the same century a movement known as Dynamic Monarchianism came into prominence. It also held an adoptionist point of view, but by the end of the third century this cause, and with it the adoptionist theory, had disappeared in the West. The Unitarians and other liberal groups revived a similar position in the last century. These groups are

---

[8] In this sense apology does not imply admission of error, but the defense and explanation of one's position.

willing to say that Jesus was a unique man or the best man but they are reluctant to say that he is more than a man.

Matthew and Luke portray a more divine Jesus. He is a unique messenger of God from his birth. These two Gospels alone tell the story of the virgin birth. They are reluctant to attribute human emotions to Jesus. Emotions described in Mark are omitted in Matthew and Luke (compare Mark 3:5 with Luke 14:10). Questions asked by Jesus in Mark are omitted in Matthew and Luke (compare Mark 5:30 with Matthew 9:20ff.). Jesus' implied denial of his own goodness, "Why do you call me good? No one is good but God alone" (Mark 10:18) is rephrased in Matthew, "Why do you ask me about the good?" (Matthew 19:17).

In the Gospel of John the human factors about Jesus are minimized even more. He is existent from the beginning of time (John 1:1), he has no need for the baptism of John and he moves through the narrative without human emotion or fallibility. Here the human Jesus has clearly become the divine Christ.

The logical extension of this development is not found in the New Testament, but it is found in parts of the early Christian community. The most extreme statement was made by the Docetists, who, during the second century A.D., maintained that Jesus was not a man at all, but only seemed to be a man. They claim that actually he was a nonphysical appearance of the divine. The position of the Monophysites, a few centuries later, closely resembled that of the Docetists. They were concerned with resolving the dual nature of Jesus, human and divine, into a single nature in which manhood and divinity were fused. In practice this fusion usually meant that the human was lost in the divine. Some would account for the growing popularity of the Virgin Mary in the Middle Ages by the resurgence of an essentially Docetic position. As Jesus was absorbed more and more into the divine, Mary took his place as a representative of God among men.[9] The Christian Church today, in all of its branches supports the early condemna-

[9] Cyrus R. Pangborn, "Christian Theology and the Dogma of the Assumption," *The Journal of Bible and Religion,* (April 1962).

tions of all of these movements and insists that Jesus was a real historical person with full humanity.

One of the main difficulties raised by the positing of a truly human nature for Jesus is that he must take on the imperfection that human nature implies. Jesus, too, must inherit original sin. The Roman Catholic Church has answered this problem with the doctrine of the Immaculate Conception which says that at the moment of Mary's conception in the womb of her mother, she was miraculously cleansed of original sin. Descended from a sinless mother and no father, Jesus avoided the inherited sin of man. Karl Barth has taken an opposite position and states that Jesus did inherit fallen human nature. Protestants have generally not devoted much thought to the question. They are inclined to say that Jesus inherited the propensity to sin and therefore the temptations are real, but that he resisted all temptation.

One attempt to solve the dilemma of two natures was posited by Arius in the early part of the fourth century and resulted in one of the more popular heresies in the history of the church. Arius said that Jesus represented neither man nor God, but was a third kind of being somewhere in between.

In 325 the bishops of the church were called to a meeting at Nicaea, largely at the instigation of Constantine, to try to resolve this basic problem regarding the nature of Jesus. Essentially they concluded by stating both sides of the issue: Jesus is truly God and truly man. The same formulation was reiterated at Chalcedon in 451 and has remained the orthodox statement on the relationship of the divine and the human in the person of Jesus: "We believe . . . in one Lord Jesus Christ . . . true God of true God . . . who was made flesh . . . and became man . . ."[10] Since this is an affirmation that defies logic, it has not been universally understood or accepted and subsequent church history has witnessed the periodic reappearance of all of the original positions with the possible exception of Docetism.

[10] Henry Bettenson, *Documents of the Christian Church,* Oxford, 1947, p. 37.

WHY DID JESUS DIE?

The fact of the Resurrection validates the work of the Crucifixion for Christians, but the nature of that work has had various interpretations. Why did Jesus die? The Greek Church, the Latin Church and the "modern" interpretation of the last century have each contributed unique insights and interpretations of this question. Christians have, as a rule, constructed their own answers incorporating some elements from each of the classical positions.

The Greek interpretation has assumed a dualism in the universe. God is in a great cosmic struggle with evil, sometimes personified as Satan or the devil. The Crucifixion represents the last event in the struggle and in that event evil loses. According to some versions of this theory, God took on the form of man (Jesus) and the devil unwittingly treated him as a man, visiting upon him the punishment of death that men indeed deserve. But God does not. For this injustice, the devil lost his job and mankind became the exclusive property of God. The most common version sees the Crucifixion as the key battle in the struggle between God and the devil. Its importance lies in the fact that when the devil has sent his full force of evil, death, humiliation, and suffering, against an innocent man, that man still emerges victorious. It finds echoes in many passages of scripture (e.g., John 16:33; I Corinthians 15:54, 57) and is beautifully manifest in Paul's great confession: "No, in all things we are more than conquerors through him who loved us. For I am sure that neither death, nor life, nor angels, nor principalities, nor things present, nor things to come, nor powers, nor height, nor depth, nor anything else in all creation, will be able to separate us from the love of God in Christ Jesus our Lord" (Romans 8:38–39).

The Greek dualistic interpretation has recently been revived in Protestant thought. Minus the dramatic battle imagery, at least in any literal sense, theologians like G. Aulen, in his work *Christus*

Victor, have represented the Christ as the embodiment of God struggling against the evil of the universe and emerging as the victorious Christ.

In considering the full depth of any of these interpretations, it is relevant to ask whether the imagery, in this case God and Satan on the battlefield, is to be understood objectively or subjectively, literally or symbolically. Many in the early church expected the Christ to lead them in a real battle either against Rome or the cosmic demons of evil. These men would have understood the battlefield imagery of the Greek interpretation in very literal and objective terms. Others, and this would be the case with Aulen, would understand the concrete picture of the battlefield to be symbolic of a spiritual battle that can only be implied by the images that are available.

The dimension of literal and symbolic may or may not correlate with the dimension of objective and subjective. Naturally if the great battle between God and evil is understood literally, it must also have an objective reality. If the battle is understood symbolically then it may have either objective or subjective reality. It may symbolize an actual struggle of good and evil forces potentially independent from the life of any given individual, such as social struggles against poverty, discrimination, and ignorance. In this case the battle is an objective reality. But it may also symbolize the struggle that takes place within the hearts of individual men against guilt, fear, and meaninglessness, in which case it is a subjective battle.

The Latin interpretation of the Crucifixion has emphasized the substitutionary nature of the work effected by Jesus. Jesus died on behalf of a sinful mankind too weak morally to effect its own salvation. Two analogies, one from the Old Testament sacrificial cultus and the other from the law court, clarify the nature of this interpretation. According to the ritual codes of the Old Testament, one had to make a guilt offering (Leviticus 5) for his various transgressions. This offering was often based on the extent of the transgression and the ability of the guilty one to pay. But what happens if the sin of man is very great and the means of man are very small? This is precisely the dilemma that all men are in according to Latin theories of the atonement which say that only the offering of a perfect being can compensate for the deep sin of man and Jesus provides the divine (perfect) sacrifice on behalf of the sins of man.

The analogy from the law court says essentially the same thing. Man stands condemned by a nature so sinful that he deserves eternal punishment. Only the compassion of the judge or the substitutionary payment of the punishment by some other being can free man. An innocent man (Jesus) takes upon himself the punishment that man deserves and mankind is eligible to be saved. In each case the atonement is understood as a supernatural cosmic drama.

Many conservative Christians understand these images as literal renderings of the drama of salvation in a space-time context. The payment has been made in a supernatural act whereby a real man has been delivered to an objective God, who, in return, will see that all men who endorse the act will spend eternal time in a heavenly place. Less conservative Christians believe that the images say something true about the drama of salvation, but they cannot be understood in a space-time setting. They reveal a dimension of human experience that can only be implied by literal symbols. The drama of salvation is a mystery that can be believed but not understood. Many liberal Christians have rejected the imagery and out of their dissatisfaction the modernist interpretation has grown.

Reluctance to accept the traditional Greek or Latin interpretations of the atonement has been based on the difficulty of resolving their implications with the suppositions of rational and scientific thought. With the growing suspicion of the supernatural, many Christians began to shift their attention from the supernatural accomplishments of Jesus to those that were compatible with the natural world. For them the ethical message and moral example of Jesus' life have become the central value of his ministry. On the one hand, it is understood that Jesus went to his death to shock men into a realization of the depth of their involvement in sin and thereby to inspire them to accept their responsibilities as set forth in the ethical demands of the New Testament. When men see that their brutality and selfishness lead to the suffering and death of an innocent man they will be sobered into repentance. On the other hand, and perhaps most important, the Crucifixion says it is better to die for a principle than to live without one. This interpretation assumes both the possibility of free will and the ability of man to do the good and may, therefore, be characterized as a liberal point of view. In baldest form, it assumes that the significance of the Crucifixion is entirely subjective. It differs from the subjective interpretations of the Greek or Latin theories in that it presumes no mysterious depths to the subjective reality. Rather than understand the Crucifixion as a symbolic way of saying something about a real change in the individual, the liberal would say that the subjective change is one wrought willfully and consciously by the individual.

SOME CONTEMPORARY INTERPRETATIONS
OF THE CHRIST SYMBOL

Through Christ men gain salvation. What is that salvation? Orthodox and conservative Christians point primarily to a place beyond death where rewards and punishments are meted out. This does not preclude the possibility that Christ can change lives in this world, too, instilling them with the fruits of the spirit: love, joy, peace, patience, kindness, goodness, faithfulness, gentleness, and self-control (Galatians 5:22–23); but primarily salvation is an experience of heaven after death. Many liberals can be quite clear about salvation, too, because they see heaven and hell as terms applicable only to this earthly life with the Kingdom of God as something men must build here.

But other liberal Christians find it hard to express such clear-cut definitions of what it means to be saved. They are reluctant to accept a heaven set in a space-time setting after death. Yet they are also reluctant to believe that eternal life has no referent other than success in this life. Generally speaking they are left with the option of understanding salvation as a subjective experience that takes place in this life, but is not measurable by the human categories of space or time.

Paul Tillich, for example, uses the term "New Being" to refer to the goal of salvation. One is continually striving to overcome the estrangement that separates one from God. To become one with God is to participate in the New Being. It is unfair to Tillich to try to reduce his symbolism to rational terms, because he insists that the reason we use symbols at all is that they are able to convey more than rational language can describe. Thus the symbol of the New Being is in a way irreducible. But the New Being implies the essence of Goodness which can grasp an individual and flood his whole being.

Rudolf Bultmann says, "The event of Jesus Christ is therefore the revelation of the love of God. It makes a man free from himself and free to be himself, free to live a life of self-commitment in faith and love."[11] Man is self-assertive and must be delivered from himself before he can live a life of self-commitment. Self-assertion drives one toward security in the things of this world. Self-commitment points one toward the future and is the only way by which the individual attains authentic existence.

Bultmann and Tillich both represent existential schools of thought, accepting validation of truths by intuitive subjective response. They differ as to whether ultimate truths need to be expressed in myths. Tillich says they do. Bultmann believes that the myths can be restated in literal language. But, in opposition to this school which has questioned the efficacy of reason in the search for truth, another line of thought has developed which has sought

[11] *Kerygma and Myth,* Harper & Row, 1961, p. 32.

to sharpen the tool of reason through the careful examination of language. In its earlier form, logical positivism, this school of language analysis would not become involved in a discussion of religious statements at all, because it believed them all to be meaningless. All intangible phenomena were rejected as meaningless. More recent schools have tried to wrestle with values, metaphysics, and other intangibles and now occasional attempts are made to apply language analysis within theological discussions.

One such attempt has been made by Paul Van Buren.[12] He begins with the assumption that theological terms of the first centuries had concrete literal referents for the people that used them and if they are to be meaningful today they must be translated into terms that have concrete literal validity today. He finds in the word "freedom" the epitome of the aspirations of men today. It is therefore an appropriate replacement for the supernatural intervention into history by the divine which was the aspiration of men of the first century. So today when a man says, "Jesus is Lord," he is saying that "Jesus' freedom has been contagious and has become the criterion for his life, public and private." The "New Being," the "authentic existence," and the "free man" are attempts to express the essence of a "Man in Christ" in contemporary terms that will not alienate those for whom old theological terms have become objectionable.

THE NEW QUEST OF THE HISTORICAL JESUS

The recognized danger in each of the contemporary interpretations is that the question of the relevance of Jesus and Christianity may be raised. Contemporary terms may become so appropriate that the necessity of associating them with any historical event or

[12] *The Secular Meaning of the Gospel,* SCM (Student Christian Movement), 1963.

tradition is dubious. Of course many individuals as well as religious groups have decided that the historical traditions are no longer meaningful or necessary and they have cut themselves off. But others insist that despite the need of contemporary expression there is still a need for historical grounding.

Tillich says, "The picture of Jesus as the Christ conquered [historical destiny and the tensions of finite freedom] through the power of a concrete reality."[13] Apart from Jesus the New Being would have no bearer. It would become as the mythology of religions that do not have an historical focus. The historical Jesus was the basis of the Christ of faith that is the criterion of the New Being. Likewise Bultmann argues that the *kerygma,* that is, the core of the Christian message, must have its grounding in history: "Here then is the crucial distinction . . . between the Christian faith and the natural understanding of Being. The New Testament speaks and faith knows of an act of God through which man becomes capable of self-commitment, capable of faith and love, of his authentic life."[14] Van Buren seems less concerned whether the Christ symbol is associated with a historical person.

Defense of the necessity of the historical Jesus has sent contemporary theologians on a new quest for that figure. Unlike the original quest which set out to throw off Pauline and creedal interpretations in favor of the original Jesus, the new quest seeks to demonstrate that the historical Jesus was the basis of the Pauline and later Christology. Far more sceptical than the previous quest, the new one, nevertheless, attempts to establish certain historical facts, particularly the arrest and Crucifixion and the sayings of Jesus. They feel that they are making a synthesis of the over-emphasis of the historical Jesus in the last century and the overemphasis on the Christ of faith in this century.

The old quest is condemned because it was impossible, since few really historical documents were available, and illegitimate because

13 *Systematic Theology,* Chicago, 1951, Vol. II, p. 151.
14 Bultmann, *op. cit.,* p. 33.

it sought security in the rational achievement of the human mind rather than in faith in the *kerygma.* The new quest is possible because history is understood in a new sense: not as a reconstruction of factual events and their causes, but as the creativity, intention, and commitment that are revealed in the documents that are left to us.[15]

However he may be interpreted, Jesus as the Christ is the mediator between man and God. Man is aware of his own limitations of character and knowledge. He is perhaps by that same knowledge also aware of the possibility of infinite dimensions of cosmic reality. The Christ is the symbol by which Christians feel a bridge unites the two.

SUGGESTED READINGS

Baillie, Donald, *God Was in Christ,* Scribners, 1948.

Goguel, Maurice, *The Life of Jesus,* Macmillan, 1945.

Henderson, Ian, *Myth in the New Testament,* SCM (Student Christian Movement), 1952.

Rahner, Hugo, *Greek Myths and Christian Mystery,* Burns and Oates, 1963.

Robinson, James, *A New Quest of the Historical Jesus,* SCM (Student Christian Movement), 1959.

Schweitzer, Albert, *The Quest of the Historical Jesus,* Macmillan, 1961.

---

[15] James Robinson, *A New Quest of the Historical Jesus,* Allenson, 1959, p. 66.

VII

The Christian Faith and Western Society

There has been a great deal of interaction between Christianity and other institutions that make up Western civilization. Much of the interaction was and is intentional. The primary activity of the church into which the secular community is called regularly to participate is the service of worship. Whatever else the church was or is, it is the place to which men go to have communion with their God. Many believe that its activity should extend no further. "Let the church be the church," they say, "and keep out of the social and personal lives of its constituents where it has no business to be." Lord Melbourne is purported to have said, "Things have come to a pretty pass when religion begins to tell a man how he ought to live his personal life."

Apart from the fact that it would be impossible to contain religion within the walls of the church, most Christians have clearly felt that the church has a responsibility to become involved in the social and personal lives of men. Numerous encyclicals of the Roman Catholic Church reflect her concern for a wide variety of social problems. No member church of the World Council of Churches, including several Eastern Orthodox bodies and most Protestant groups, held back its endorsement of the concept of a responsible society and the churches' role in the creation of such a society.

Despite this unanimity, there is a real question as to when and how the church should speak to society. The story is told of the old woman who sat in church taking her snuff and listening to the sermon. As the preacher swung into a colorful condemnation of drinking, the woman shouted, "Amen!" When the preacher deplored the sin of smoking the old woman sounded another, "Amen!" Then the preacher described the horrible consequences awaiting those who practice the vice of taking snuff. The woman was startled and thought to herself, "Preacher's stopped preachin' and started meddlin'." The line between prophetic condemnation and legalistic meddling is a difficult one to draw. Civil liberties, discrimination, drinking, and dancing have fallen on one side or the other of that line, depending upon the suppositions of particular churches. But for the most part, the church has felt a responsibility to speak and act on issues that face men in all aspects of their lives.

This is not to say that the church has always been wise or good when it has moved into the lives of men. No halo can be cast over the practice of selling high clerical positions to the highest bidder as became prevalent in the Middle Ages; Christians today can only wince at the boast of the crusaders that the streets of Jerusalem flowed with the blood of 40,000 slaughtered Arabs; it is a continuing embarrassment to the church that she contradicted and condemned the astronomical observations of Galileo. The church, like other institutions, has often too well reflected the fallibility of its constituents. But the church has in her higher moments influenced individuals and societies in profound and lasting ways and no study of Christianity is complete without a survey of these accomplishments.

Some words of caution are necessary before such a survey can begin. Influence is difficult to measure. Many forces are at work in any given social phenomenon and their direction and significance is often quite ambiguous. For example, did the affirmation of the individual rights of man originate in the sixteenth century in social forces other than the church and penetrate into religious institutions, or did it originate in the spirit of the Reformation and move out into other spheres? It seems that when relationships between various institutions in society are so intricate, they are better described in terms of correlation rather than cause and effect.

RELIGION AND CULTURE

The relationship of religion and culture is, therefore, very difficult to assess. Both terms are difficult enough in themselves. In this discussion culture refers to all of the artifacts and conceptual patterns created by man. It is possible to speak of human culture, national culture, regional culture, suburban culture, religious culture, and many other subcultures, but in each case the reference is to the describable aspects of the society. Anything that man produces, from a needle to an educational institution, is part of his culture. In this sense religion is also a part of culture in that it is a man-made institution associated with many artifacts. Many social scientists would treat religion exclusively as one subheading of culture.

When religion refers to any particular institution like the Roman Catholic Church or the Baptist Church it may be conceived narrowly as a subdivision of culture. In a broader sense, religion refers to the basic human experiences of awe, creativity, intuition, guilt, fear, and other emotive responses to life. Some social scientists would say that these phenomena, too, are determined by the culture of the individual and are still to be considered as subdivisions of culture. But it is more likely that these experiences are the wellspring rather than the product of culture. These experiences influence the shape and form of culture rather than the reverse. Paul Tillich suggests that "Religion as ultimate concern is the meaning-giving substance of culture, and culture is the totality of forms in which the basic concern of religion expresses itself. In abbreviation: religion is the substance of culture, culture is the form of religion."[1]

Religion is the intuitive perception of what will bring meaning to life. Culture is the social heritage of alternative ways of accomplishing it. A religious experience may inform one that he ought to help his fellowman; culture defines the various institutions through which such help may be proferred. The culture may present a wide or narrow range of alternative. It may highly sanction one set of values over another, but ultimately the choice is with the individual. Americans believe in God, seek success, and live in ranch-style houses in the suburbs. Individual Americans, on the basis of their intuitive convictions, may choose or reject any of these highly sanctioned characteristics.

There are "oughts" that are not religious. One may feel he ought to polish his shoes or go to the movies or buy a new hat. It is not likely that such an ought is involved in an issue sufficiently basic to be called religious. Only when oughts relate to the basic purpose of life and its attainment are they religious. Certainly culture, too, has an influence on the basic values that an individual holds. The legal codes which cultures transmit are very explicit regarding the obligations of men. But the individual must accept or reject any given cultural value and none bind him in a religious sense unless he affirms it intuitively. When law goes against

[1] Paul Tillich, *Theology of Culture*, Oxford, 1959, p. 42.

what one intuitively believes to be right, one may, for the sake of conscience, break the law. Conscientious objectors to military conscription and sit-in demonstrators in the early 1960's did just this.

The unique revelations of particular individuals may alter a given culture either by forcing it to adopt a wider range of values or replace the values it has. Moses, Jesus, and Gandhi are three examples from chronologically different periods. The spirit initiated by such men is often institutionalized and the institution continues to promote the influence of the man long after his time. The Christian Church is one such institution.

Richard Niebuhr has done much to help categorize positions of various theologians regarding the relationship Christians ought to have with their culture.[2] The position of the first group he calls, "Christ against Culture." It represents all the groups and individuals who believe that this world is essentially evil and man must withdraw from it in order to purify himself. It condemns politics, art, and all other aspects of secular culture. The hermit, the monastery, and the utopian community are products of this belief as individuals and groups seek to extricate themselves from society. Religion and secular culture are seen as incompatible spheres between which men must choose.

The second position is characterized as "the Christ of culture" and points to those groups who see religion and culture as essentially the same. This is the predominant thought today in America where the American way of life and the Christian way are equated. Culture can be Christian and Christianity can participate in the culture.

The third position, "Christ above culture," agrees that there is a large area in which culture and religion can meaningfully interact, but it also argues that there is an area into which culture cannot reach. Although religion permeates culture, it also is above culture "like a cathedral . . . solidly planted among the streets and

[2] Richard Niebuhr, *Christ and Culture,* Harper & Row, 1951.

marketplaces, the houses, the palaces, and universities that represent human culture, but which, when one had passed through its doors, presented a strange new world of quiet spaciousness, of sounds and colors, actions and figures, symbolic of a life beyond all secular concerns."[3] Niebuhr claims that this is the majority position within Christianity.

The last position, descriptive of the neo-orthodox or new reformation theology, is called, "Christ and culture in paradox." At first glance it looks like the first position because it also sees evil in culture. But unlike the first position, it insists that man must live in culture. While religion may always pose an idealistic norm and culture must always partake of evil, man cannot extricate himself from culture nor attain the idealistic norm.

These positions describe how men do view culture and religion. There is another dimension to the same problem that also divides Christians. For those who believe that religion can create some reformation within culture (and only those who fall into Niebuhr's first position flatly deny such a possibility), the question of basic strategy is raised. The more liberal position has been that the church ought to set out actively to reform the political and economic institutions of society. More conservative Christians have felt that the church ought to begin with individuals and when enough individuals are won, they will make the reformation in society. In any case, it is a rare Christian that believes that the church has no responsibility to secular society. Christianity has always thought of itself as an institution with a mission.

THE CHURCH'S SOCIAL MISSION
IN HISTORICAL PERSPECTIVE

Ascetic hermits and the rich monastic tradition of the church dramatically portray the transcendent and otherworldly nature of the church. But whatever conviction the church has had about

[3] *Ibid.,* p. 130.

transcending the world, the Judeo-Christian tradition has also strongly affirmed its participation in the world. The prophet of the Old Testament was sent to speak to the worldly affairs of men: their political (e.g., Hosea 7:11ff.), economic (e.g., Amos 2:6ff.), and personal (e.g., Micah 2:1ff.) life. Jesus announces that he has come that man might have life and have it more abundantly (John 10:10). Although Jesus did not seek to reform the political and economic institutions of his society, because they were no longer in the control of the men he addressed, he did speak to their personal concerns. He healed their illnesses, condemned their shortcomings, and offered them ethical injunctions for their personal lives.

His followers did not flee the world after his death. They made themselves felt in it. They went to both the Gentiles and the Jews. They spoke about the government (Romans 13), they healed the sick (Acts of the Apostles 5), they commented on marriage (I Corinthians 7), wealth (James), and morality. As evidence that the world was responding to them, thousands of them went to their deaths as martyrs.

Throughout the early centuries the Western world could not help but be aware of Christians because their faith made a difference in the way they lived. "See how these Christians love one another," exclaimed one non-Christian witness in the early centuries. They refused to go to war. They bore one another's physical and financial burdens, they proclaimed their faith to the non-Christian world, and they died at the stake.

Constantine's official recognition of the Christian Church marks a transition from the early church into the church of the Middle Ages. At this point the church became highly institutionalized and stable. It was during this period, also, that the monastic movement began to flourish, drawing many men out of the normal life of society. By contrast the church moved in the opposite direction, too, and took over many of the responsibilities for social welfare that had been abandoned by the weakened political structure or had not been recognized as civil obligations. Many churches had hospitals attached to them, service brotherhoods arose to work in the hospitals, and monasteries were likely to maintain houses for lepers. The church sent forth the crusaders to bring the Holy Land under the political control of the West, it gained political power in Europe itself, it established schools, and it continued to send missionaries in ever widening fields.

With the Reformation the Middle Ages end. The advent of Protestantism modified the church's dialogue with the world. Luther wrote on political and economic questions as well as on personal morality. Calvin established a community at Geneva which he believed to be patterned after the Old Testament theocracy. Missionaries continued to sail to far outposts. Hospitals, schools, and orphanages were built. The so-called "enthusiastic" manifestations of Protestantism: the Anabaptists, the Prophets, the Moravians, and the Methodists spoke particularly to the social abuses of the day: slavery, drinking, and sexual immorality.

It has already been seen that the church was divided on the issue whether change in society was best achieved by reforming institutions or reforming individuals. The nineteenth century witnessed the efforts of both sides. The more conservative position believed that the best way to social transformation was through the conversion of individuals. Conservative Christians established social agencies to care for individuals who had been cast out by society, but felt these individuals were better served through charity than social reform. The liberal school of thought felt that social evils must be met in a much more comprehensive way and advocated a restructuring of the social order. They felt that the church should bring pressure to bear on government to create a just society.

Economic and political stability as characterized in this century has narrowed the need for church participation in many areas. Governments are more and more supporting educational and welfare programs that were previously carried on by the church. Non-Christian nations are becoming more and more wary of the presence of missionaries. These new phenomena have forced a modification of the church's role in society. Nevertheless, it has by no means withdrawn from participation. It continues to support educational and welfare programs. It continues to send experts equipped with the skills that the emerging nations can use. It engages active lobbies to influence legislative action and through its periodicals and pulpits it makes commentary on all phases of life encouraging Christians to participate in the decisions of their society. Perhaps most important are the various social agencies that are part of the structure of almost every church organization from local to national or international level. These agencies have been instrumental in disseminating literature on current issues, organizing meetings for information or social protest, and preparing policy statements for the guidance of their members. The church speaks both to the problems of individuals and the problems of society.

PERSONAL BELIEFS AND ETHICS

Even those churches that believe that social problems would be best alleviated by changing or reforming social institutions, also believe that the church has a responsibility directly to individuals. This responsibility lies primarily in two major areas: belief and ethics.

Religion communicates beliefs that bring meaning into life. Thomas Aquinas said that death makes our lives unhappy. Albert Camus has said that death makes life absurd. Religion has helped men find meaning in life in spite of death. It provides man with a vision to instill him with the courage to live and die under the threat of boredom, fear, and despair.

The key question in each man's life, however he may ask it, is "What must I do to be saved?" It was asked of Jesus (Mark 10:17). It was asked of Paul (Acts of the Apostles 16:30), and it is continually asked of the church. The church is the keeper of the great symbols of Western civilization that speak to this question.

They are found in the Bible and the creeds. The success of these symbols is seen in the extent to which they have influenced the art as well as religion in the West. The sculptor, the painter, the composer, and the writer have all found the themes and symbols of Christianity appropriate vehicles for their thought.

The success of the Christian symbols is also seen in the lives of individuals. They influence the genius of such divergent personalities as Augustine, Aquinas, Bach, Michelangelo, Lincoln, and Schweitzer. They led to triumphant deaths for Joan of Arc, Polycarp, Servetus, and a host of Christian martyrs. From the beginning, Christianity, like other religions, has had tremendous impact among the common people as well as the great. The real depth of Christianity's impact is seen by examining what it has meant to the multitudes through the ages.

Any belief has certain contingencies. When one is assured that there is some meaning to life, there follows a development of practices that either assure or manifest that meaning. The religious beliefs of the individual become externalized in his decisions and actions. Theologians are reluctant to talk about ethics apart from theology because ethics would have no meaning apart from the theological presuppositions from which it springs. But conversely, there is no theology without ethical implications. From a creed of beliefs an ethical code follows.

All ethical questions rest on a basic dilemma which is expressed in several of the major ethical controversies. Perhaps chief among them is the controversy of free will versus determinism. It is difficult to argue for free will. If there is a reason for making a decision, then there is no freedom because it would be strange to say that one can choose to be unreasonable. On the other hand, if there is no reason to choose one way or the other, there is no act of real will involved. Yet most of us affirm free will. What we think of man's freedom is relevant to any consideration of ethics.[4]

The dilemma is frequently expressed in Christian theology in

[4] For a more extended discussion of free will, see Chapter IV.

the "faith versus works" controversy. Generally speaking those who believe justification is by faith say that one does the good because he is saved and salvation is a gift from God. Those who say justification is by works say one is saved because he is good by virtue of having fulfilled either the sacramental or ethical obligations of his faith. The former clearly leaves the initiative for salvation outside of the individual and is thereby deterministic, while the latter makes the individual responsible and presupposes freedom. Neither group denies the need for confession, punishment, and forgiveness through community worship or personal prayer.

A similar question is reflected in the continuing controversy between the spirit of the law and the letter of the law. The law implies overt action that can be observed by others and presumably controlled by the individual. The spirit of the law may be impossible to legislate. After listing several characteristics of the spirit of the law: love, joy, peace, patience, kindness, goodness, faithfulness, gentleness, and self-control, Paul states that "against these there is no law" (Galatians 5:23). The law can define that one ought not kill, but it cannot enforce love.

Free will, salvation by works, and legalism tend to join together on one end of the continuum of this dilemma. Determinism, salvation by faith, and the spirit of the law congregate on the other end. Each end of the continuum has certain implications for the resolution of ethical questions.

Perhaps the most important of the implications pertains to the manner in which knowledge of right and wrong is acquired. The main alternatives are reason and intuition. By observation and reason men can deduce a moral code, put it in legal form and live up to it, if the presuppositions of the free will end of the continuum are assumed. For example, one may logically assume that chaos would result in a society if there were a great amount of theft. The law, "Do not steal," is inevitable. If man has free will he can then obey the law and if he believes his salvation lies in the doing of the law he will want to obey. Such an approach to ethics can be very explicit about moral obligations for all men. The law of the church from this point of view can be understood as binding on each individual. Even exceptions to the law may be explicitly stated (e.g., prohibition of divorce, *except* in cases . . .). The Ten Commandments are the epitome of legalism in the Judeo-Christian tradition.

An intuition that speaks to us about some ultimate question in our life is referred to theologically as a revelation. Ethical decisions can be made on the basis of revelation. The revelation of a revered man may be put into the form of a law, in which case it is passed into a legalism. But individuals may act directly on their own revelation. A revealed ethic is naturally relative. One man may feel called to participate in a war in which he feels moral issues are at stake. Another man may feel that it is morally wrong for him to participate in the same war. It is impossible to establish an objective universal morality on the basis of revelation alone. It defies the law. Nevertheless there is strong biblical support for a subjective basis of morality. In the Old Testament, Jeremiah implies such an ethic when he describes the new covenant that will be written in the hearts of men rather than on tablets (Jeremiah 31:31). Paul is quite explicit in his renunciation of the law. The Sermon on the Mount presents an imprecise ethic capable of alternative interpretations.

Such an ethic has its difficulties. Sanction of subjectivity has often led to licentiousness and it is impossible for one man to judge whether or not another man is acting on the basis of a real revelation. Forsaking the law is valid only if one is true to his intuition. If one Holy Spirit reveals the will of one God, presumably there will be consistency if not agreement among the things revealed to all men.

A legalism can emerge either from rational deduction or revelation. The law for Christianity has been preserved in the Bible and in the traditions of the church. Thus an individual Christian is left with two major guides to help him in making ethical decisions. He has the law as expressed in the Bible and in the rules and tradition of his church, and he has his own resources derived from his reason and intuition. Any Christian, for example, may resist stealing because of the biblical condemnation in the Ten Commandments; a Roman Catholic will reject mechanical contraceptives and a Methodist refrain from drinking because of the rules of their particular churches; and again any Christian might become a conscientious objector in wartime because he believes it is God's will for him.

The personal decisions that an individual must make generally revolve around his work, his family responsibilities, and the way in which he uses his leisure time. Work, family, and recreation provide a focus for a discussion of personal ethics.

WORK AND PROPERTY

The Christian tradition has been ambiguous in its evaluation of the inherent virtue of work. There is a strong current of Christian thought that considers work to be a curse. Biblically supported by the Genesis story describing the expulsion of Adam and Eve from the Garden of Eden, "Because you have listened to the voice of your wife, and have eaten of the tree of which I commanded you, 'You shall not eat of it,' cursed is the ground because of you; in toil you shall eat of it all the days of your life" (Genesis 3:17), it has left its marks on major movements within the church. This has been most commonly expressed in the implied superiority of religious over secular vocations. The stigma of dirty hands is a rather universal phenomena around the world. Ecclesiastical and white-collar workers look down upon farmers and artisans.

But there is also a strong tradition within the church that sees all work as potentially a high Christian calling. It too has biblical support. Even before the fall Adam had to work; indeed he had been called to till and look after the Garden (Genesis 2:15). Although the new status of labor is usually attributed to the Reformation, Pope Leo XIII in a classic statement of the position of the Roman Catholic Church on labor also reflected the view that "even had man never fallen from the state of innocence, he would not have remained wholly unoccupied."[5] Calvin, picking up a line of thought from Luther, developed a theology of work that enabled almost any kind of work to become a Christian vocation and certainly since the Reformation Christianity has expressed itself positively toward labor.

Naturally some vocations have been considered unfit. Luther particularly saw fit to exclude prostitution and robbery. In later years as alcoholism became a problem in areas hit by the industrial revolution or in the lonely wastes of the frontier, churches such as the Baptists and Methodists condemned vocations related to the brewing or distribution of alcohol. But Luther condoned the soldier and the hangman despite the consequences of their labor. In discussing the question: "Is any vocation inherently un-Christian?" the authors have never found a class of students that would unanimously agree on any vocation. Despite the condemnation of some few vocations by some Christians, the overwhelming affirmation of the church is that work is good.

Papal encyclicals and pronouncements by various church bodies have sought to protect the worker from becoming simply a commodity. Clergymen were instrumental in the formation of the early trade unions when workers needed such help to protect themselves from exploitation. The churches of all faiths have argued for the fair distribution of profits and the banning of monopolistic practices that might take from the worker his fair share.

Presuming that men work to acquire property in the broad sense of the word, the church has condoned the right to own property. One of the major objections to communism made by some of the churches is that it interferes with the rights of individuals to own

[5] Anne Fremantle, *The Papal Encyclicals,* Mentor Books, 1956, p. 173.

property. However, the church is also insistent that ownership involves responsibility. One may not use his property as a means of invading the property rights of others; one must handle all property as belonging ultimately to God and one is entitled only to such property as is necessary for his own well-being. Out of the surplus one has a responsibility to care for the needy.[6]

SEX AND FAMILY

The moral questions that are related uniquely to the family for the most part involve sex. There is no question in Christianity of the legitimacy of the family. It is condoned and encouraged by scripture (Genesis 2:24; Matthew 19:5–6), church tradition, and natural law. The one dissenting word by Paul (I Corinthians 1:7) must be understood in the context of his presupposition that the world was soon to end and there were more urgent concerns than marriage. Jesus at times makes light of family responsibility (Matthew 12:48–49, 23:9; Luke 14:26), but generally gives it his strong sanction.

The unique purpose of the family, at least in the Judeo-Christian tradition, is for procreation and the rearing of children. Economic, hedonistic, or therapeutic rationalizations for the family are practically never discussed in classic Christian documents. It is at this point that the problems related to sex become relevant. For sex is also seen primarily in its functional use of procreation in Christian thought. Immediately a stigma is placed on many sex practices.

Masturbation, sodomy, and homosexuality are immediately condemned either as sinful or reflections of mental difficulties, since they pervert the normal end of sex. Each is explicitly condemned in the Bible (Leviticus 18:23, 21:13), or in church tradition. Roman Catholics and conservative Protestants have been inclined to think

[6] This sentiment is expressed in many denominational statements and in the Papal Encyclical, *Rerum Novarum*.

of these acts as sinful. Anglicans and more liberal Protestants have been inclined to think of them as reflecting psychological rather than moral difficulty.

Likewise premarital sex relationships are considered immoral. Procreation still provides the criterion. In most premarital experiences, procreation is deliberately avoided and, since the couple have not made any ultimate commitment to each other, they cannot accept the role of responsible parenthood. Further, the church has felt that premarital sex experience makes light and superficial use of a profound phenomena, exploiting a potentially deep experience for the sake of pleasure, prestige, or acceptance. In the biblical world, marriage occurred at such a young age that premarital sex was seldom a problem and Christian thought on this question evolves primarily in the tradition of the church. The necessity of late marriage and knowledge derived from studies of sexual behaviour have led some liberal Protestant churchmen to the conclusion that "not every act that is, technically, pre-marital intercourse (in the sense of pre-wedding) is a distortion of the nature of sex." They are reluctant to insist upon a legalism although they argue for responsibility and awareness of the nature of cultural, ethical, and biological pressures involved.[7]

For those who accept the condemnation of premarital sex that is characteristic of most Christians, a further question arises. If sexual intercourse is wrong, how far may one go? At this point the Christian Church has been of little help. Partly because the preliminary possibilities are so varied and difficult to define, and partly because it is a rather awkward subject matter, none of the churches has made any effort to be very explicit. Prohibition of dancing by several Protestant groups and the discouragement of "going steady" by the Roman Catholics, the Missouri Synod Lutherans, and others represent an attempt to keep couples out of situations where the issue comes up, but when the issue does come

[7] Seward Hiltner, *Sex Ethics and the Kinsey Reports,* Association Press, 1953, p. 230.

up, Christian young people are left to their consciences, since the legalism of neither the Bible nor the church offers explicit advice.

Sex within marriage is considered a natural part of the creation instituted by God. This is not to say that there is unanimity among Christians regarding the value of sex. There are Christians who associate sex with the sin of Adam and Eve and believe it involves a stigma that can never be wholly obliterated. After Paul, Tertullian, Jerome, and Augustine, for example, reiterated the greater virtue of abstinence. Pope Pius XII in 1954 wrote in his encyclical *Sacra Virginitas:* "Virginity is preferable to marriage then, as We have said, above all else because it has a higher aim: that is to say, it is a very efficacious means for devoting oneself wholly to the service of God, while the heart of married persons will always remain more or less 'divided.' " Even for those who marry, abstinence is advocated by the Roman Catholic Church as the best means of birth control as well as a means of accruing special merit. Almost all Protestant bodies leave the question of sex within marriage to the individual. Adultery is unanimously condemned by all Christian churches, both on the basis of biblical texts (Deuteronomy 5:18) and church tradition.

Roman Catholics and some Protestants condemn the use of artificial means of contraception. The argument is based on biblical readings and natural law. The two primary biblical readings are the injunction to Adam to be fruitful and multiply (Genesis 1:29) and the condemnation of Onan for interrupting intercourse with Tamar in order to prevent conception (Genesis 38:9–10). It is then argued that contraception is unnatural. For Roman Catholics conception may be prevented for certain reasons like ill health, but it should be prevented by abstinence from intercourse or observation of the infertile periods in the menstrual cycle. The development of the pill to stop ovulation and conception leaves the Roman Catholic Church with something of an enigma. The pill was primarily designed as a contraceptive measure, but in a sense it is neither mechanical nor artificial. It modifies the natural functioning of the body and may be used simply to stabilize the menstrual cycle so that the rhythm method is possible. As a result, considerable difference of opinion has risen within the Catholic Church as to whether or not Roman Catholics may use the pills.

Birth control is a matter that Protestants have left up to the individual conscience. While they would not condone the use of contraceptives to facilitate extramarital sexual experiences, they do believe that there are times when moral responsibility requires family planning. Persons of limited means or certain physical deformities may be morally obligated not to bear children. The means of contraception is a personal choice. There is a general emphasis that contraceptives ought not be used for selfish ends. Many Protestant clergy feel a responsibility to see that families are educated in the use of contraception.

Divorce is the last of the major ethical questions directly related to the family. The Bible is quite emphatic in its condemnation of divorce except in cases of adultery. Most church bodies have expressed concern at the pattern of divorce as it has developed in the United States. In keeping with biblical tradition most churches hold adultery to be the only legitimate ground and many clergymen will not remarry a divorced person unless they were clearly an innocent party. The Anglican, Eastern, and Roman Catholic churches are the most strict in their condemnation of divorce. However, they have the practice of annulment to cancel out marriages that they believe have never really taken place.

RECREATION, LEISURE, AND PLEASURE

The influence of the church is probably more apparent in the area of recreation than any other area. Although she may have an equally adamant interest in questions of marriage and sex, her attitudes so closely parallel the civil codes of Western civilization that responsibility of sanction is shared and the church is not so central. The church's activity in political and economic life is considerably more peripheral and attracts proportionately less attention. But since the morality of various types of recreation is a real issue and since opinions vary greatly among churches, the civil codes have never had a consensus to reflect and the moral evaluation of recreational possibilities has been left to the various churches.

At various times and by various denominations many forms of recreation have been condemned. This has led to an image of the church as an institution that is determined that people will not enjoy life. In part this is due to the fact that the church is trying to face the great and grave issues of life—which requires a serious posture. Much of the enjoyment that men pursue has the opposite end in mind: escape from the real issues of life. Such an image is also due in part to a failure to recognize that not all churches condemn all pleasures. Each church endorses many forms of recreation which it views as wholesome and creative. The image is also perpetuated by the fact that as a matter of fact some churches are pretty zealous in the condemnation of pleasure.

It is fruitful to examine the reasons why the churches condemn various activities. There are and have been churchmen who believe that all the things of this world are evil and man may not morally participate in any activity of society. This is position one of Richard Niebuhr's analysis. Since man must choose between religion and the world, he chooses against religion whenever he attends the theater, sports activities, or enjoys art. Men and women joined monastic movements and utopian communities to avoid these forms of pleasure and concentrate on what they considered to be holy. From this point of view the pleasures of this world are universally condemned.

The classical Protestant posture from the time of Calvin through New England Puritanism was essentially the same. It did not make a blanket condemnation of culture, but it developed a theology of work that left little place for anything else. Recreation was a frivolity. Pleasures were not so much evil in themselves, but evil because they distracted from the one good, work.

All Christians have condemned pleasures which they feel lead to abuse of other people. Probably most notable is the condemnation by Protestants of excessive drinking which deprives the family of income and sober companionship. Likewise gambling has been condemned by Protestants because it drains off needed family income and condones a philosophy of getting something for nothing. Sports involving cruelty to animals have been generally condemned and some Christians are opposed to boxing for the same reason. Nor does Christianity sanction self-abuse and on this basis it has counselled against drinking, smoking, and the use of dope. Some churches, like the Methodist and the Baptist counsel total abstinence. Most Christians counsel moderation.

The church has been concerned about recreational activities that lead to immoral behavior whether or not they are otherwise immoral in themselves. One of the major criticisms of dancing has been that it is conducive to intimate relationships between the sexes. Drinking is often condemned because it may lead to sexual irresponsibility or violence. Certain literature, art, and drama have been proscribed because they may stimulate sex or violence.

In general, the control of the church in these matters has been primarily advisory, although it has provided strong sanctions by associating moral behavior with salvation. Some churches have tried more explicit means of repressing immoral behaviour. Since 1571 the Roman Catholic Church has had the Congregation of the Index, which censors books which may not be read by Roman Catholics without special dispensation. The Roman Catholic Church has also evaluated current literature and movies in its various periodicals.

Methodists and Baptists and supporting smaller denominations were sufficiently powerful to push through the Eighteenth Amendment to the Constitution, prohibiting the manufacture and sale of alcoholic beverages. For many years Roman Catholic support kept laws prohibiting the sale of contraceptives on the books in Massachusetts and Connecticut. Neither of these ventures was very successful. The Eighteenth Amendment was repealed in 1932 and the birth control legislation was overruled by the Supreme Court in

1965. More recent has been the lobbying of church groups for the so-called Blue Laws in various states to prohibit certain businesses from operating on Sunday, thereby detracting from religious activities and attitudes of the day.

SOCIAL ETHICS

In addition to advising men how they ought to live their personal lives, the Christian Church has been involved in attempts to modify social institutions in such a way that they may better serve man and lead to his salvation. It has already been noted that many churches have felt that the church ought to stay out of social questions either because secular culture is evil and ought not be entered by any Christian or because they believe that the work of the church ought to be aimed exclusively at individuals.

In a sense the distinction between individual ethics and social ethics is artificial. Any individual ethic has social implications and any social ethic has individual implications. In this discussion individual ethics are those that can be relevant to an individual whether or not they are adopted by his society. Social ethics must have a broader base and be accepted by one or more social institutions.

There have been times when the church has been a minority in a hostile culture and has been helpless to affect any institution other than herself. Nevertheless, the great majority of churches have been willfully or accidentally entangled in the social institutions of their times. The churches have built and maintained hospitals, schools, orphanages, and homes for the aged, and the church has affected the life of the community by its involvement in her political and economic institutions.

RELATIONSHIP TO GOVERNMENT

Concerning the political power, Jesus said, "Render therefore to Caesar the things that are Caesar's, and to God the things that are

God's" (Matthew 22:21). Paul continued, "Let every person be subject to the governing authorities. For there is no authority except from God, and those that exist have been instituted by God. Therefore he who resists the authorities resists what God has appointed . . . ," (Romans 13:1–2). On the one hand the early Christians did not see the political powers as their basic enemy. They were willing to pay their taxes and generally submit to the rule of local governments. On the other hand they did not see the political structure as a means to Christian goals and tolerated rather than supported it. They refused to take their differences to court, they refused to hold public office, and they would not serve in the army.

In part their attitude was determined by the fact that since they had no access to the real power of government, it was impractical for them to look to political life as a means of serving their mission. In part their attitude was determined by their "otherworldly" orientation, whether that other world was to be understood as geographically in a different place or conceptually on a different level of experience.

With the conversion of the Emperor Constantine and the subsequent rise of Christianity to a place of power, her indifference to political life became less pronounced, although the basic philosophy remained the same. The church during the Middle Ages became very much involved in political life and there evolved a major struggle between the church and the state for supreme power. At times this struggle represented crass selfishness on both sides, but at times it produced eloquent statements of the judgment of God upon the institutions of men; rulers have their power only by divine fiat. Some specific historical instances are presented at the beginning of the next section of this chapter. Of course, the converse was that men should submit to their rulers because they do have the divine fiat.

A positive if qualified appraisal of government was endorsed by both of the great leaders of the reformation, Calvin and Luther.

They endorsed the necessity of government in order to restrain the evil nature of man.[8]

No particular form of government has ever had the exclusive endorsement of the Christian Church. Tyranny has been universally condemned and the philosophy of such men as Calvin and the sixteenth-century Roman Catholic Cardinal, Bellarmine, has supported a constitutional and parliamentary form of government, but the church has been reluctant to endorse any one form. Pope Leo XIII taught that men are free to choose any just form of government.

The church has not been quite so reluctant to condemn forms of government which it considers unjust. Bishops of the Roman Catholic Church have repeatedly warned their congregations to vote against Communists and many Protestant periodicals are outspoken in their denunciation of communism. The Oxford meeting of the World Council of Churches in 1937 passed a resolution calling upon the churches to persuade their people to oppose nationalistic tendencies.

War

The primary moral problem for political, if not all, life is the problem of war. Despite the pacifistic stance of the early church, a Roman soldier, Cornelius, was admitted to the church without difficulty (Acts of the Apostles 10) and by the fourth century attitudes had changed considerably. The Council of Arles in A.D. 314, the first general council of the Western Church condemned conscientious objectors who deserted their colors, and since that time the position of Christian churches has been divided. Augustine felt war was a necessary tool of the state and later Thomas Aquinas agreed. The church encouraged the crusades to forcefully reclaim the Holy Land. Luther argued that self-defense is a

---

[8] Waldo Beach and H. Richard Niebuhr, *Christian Ethics*, Ronald, 1955, p. 273.

natural right. Calvin appealed to the Old Testament example of David to support the justification of war. The English theologian, Jeremy Taylor, characterized war as "the rod of God in the hands of princes." Christians of most persuasions participated in the great wars of this century with the full support of their churches.

But even those who have supported war have seen the stigma of evil attached to it. Basil, an early Church Father, insisted that soldiers after their discharge be excluded from communion for three years. During the time of William the Conqueror it was stated that soldiers must do a year's penance for each man killed in battle. Clergy were often forbidden to fight and in America they still are automatically exempt from military service.

Many Christians have been and continue to be adamant in their opposition to war. In the reformation period Erasmus declared: "Nothing is more impious, more calamitous, more widely pernicious, more inveterate, more base, or in sum more unworthy of a man, not to say of a Christian, than war. . . . The man who engages in war by choice, whoever he is, is a wicked man; he sins against nature, against God, and against man, and is guilty of the most aggravated impiety."[9] The Quakers, the Mennonites, and various other groups have maintained a position of conscientious objection to war.

The added terror of nuclear weapons has evoked a great number of statements from all faiths advocating peaceful means of resolving international difficulties. "War," declared the Oxford meeting of the World Council of Churches, "is a particular demonstration of the power of sin in this world."[10]

DISCRIMINATION AND RACE

If war is the major ethical question confronting Christianity, discrimination is a close second. In the story of the Good Samari-

[9] Quoted from W. R. Inge, *Christian Ethics and Modern Problems,* Knickerbocker, 1930, p. 320.
[10] Beach and Niebuhr, *op. cit.,* p. 486.

tan Jesus probably makes his most direct statement on minority group discrimination. The Samaritan, despised outcast in a community to the north of Jerusalem, is also one's neighbor. Paul follows close behind both in time and theme: "For there is no distinction between Jew and Greek; the same Lord is Lord of all and bestows his riches upon all who call upon him" (Romans 10:12).

On the basis of Old Testament tradition Christianity could have moved in either direction. The doctrine of the "Chosen People" hedged Judaism into a position of exclusiveness. Although in its best sense this has been understood as a doctrine of mission—that is, Israel is chosen for a task rather than a privilege—it also resulted in feelings of superiority. The Samaritan community was excluded from any heritage in the new temple after the Babylonian exile because it was no longer racially pure, having mixed with the Assyrian population. Nehemiah physically beat his countrymen (Nehemiah 13:25ff.) and Ezra tore out his hair (Ezra 9:3) when they saw that Jews were marrying non-Jews.

But there was another trend of thought prevalent in Judaism. The Old Testament pointed men to a common ancestry of two parents, Adam and Eve, thus implying that biologically all men are brothers. The prophets of the eighth century recognized Yahweh as a God of all men. The books of Ruth and Jonah were written to combat the nationalism reflected in Ezra and Nehemiah.

In its theory, Christianity followed the second line of thought. In practice it was often bound by the culture in which it resided. In the early centuries it made no condemnation of slavery with its implicit assumption of different levels of worth among men. Slavery was an established institution and it was difficult to realize that it was not a part of the natural order. When Christian nations colonized much of the rest of the world, they were quick to characterize other peoples and cultures as inferior. It was Christian nations that carried on the slave trade between Africa and the United States. During the Civil War political ties were stronger than religious ties and northern churches took abolitionist stands, while southern churches sided with the Confederacy. The split still remains. Northern churches, where the race question has only recently become intense, have been able to be quite free in their affirmation of brotherhood. Southern churches have often spent much time seeking biblical justification for discrimination. It is common, for example, to identify Negroes as descendants of Ham who inherit the curse of his son Canaan: "Cursed be Canaan; a slave of slaves shall he be to his brothers" (Genesis 9:25). There have been some strong antidiscrimination statements by a few southern churches and many discriminating practices among northern churches.

Several churches made antislavery statements before the Civil War and it was no doubt the moral support of the church that in part made the war inevitable. Roman Catholic popes have spoken against slavery[11] and race hatred,[12] and one of the strongest church stands in the United States was made by the Roman Catholic bishop of Louisiana.[13] When Negroes began their strong bid for equal rights in the 1950s it was largely organized through the churches and a clergyman, Martin Luther King, became a chief spokesman.

OTHER POLITICAL ISSUES

By contrast the involvement of the church in other political institutions has been considerably less significant. As soon as civil governments have taken over educational institutions, the churches have ceased to have a strong say in those institutions, and in the United States the churches have been encouraged to stay out of public education. Religion has played various roles in prison reform. For many centuries, the church considered that it was doing enough for imprisoned or condemned men if it brought them the sacraments and worked for their conversion. In the last

[11] Fremantle, *op. cit.*, p. 80.
[12] *Ibid.*, p. 215.
[13] *The Christian Century*, April 11, 1962, pp. 448–449.

hundred years, liberal Protestant groups in particular have pushed for changes in penology and the prison chaplaincy has become a specialized form of the ministry. The church regularly supplies chaplains for the armed services and federal and local governing bodies.

In many parts of Europe national churches have continued to have a substantial voice in government. In America, which has no such homogeneity of denominations, the doctrine of the separation of church and state has emerged. The intent of the doctrine is to assure that no particular church can gain overt or subtle advantage over any other religious community. As a result, American Christians have been faced with a real dilemma. On the one hand, most of the Founders were very much involved in their religious communities and assumed that they were establishing a Christian nation. On the other hand, they did not want to give official recognition to any religious group. So some men argued that there was not enough explicit reference to Christianity in the Constitution and other men argued that there ought not be any explicit references to religion. Yet both argued from a strongly Christian background.

ECONOMIC LIFE

The church could no more avoid involvement in the economic life of society than it could avoid involvement in her political life. "Now the company of those who believed were of one heart and soul, and no one said that any of the things which he possessed was his own, but they had everything in common. There was not a needy person among them, for as many as were possessors of lands or houses sold them, and brought the proceeds of what was sold and laid it at the apostles' feet; and distribution was made to each as any had need" (Acts of the Apostles, 4:32, 34–37). In such a startling economic setting, the life of the early Christian community began. It is startling because it reflects a socialism that is an anathema to almost all of Christendom today. Yet it is not out of keeping with the general tenor of New Testament teaching which advocated a strong divorce from the material world. How much of this attitude was fostered because of the expected end of the world is difficult to measure, but with time Christians became more interested in property and the things of the world. Clement of Alexandria in the second century outlined the reasoning by which the Christian could resolve his wealth with the teachings of the New Testament. The man of possessions must not be inwardly attached to his belongings and he must recognize his responsibility in handling these gifts of God.

The monastic movement within the church continued to look with wary eye upon the dangers of riches and in their eyes poverty was a necessary virtue. In the thirteenth century St. Francis of Assisi founded an order, embraced "Lady Poverty," and spent the rest of his life trying to keep the order itself from concern with property, uniforms, books, and other belongings that might lure it into worldly concerns.

Calvin provided a theological base for a high valuation of work which many believe was directly responsible for the ethic of free enterprise that developed in the West. With it he combined a kind of asceticism that forbade irresponsible use of the wealth so derived. Poverty was by no means considered a virtue, but a vice, since it implied that the poor were unwilling to work. Such an ethic flourished in Puritan New England and from that base became deeply embedded in American economic thought: "To secure wealth is an honorable ambition, and is one great test of a person's usefulness to others. . . . I say, get rich, get rich! . . . 98 out of 100 of the rich men of America are honest. That is why they are rich. . . . I won't give in but what I sympathize with the poor, but the number of poor who are to be sympathized with is very small. To sympathize with a man whom God has punished for his sins, thus to help him when God would still continue a just punishment, is to do wrong, no doubt about it. . . .[14] The so-called "Protestant ethic" drove men to work, so that they accumulated riches which the New Testament forbade them to have. John Wesley suggested: Gain all you can without hurting body, mind, or neighbor; save all you can and give all you can. There was a growing concept of the rich man as the man appointed to be a special steward of God's goods and upon him fell the responsibility to render charity to society.

The liberal Protestant movements of the end of the nineteenth and beginning of the twentieth centuries condemned capitalism as an economic system glorifying greed and competition. Under the leadership of men like Walter Rauschenbush they sought to construct a system of cooperative economic life more in keeping with what they understood to be the teachings of Jesus.

But capitalism continued to intrigue the Christian Church. Bruce Barton wrote a book, *The Man Nobody Knows,* in which Jesus is depicted as an ancient man in a grey flannel suit who with his 12-man board went about his father's business. Protestantism, in particular, has become identified with the successful businessman rather than with labor. As issues like automation and the price-wage spiral come up, Protestant periodicals tend to side with the position of management. Roman Catholicism, which until recently was primarily a church of the immigrants who were in the laboring classes, has been more sympathetic with the cause of labor.

CONFLICTS BETWEEN CHURCH AND SOCIETY

The early church found itself in a hostile and unsympathetic environment and it is not surprising that there was considerable conflict between Christian and secular authorities. Many Christians

---

[14] The nineteenth-century preacher, Russell Conwell, quoted in Marquis W. Childs and Douglass Cater, *Ethics in a Business Society,* Mentor Books, 1954, p. 137.

became ascetics and withdrew from society altogether. Most Christians refused to pay homage to the emperor or serve in his army. As a result many were arrested and not a few were martyred.

A brief respite in the battle between church and state was possible under Constantine and for a few years afterward. Christianity became the official religion of the empire and for a short time had little quarrel with secular officials. But once established, it began to compete with secular leadership for ultimate control in a battle which reached its climax in the time of Innocent III in the thirteenth century. In 1198 Innocent proclaimed: "The creator of the universe set up two great luminaries in the firmament of heaven; the greater light to rule the day, the lesser light to rule the night. . . . These dignitaries are the pontifical authority and the royal power. Furthermore, the moon derives her light from the sun, and is in truth inferior to the sun in both size and quality. . . . In the same way the royal power derives its dignity from the pontifical authority. . . ."[15] By threat of crusade, excommunication, and withholding the sacraments, he was successful in making good his claim.

His successor, Boniface VIII, fought the climactic battle in the struggle between church and state with Philip IV of France. The early skirmishes went to Philip. Boniface, incensed, issued a papal bull which said in part: "Let none persuade you . . . that you are not subordinate to the head of the ecclesiastical hierarchy, for he is a fool who thinks so. . . ."[16] Philip replied: "Philip by the Grace of God, King of the Franks, to Boniface who gives himself out for Supreme Pontiff, little or no greeting. . . . Let your great fatuousness know that in temporalities we are subject to none. . . . Such as believe otherwise are fools or madmen."[17] The church was to lose by default. Boniface died and was succeeded by a weak pope who was easily put under the control of Philip. The

[15] Henry Bettenson, *Documents of the Christian Church,* Oxford, 1950, p. 157–158.
[16] Thomas Boase, *Boniface the Eighth,* Constable, 1933, p. 302.
[17] *Ibid.,* p. 305.

battle continued, but the church had passed its zenith of political power.

The Reformation greatly changed the complexion of church-state relations. Europe had long been divided politically and now the church lost its monolithic structure. Churches continued to have official government recognition, but there were now several churches and their influence often did not go beyond the political frontiers. They recognized their political limitations and established amiable relations with secular authorities.

CHURCH AND STATE IN AMERICA

In America quite a different pattern emerged. Since it had been settled by a number of religious groups, each refused to make a union unless its rights were guaranteed against the power of any state church. As a result an attempt has been made to draw a careful distinction between church and state. The biggest problem for the American churches has been defining the place of religion in politics and education.

There was general agreement among the churches in America that no one faith should be able to gain priority. In order to avoid official recognition of any particular faith, the Constitution made no mention of religion at all. This was only a partial assurance that no one faith could gain ascendancy and some groups, like the Presbyterians and the Baptists tended to oppose ratification of the Constitution unless it included more explicit safeguards for religious freedom. Others lamented the omission of any mention of God or the Christian religion.

Pressure mounted for a Bill of Rights and when it came it included more specific mention of religion. The First Amendment to the Constitution stated: "Congress shall make no law respecting an establishment of religion or prohibiting the free exercise thereof; or abridging the freedom of speech, or of the press; or the right of the people peaceably to assemble and to petition the Government for a redress of grievances." The purpose of the Amendment was to create a "wall of separation between church and state" as Thomas Jefferson explained. It has been a difficult wall to defend and many obvious facts contradict the law: tax exemption for church property, release of students to attend religious classes, free lunch programs and transportation for parochial school children, maintenance of chapels and chaplains at military installations, and Sunday closing laws.

The Sixth Amendment also pertained to a religious question: "No religious test shall ever be required as a qualification to any office or public trust under the United States." The 1960s brought two tests to this Amendment. In the first, a man was denied a notary public commission by the State of Maryland because he was an avowed atheist. The case was carried to the state supreme court where the decision of the lower court was declared unconstitutional. More subtle was the presidential campaign of 1960. A Roman Catholic had never held the office of President, although Alfred Smith had run unsuccessfully in 1928. Technically there could be no law prohibiting a Roman Catholic president, but *de facto,* much of Protestant America had such a rule. Protestants were caught in the paradoxical position of advocating bigotry to protect the country from a candidate they feared would give support to bigotry. Nevertheless the Roman Catholic, John F. Kennedy, won and the issue lost all importance.

In recent years the political structure of the United States has looked to the religious institutions for a new kind of support. Many have understood the conflict with communism to be a basically religious question. As a consequence many religious items have cropped up in political settings. The phrase "under God" was inserted into the pledge to the flag. "In God we trust," long the official motto of the United States, became more conspicuous, and politicians have gone out of their way to adopt a religious stance.

Education has been the other major battleground of church-state relations. For many centuries the churches founded and maintained educational institutions both at university (Harvard, Yale, Princeton, Dartmouth, for example) and grammar school levels. As the public school program developed in America, it soon assumed the major responsibility for primary and secondary schools and is on the way toward educating the majority of university-level students. A good many parochial schools still exist and any parent is free to send his children to them.

The public schools who enroll the vast majority of students in the United States are rapidly cutting themselves off from any religious traditions. At one time, the United States was so exclusively Protestant in makeup that the public schools were practically Protestant parochial schools. Bible readings and prayers were a part of the daily exercises and the religious holidays were celebrated in the assembly programs. As the number of Roman Catholic and other non-Protestants grew, pressures increased for a more literal rendering of the First Amendment in regard to public schools.

As early as 1786 the Virginia state legislature tried to resolve the difficulty of providing religious education for a pluralistic community within the confines of the Constitution. A bill was proposed that would use tax monies for religious education on a nonpreferential basis. The individual taxpayer could specify which faith should be the recipient of his money, or if he wished to support no faith, his money could go to some other kind of institution. The bill was defeated largely through the efforts of James Madison who argued that religion should be strictly voluntary and the government should stay out of religious questions.

Another tack was tried. In many schools a certain period was set aside each week for religious education. At that time church teachers from outside came in to conduct the classes. Students could elect to learn about any faith represented or they could remain in their classroom. The test of the validity of this procedure was put to the Supreme Court in 1948. The Court in the *McCollum* v. *Board of Education* case ruled in favor of a professed atheist who claimed that her son was placed in an awkward position by the practice. Justice Black commented: "Here not only are the state's tax-supported public school buildings used for the dissemination of religious doctrine. The State also affords sectarian groups an invaluable aid in that it helps to provide pupils for their religious classes through use of the State's compulsory public school machinery."[18]

In other schools the children were released from classes to leave the school building and attend religious instruction in local churches. This practice, too, was brought to the Supreme Court and this time the Court ruled against the plaintiff and defended the practice.[19]

In 1962 the Supreme Court ruled against the practice of having any set prayer read in the classroom. The ruling was in itself not particularly sweeping. It even allowed room for some types of prayer. But it was probably far more effective in making a final break between religious and public instruction than any previous ruling. School administrators became anxious as many cases were taken to the Court. Since they preferred to allow no room for question, classroom prayer, Bible readings, and holiday assembly programs rapidly disappeared.

Since most of the parochial schools are run by the Roman Catholic Church, its increasing numbers and status have resulted in increasing pressure for public support of parochial schools. These schools argue that they serve a legitimate function in attempting to bring a religious education to their constituents. They give considerable relief to overcrowded conditions in public schools since they enroll something like 12 percent of the school children in America and for their efforts they find themselves taxed both by the state and the church.

Opponents argue that public support of parochial schools would

[18] Joseph Tussman, *The Supreme Court on Church and State,* Oxford, 1962, p. 241.
[19] *Ibid.,* p. 264.

violate the Constitution, undermine public schools, and offer federal support without federal control. The most famous case in which this issue has come to the Supreme Court is *Everson* v. *Board of Education*. The question at issue was state support of bus transportation. The Court ruled that tax money could be used for transportation to parochial schools in some circumstances. A distinction was made between support of individuals and support of religious institutions.

With the growing percentage of students seeking higher education at state universities, the question of teaching religion in these institutions is becoming quite important. Most state universities offer some courses in religion, if only a course on Bible offered in the English department.[20] Several state universities have full academic departments offering degrees in religion. No court case has ever arisen on this question. For one thing, religion as taught in a university is taught from an academic rather than a persuasive point of view. Professors of religion, like those in any other field, have Ph.D.'s belong to learned societies, and publish in scholarly journals. The rapid elimination of religious practices in public schools may be accompanied by an increasing acceptance of the academic study of religion already well established at a university level.

Conflict is inevitable as responsibilities shift among the institutions of society. For various reasons education and social welfare have sometimes been primarily the concern of the state and at other times the concern of religious or other private institutions. There is no obvious single institution to which these concerns belong. The church ought to be assured that these needs are being filled, but the church is not necessarily the agency that must do it.

There is, however, an area in which the church has a prerogative that it cannot neglect because no other institution in society will take it up. It is the concern for the basic questions of meaning in

20 Milton McLean and Harry H. Kimber, *The Teaching of Religion in State Universities,* University of Michigan, 1960.

life, the question of value and salvation. The Christian Church is the custodian of the wisdom and revelation of three millennia of Western civilization. It is the content of that depository and its effect on Western civilization that has been the subject of this book.

SUGGESTED READINGS

Niebuhr, Reinhold, *An Interpretation of Christian Ethics,* Harper & Row, 1935.

Tillich, Paul, *Theology of Culture,* Oxford, 1959.

Troeltsch, Ernest, *The Social Teachings of the Christian Churches,* Macmillan, 1949.

Tussman, Joseph, *The Supreme Court on Church and State,* Oxford, 1962.

Vernon, Glenn, *Sociology of Religion,* McGraw-Hill, 1962.

Walter, Erich A., *Religion and the State University,* University of Michigan, 1958.

Index

Format by Jeanne Ray Juster
Set in Intertype Garamond
Composed, printed and bound by American Book–Stratford Press, Inc.
HARPER & ROW, PUBLISHERS, INCORPORATED

73 74 75 76   8 7 6 5